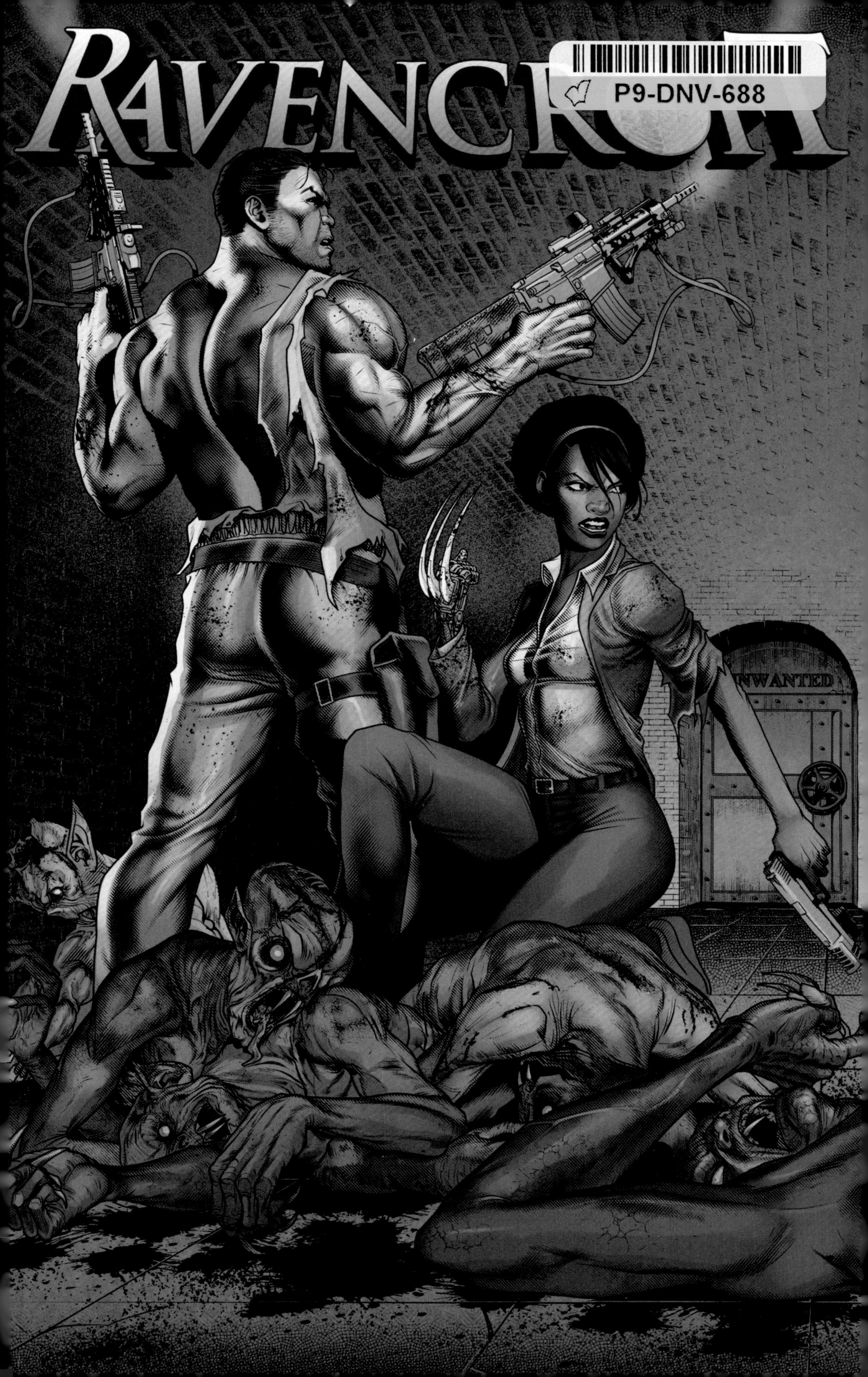
RAVENCR
NWANTED

RAVENCROFT

WRITER: **FRANK TIERI**

ARTISTS: **ANGEL UNZUETA** (#1-5) &
JOSÉ LUIS (#2-3) WITH
SCOTT HANNA (#2-3)

COLOR ARTISTS: **RACHELLE ROSENBERG** WITH
DONO SÁNCHEZ-ALMARA (#1)

LETTERER: **VC's JOE SABINO**

COVER ART: **KYLE HOTZ**
& **DAN BROWN**

ASSISTANT EDITOR: **DANNY KHAZEM**

EDITOR: **DEVIN LEWIS**

COLLECTION EDITOR: **JENNIFER GRÜNWALD**
ASSISTANT MANAGING EDITOR: **MAIA LOY**   ASSISTANT MANAGING EDITOR: **LISA MONTALBANO**
VP PRODUCTION & SPECIAL PROJECTS: **JEFF YOUNGQUIST**   BOOK DESIGNERS: **STACIE ZUCKER** WITH **JAY BOWEN**
SVP PRINT, SALES & MARKETING: **DAVID GABRIEL**   EDITOR IN CHIEF: **C.B. CEBULSKI**

RAVENCROFT. Contains material originally published in magazine form as RAVENCROFT (2020) #1-5. First printing 2020. ISBN 978-1-302-92260-3. Published by MARVEL WORLDWIDE, INC., a subsidiary of MARVEL ENTERTAINMENT, LLC. OFFICE OF PUBLICATION: 1290 Avenue of the Americas, New York, NY 10104. © 2020 MARVEL No similarity between any of the names, characters, persons, and/or institutions in this magazine with those of any living or dead person or institution is intended, and any such similarity which may exist is purely coincidental. **Printed in Canada.** KEVIN FEIGE, Chief Creative Officer; DAN BUCKLEY, President, Marvel Entertainment; JOHN NEE, Publisher; JOE QUESADA, EVP & Creative Director; TOM BREVOORT, SVP of Publishing; DAVID BOGART, Associate Publisher & SVP of Talent Affairs; Publishing & Partnership; DAVID GABRIEL, VP of Print & Digital Publishing; JEFF YOUNGQUIST, VP of Production & Special Projects; DAN CARR, Executive Director of Publishing Technology; ALEX MORALES, Director of Publishing Operations; DAN EDINGTON, Managing Editor; RICKEY PURDIN, Director of Talent Relations; SUSAN CRESPI, Production Manager; STAN LEE, Chairman Emeritus. For information regarding advertising in Marvel Comics or on Marvel.com, please contact Vit DeBellis, Custom Solutions & Integrated Advertising Manager, at vdebellis@marvel.com. For Marvel subscription inquiries, please call 888-511-5480. **Manufactured between 10/23/2020 and 11/24/2020 by SOLISCO PRINTERS, SCOTT, QC, CANADA.**

10 9 8 7 6 5 4 3 2 1

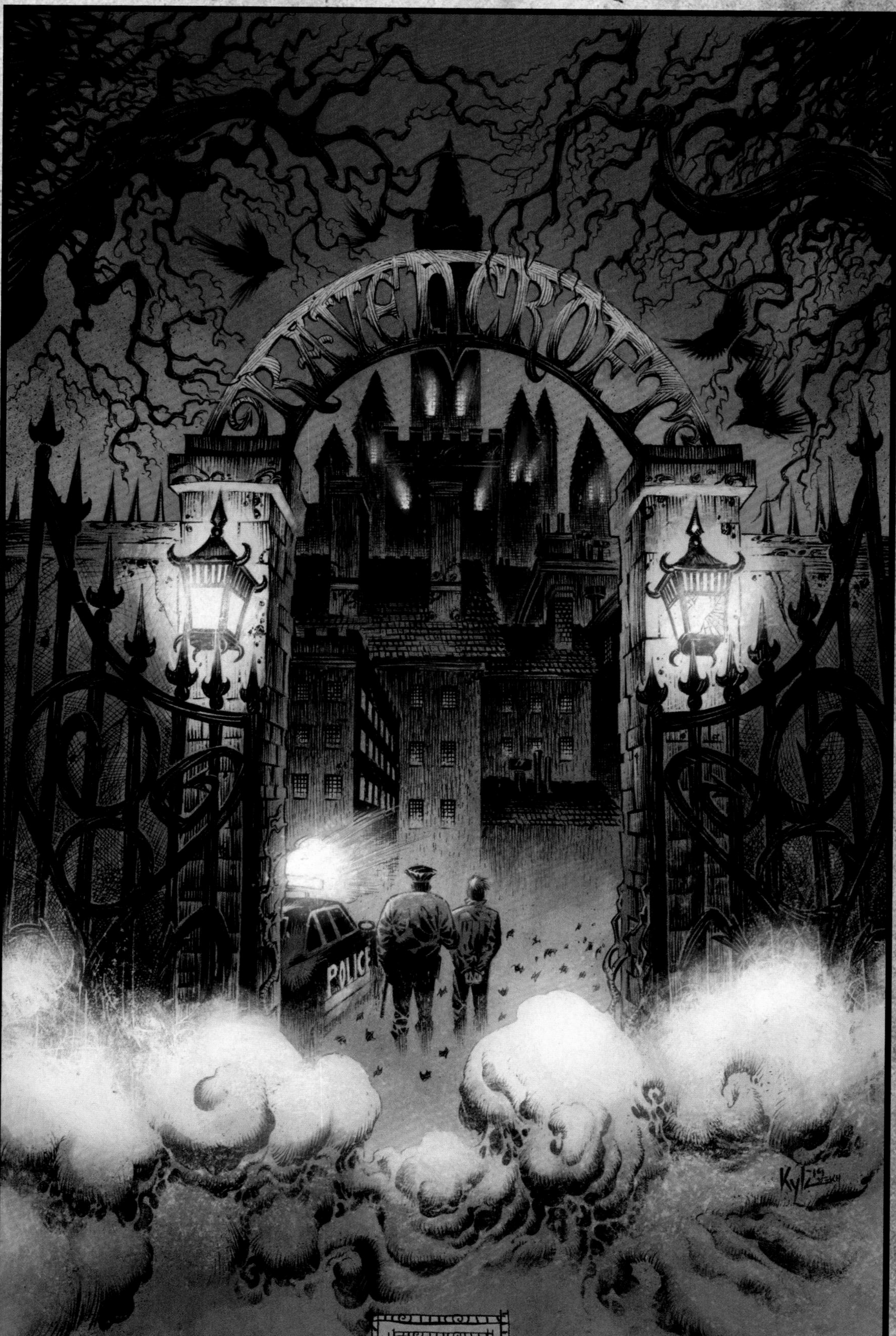
RAVENCROFT
POLICE

1

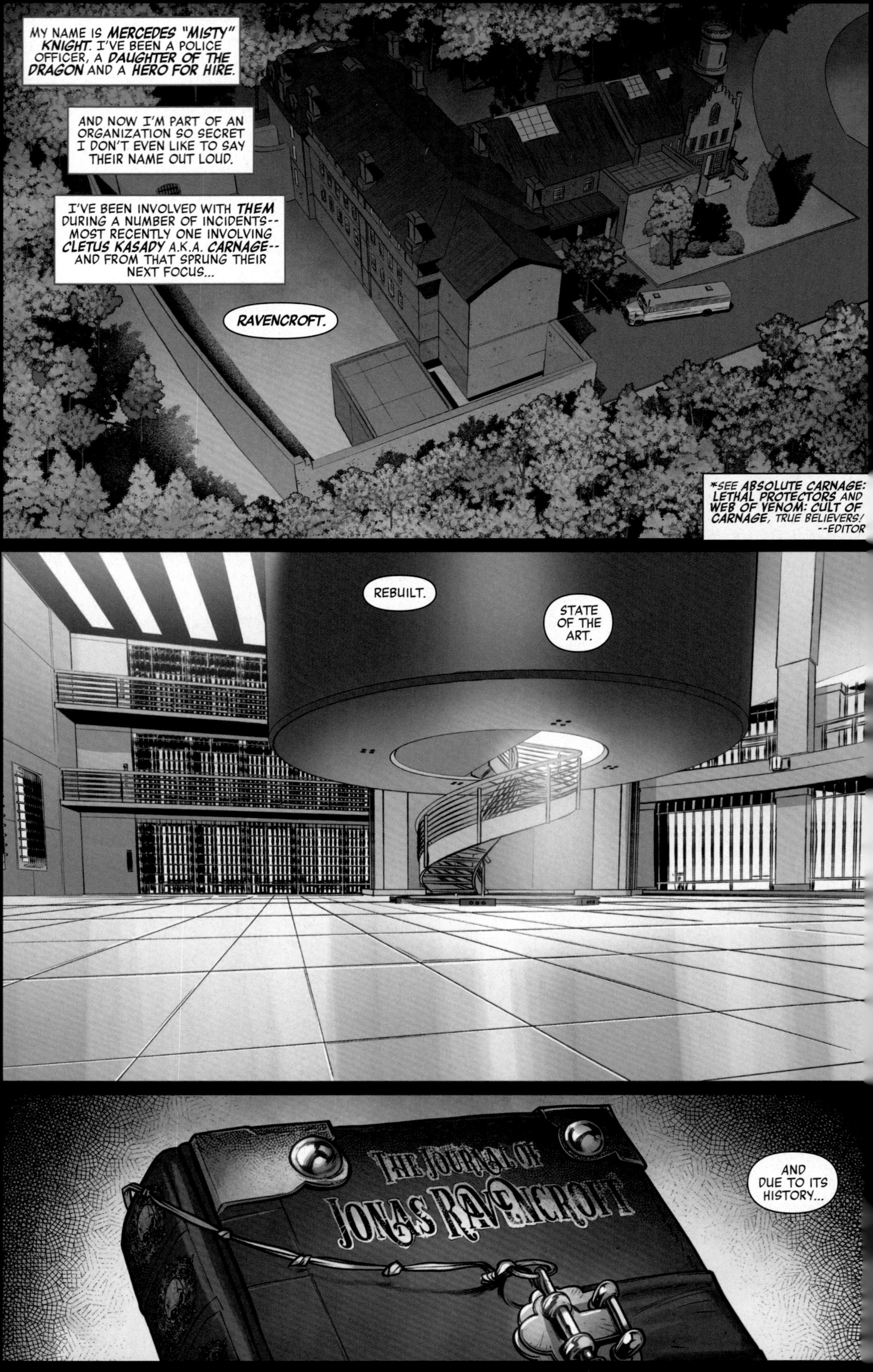
MY NAME IS MERCEDES "MISTY" KNIGHT. I'VE BEEN A POLICE OFFICER, A DAUGHTER OF THE DRAGON AND A HERO FOR HIRE.
AND NOW I'M PART OF AN ORGANIZATION SO SECRET I DON'T EVEN LIKE TO SAY THEIR NAME OUT LOUD.
I'VE BEEN INVOLVED WITH THEM DURING A NUMBER OF INCIDENTS-- MOST RECENTLY ONE INVOLVING CLETUS KASADY A.K.A. CARNAGE-- AND FROM THAT SPRUNG THEIR NEXT FOCUS...
RAVENCROFT.
*SEE ABSOLUTE CARNAGE: LETHAL PROTECTORS AND WEB OF VENOM: CULT OF CARNAGE, TRUE BELIEVERS! --EDITOR
REBUILT.
STATE OF THE ART.
THE JOURNAL OF JONAS RAVENCROFT
AND DUE TO ITS HISTORY...

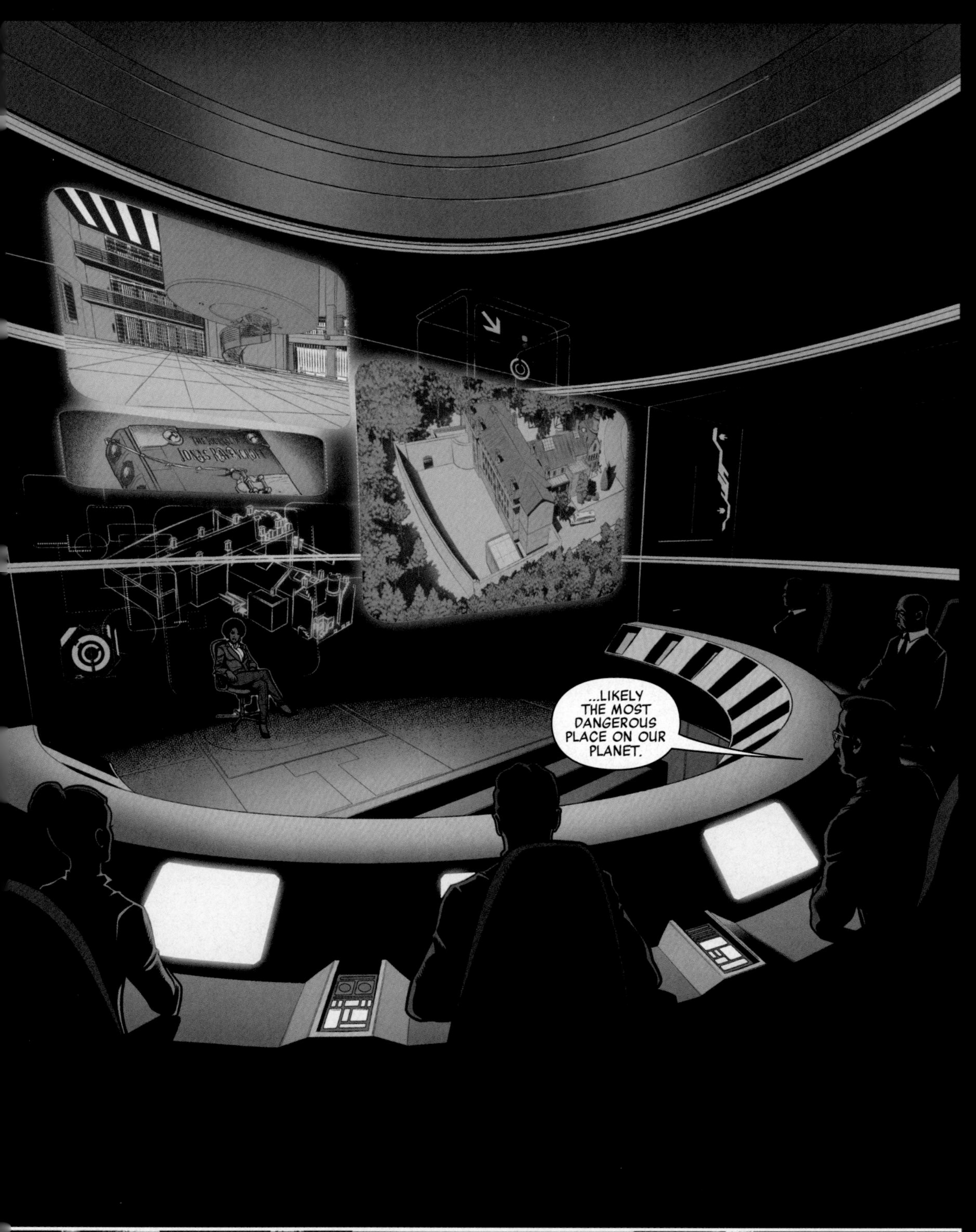
...LIKELY THE MOST DANGEROUS PLACE ON OUR PLANET.

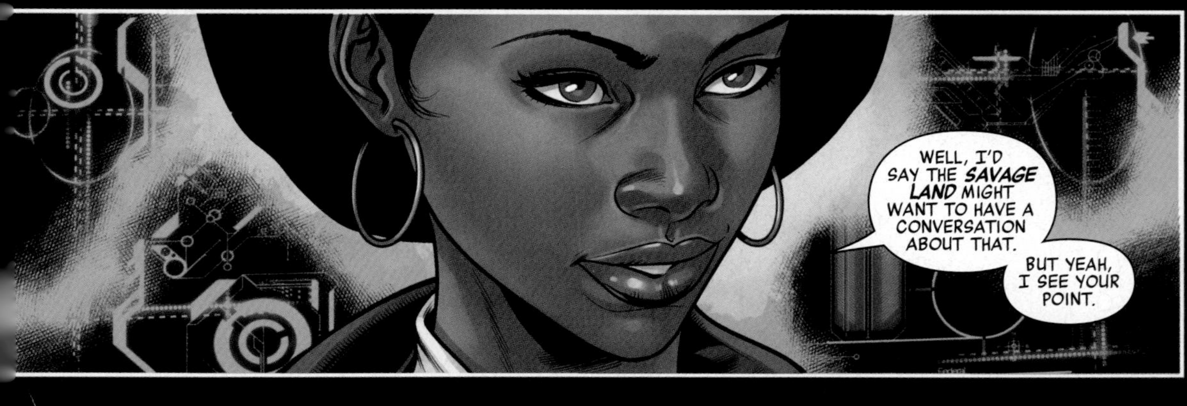
WELL, I'D SAY THE SAVAGE LAND MIGHT WANT TO HAVE A CONVERSATION ABOUT THAT.
BUT YEAH, I SEE YOUR POINT.

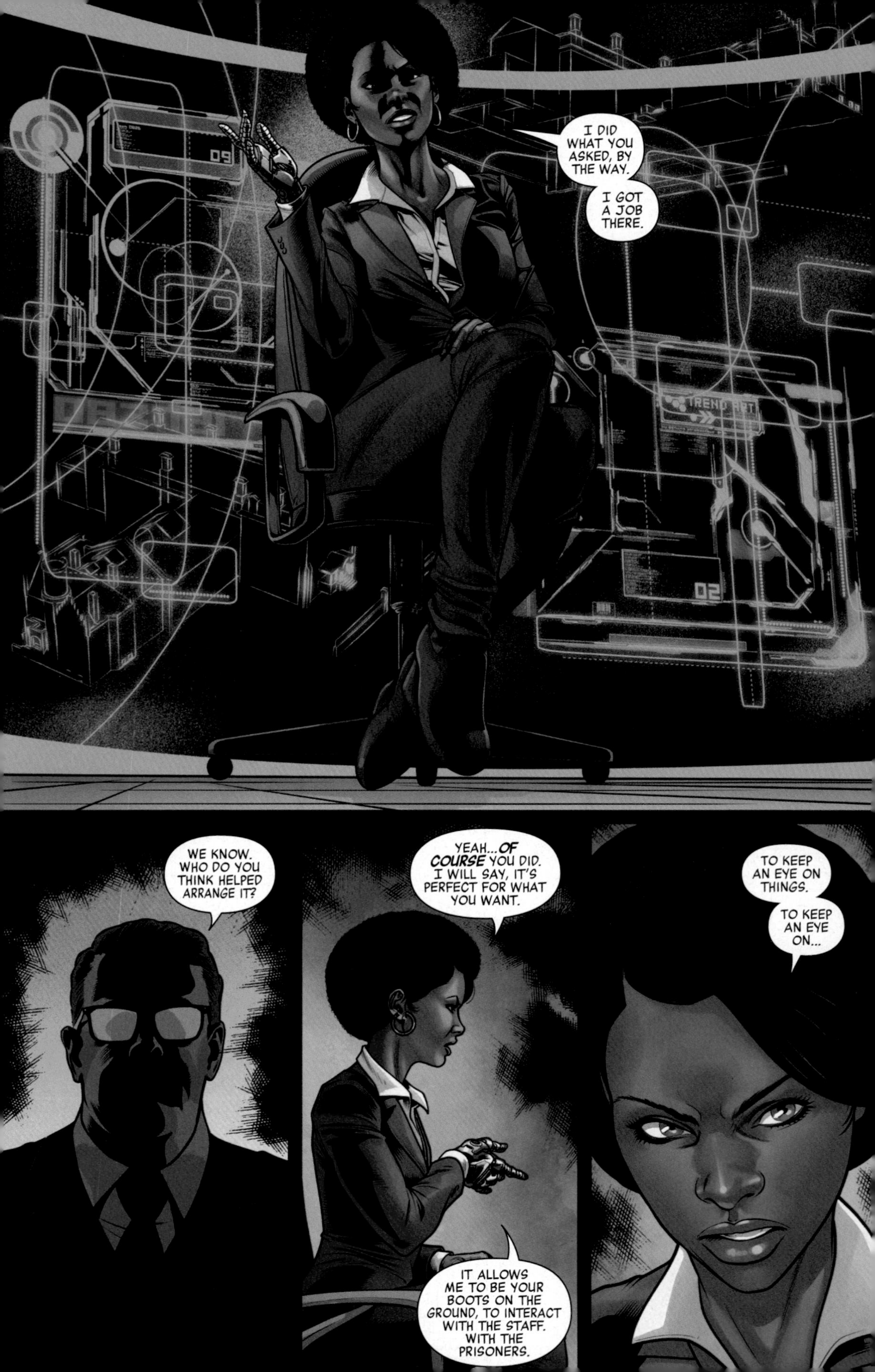
I DID WHAT YOU ASKED, BY THE WAY.
I GOT A JOB THERE.
WE KNOW. WHO DO YOU THINK HELPED ARRANGE IT?
YEAH...*OF COURSE* YOU DID. I WILL SAY, IT'S PERFECT FOR WHAT YOU WANT.
IT ALLOWS ME TO BE YOUR BOOTS ON THE GROUND, TO INTERACT WITH THE STAFF. WITH THE PRISONERS.
TO KEEP AN EYE ON THINGS.
TO KEEP AN EYE ON...

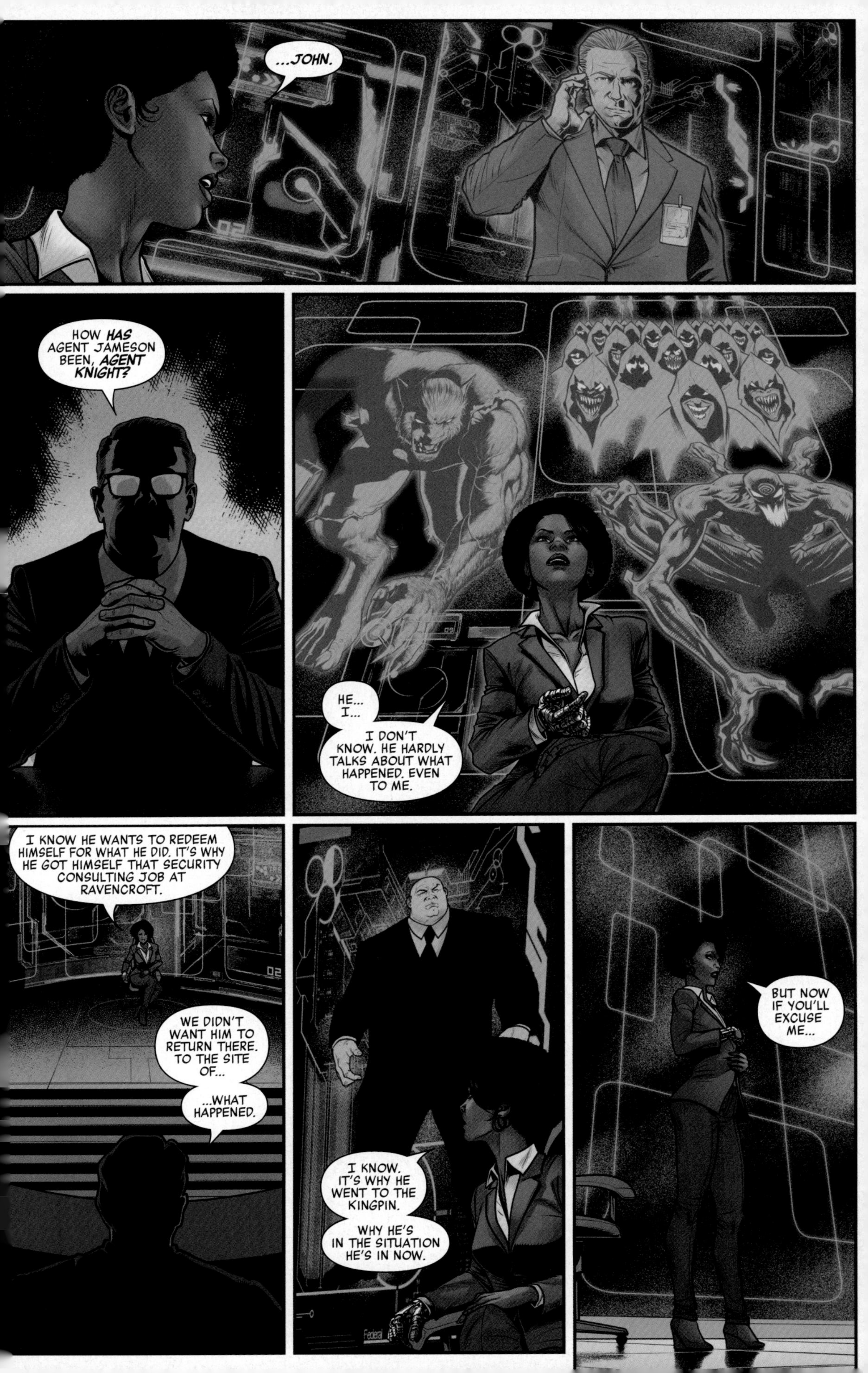
...JOHN.
HOW HAS AGENT JAMESON BEEN, AGENT KNIGHT?
HE... I...
I DON'T KNOW. HE HARDLY TALKS ABOUT WHAT HAPPENED. EVEN TO ME.
I KNOW HE WANTS TO REDEEM HIMSELF FOR WHAT HE DID. IT'S WHY HE GOT HIMSELF THAT SECURITY CONSULTING JOB AT RAVENCROFT.
WE DIDN'T WANT HIM TO RETURN THERE. TO THE SITE OF...
...WHAT HAPPENED.
I KNOW. IT'S WHY HE WENT TO THE KINGPIN.
WHY HE'S IN THE SITUATION HE'S IN NOW.
BUT NOW IF YOU'LL EXCUSE ME...

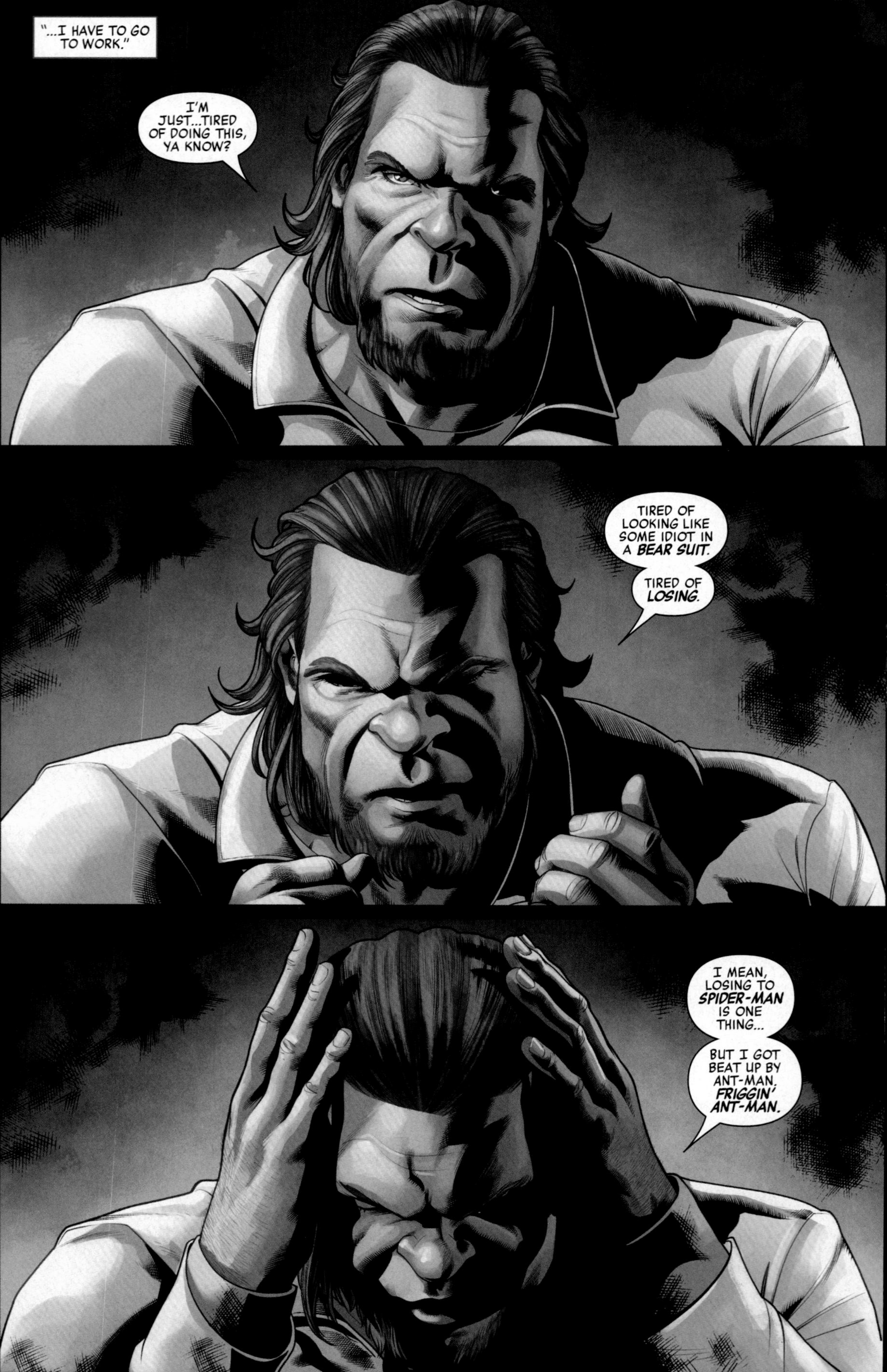
"...I HAVE TO GO TO WORK."
I'M JUST...TIRED OF DOING THIS, YA KNOW?
TIRED OF LOOKING LIKE SOME IDIOT IN A BEAR SUIT.
TIRED OF LOSING.
I MEAN, LOSING TO SPIDER-MAN IS ONE THING...
BUT I GOT BEAT UP BY ANT-MAN. FRIGGIN' ANT-MAN.

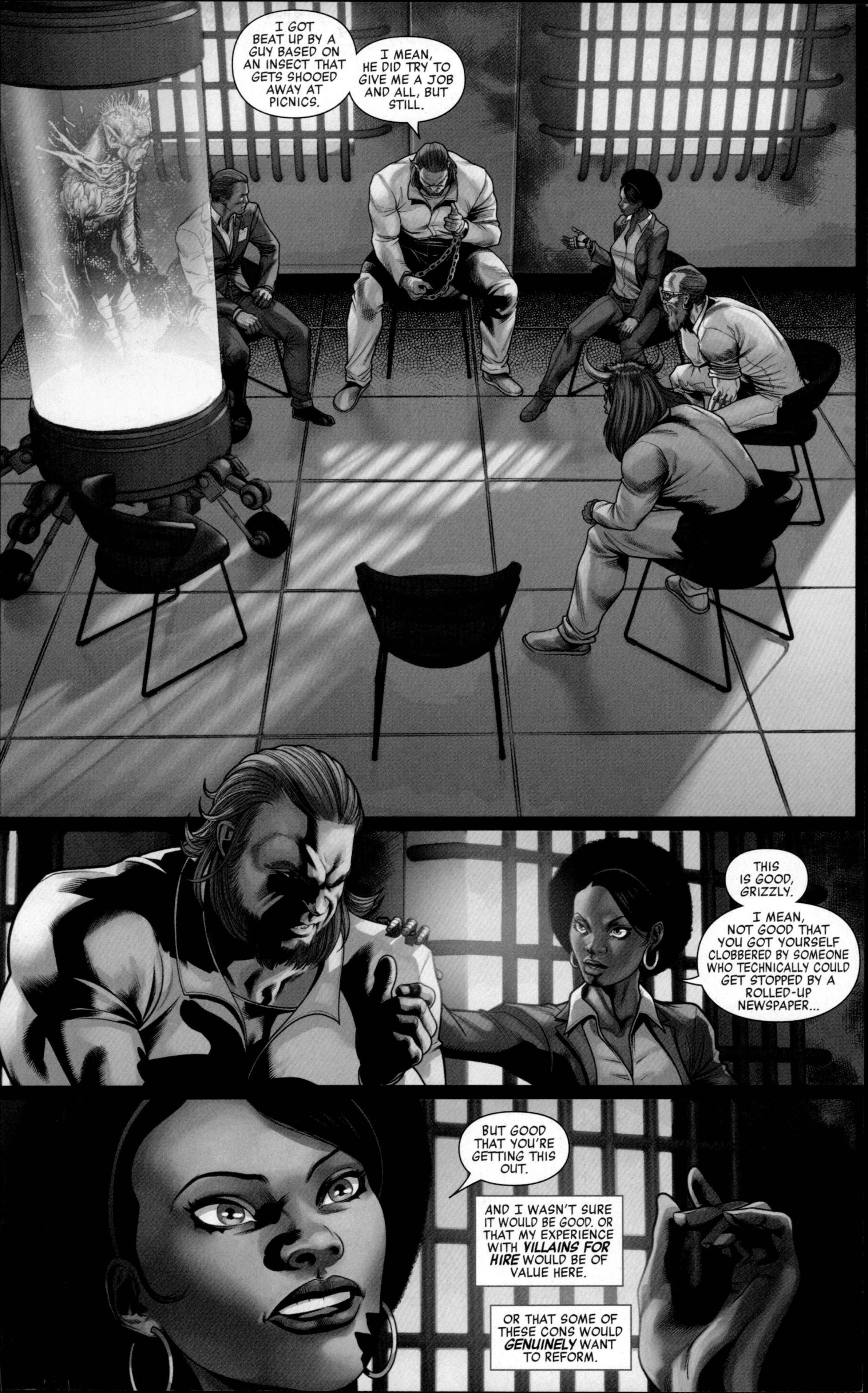
I GOT BEAT UP BY A GUY BASED ON AN INSECT THAT GETS SHOOED AWAY AT PICNICS.
I MEAN, HE DID TRY TO GIVE ME A JOB AND ALL, BUT STILL.
THIS IS GOOD, GRIZZLY.
I MEAN, NOT GOOD THAT YOU GOT YOURSELF CLOBBERED BY SOMEONE WHO TECHNICALLY COULD GET STOPPED BY A ROLLED-UP NEWSPAPER...
BUT GOOD THAT YOU'RE GETTING THIS OUT.
AND I WASN'T SURE IT WOULD BE GOOD. OR THAT MY EXPERIENCE WITH ***VILLAINS FOR HIRE*** WOULD BE OF VALUE HERE.
OR THAT SOME OF THESE CONS WOULD ***GENUINELY*** WANT TO REFORM.

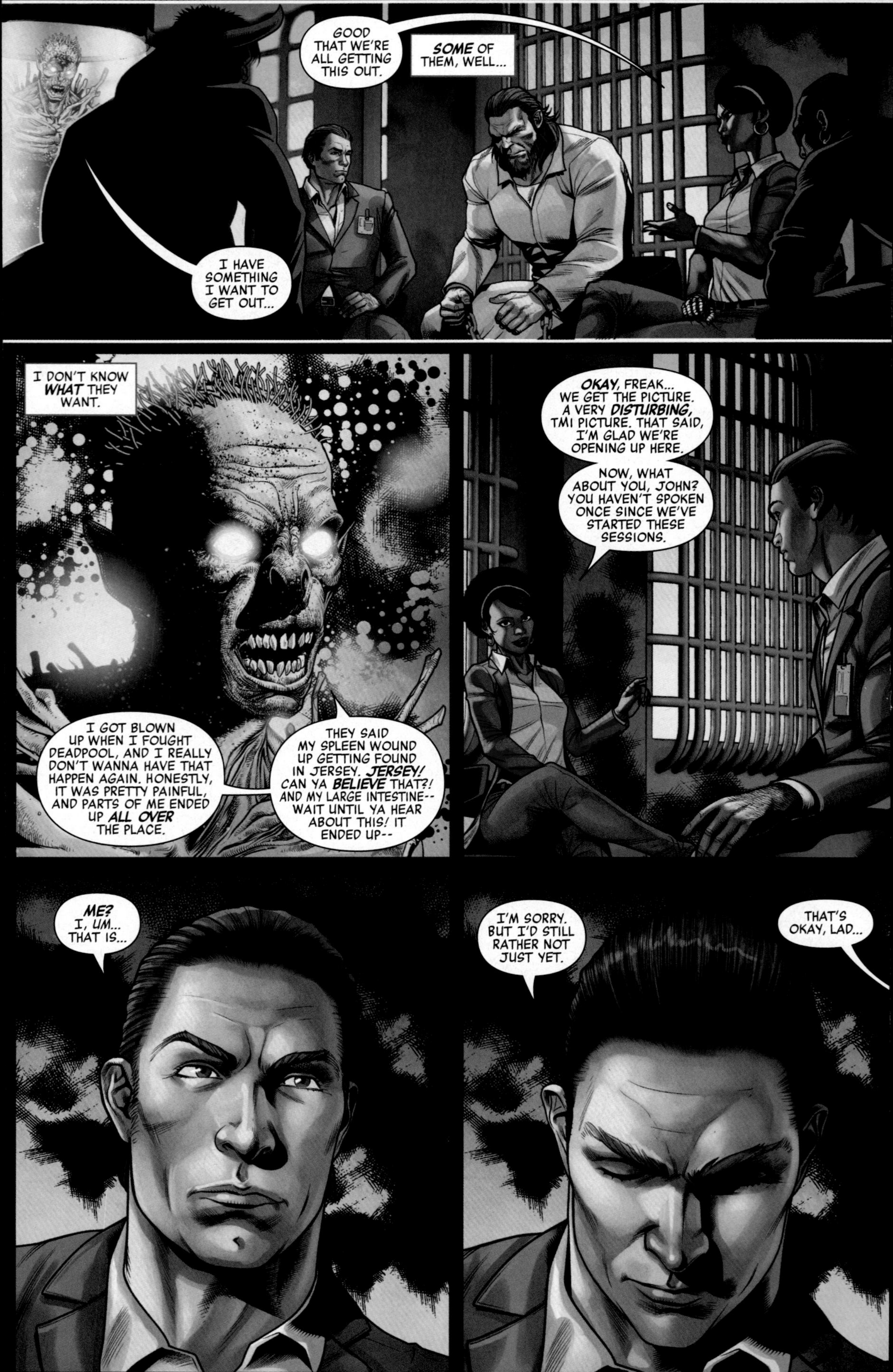
GOOD THAT WE'RE ALL GETTING THIS OUT.
SOME OF THEM, WELL...
I HAVE SOMETHING I WANT TO GET OUT...
I DON'T KNOW WHAT THEY WANT.
I GOT BLOWN UP WHEN I FOUGHT DEADPOOL, AND I REALLY DON'T WANNA HAVE THAT HAPPEN AGAIN. HONESTLY, IT WAS PRETTY PAINFUL, AND PARTS OF ME ENDED UP ALL OVER THE PLACE.
THEY SAID MY SPLEEN WOUND UP GETTING FOUND IN JERSEY. JERSEY! CAN YA BELIEVE THAT?! AND MY LARGE INTESTINE-- WAIT UNTIL YA HEAR ABOUT THIS! IT ENDED UP--
OKAY, FREAK... WE GET THE PICTURE. A VERY DISTURBING, TMI PICTURE. THAT SAID, I'M GLAD WE'RE OPENING UP HERE.
NOW, WHAT ABOUT YOU, JOHN? YOU HAVEN'T SPOKEN ONCE SINCE WE'VE STARTED THESE SESSIONS.
ME? I, UM... THAT IS...
I'M SORRY. BUT I'D STILL RATHER NOT JUST YET.
THAT'S OKAY, LAD...

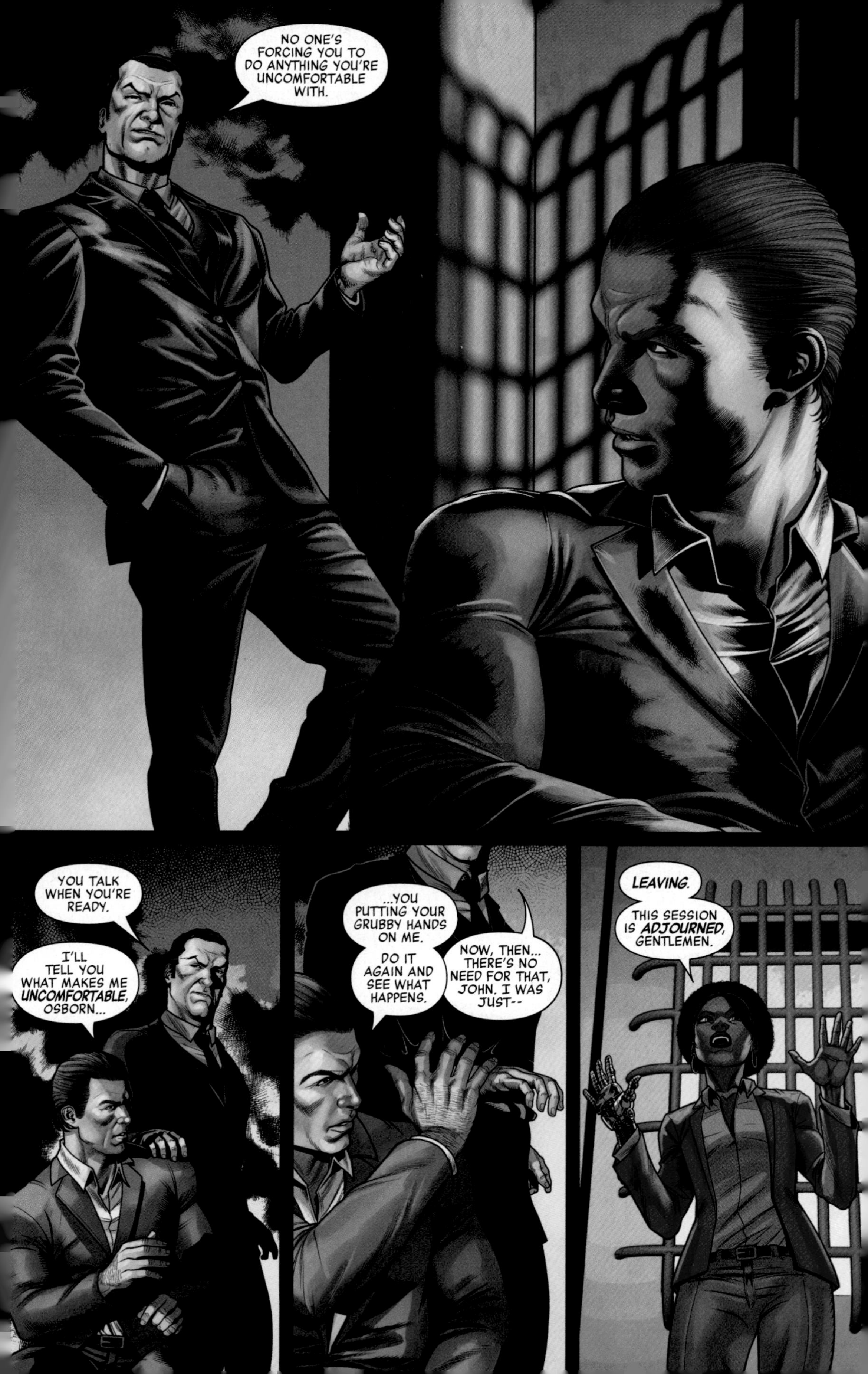
NO ONE'S FORCING YOU TO DO ANYTHING YOU'RE UNCOMFORTABLE WITH.
YOU TALK WHEN YOU'RE READY.
I'LL TELL YOU WHAT MAKES ME *UNCOMFORTABLE*, OSBORN...
...YOU PUTTING YOUR GRUBBY HANDS ON ME.
DO IT AGAIN AND SEE WHAT HAPPENS.
NOW, THEN... THERE'S NO NEED FOR THAT, JOHN. I WAS JUST--
LEAVING.
THIS SESSION IS *ADJOURNED*, GENTLEMEN.

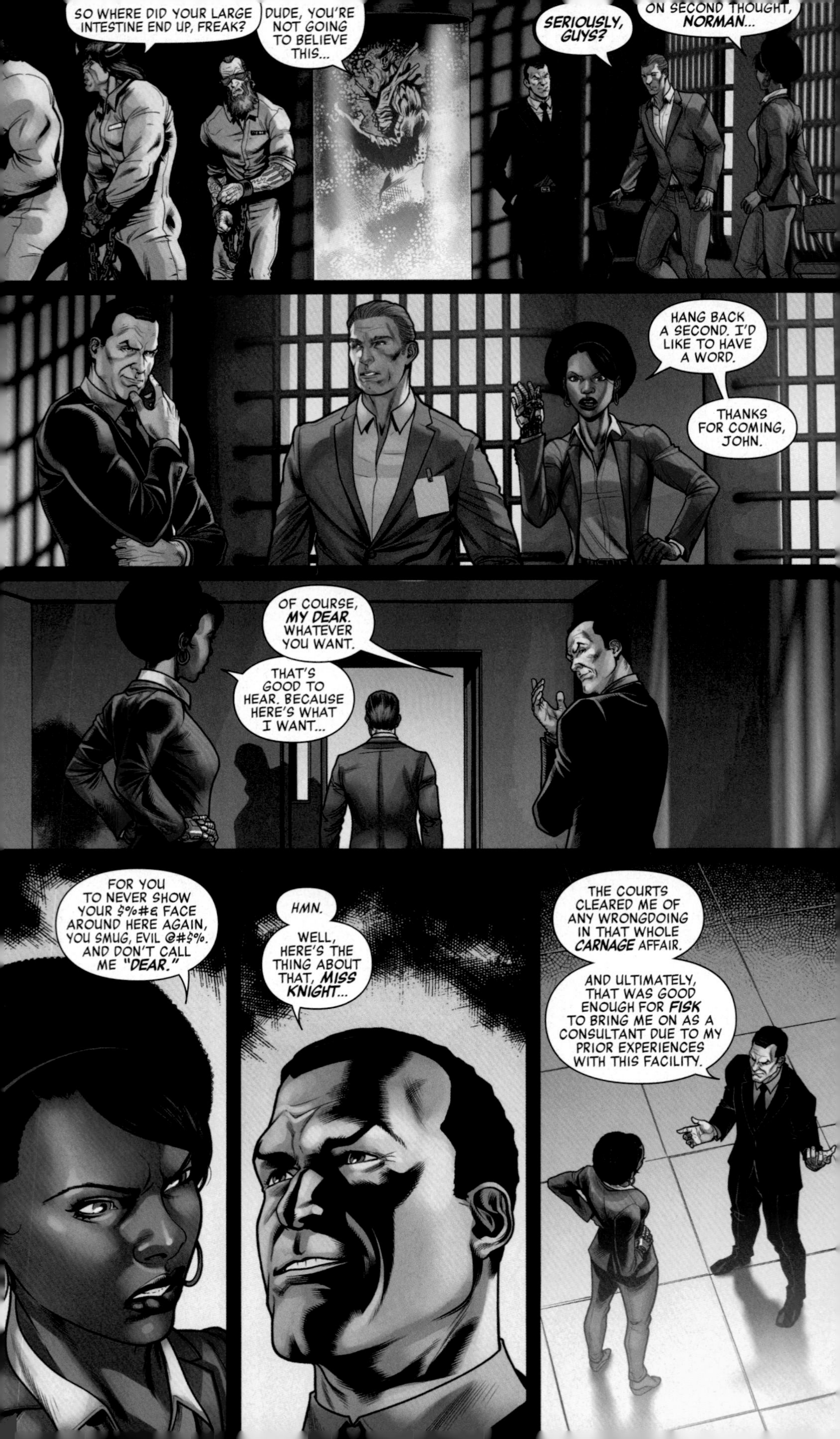
SO WHERE DID YOUR LARGE INTESTINE END UP, FREAK?
DUDE, YOU'RE NOT GOING TO BELIEVE THIS...
SERIOUSLY, GUYS?
ON SECOND THOUGHT, NORMAN...
HANG BACK A SECOND. I'D LIKE TO HAVE A WORD.
THANKS FOR COMING, JOHN.
OF COURSE, MY DEAR. WHATEVER YOU WANT.
THAT'S GOOD TO HEAR. BECAUSE HERE'S WHAT I WANT...
FOR YOU TO NEVER SHOW YOUR $%#& FACE AROUND HERE AGAIN, YOU SMUG, EVIL @#$%. AND DON'T CALL ME "DEAR."
HMN.
WELL, HERE'S THE THING ABOUT THAT, MISS KNIGHT...
THE COURTS CLEARED ME OF ANY WRONGDOING IN THAT WHOLE CARNAGE AFFAIR.
AND ULTIMATELY, THAT WAS GOOD ENOUGH FOR FISK TO BRING ME ON AS A CONSULTANT DUE TO MY PRIOR EXPERIENCES WITH THIS FACILITY.

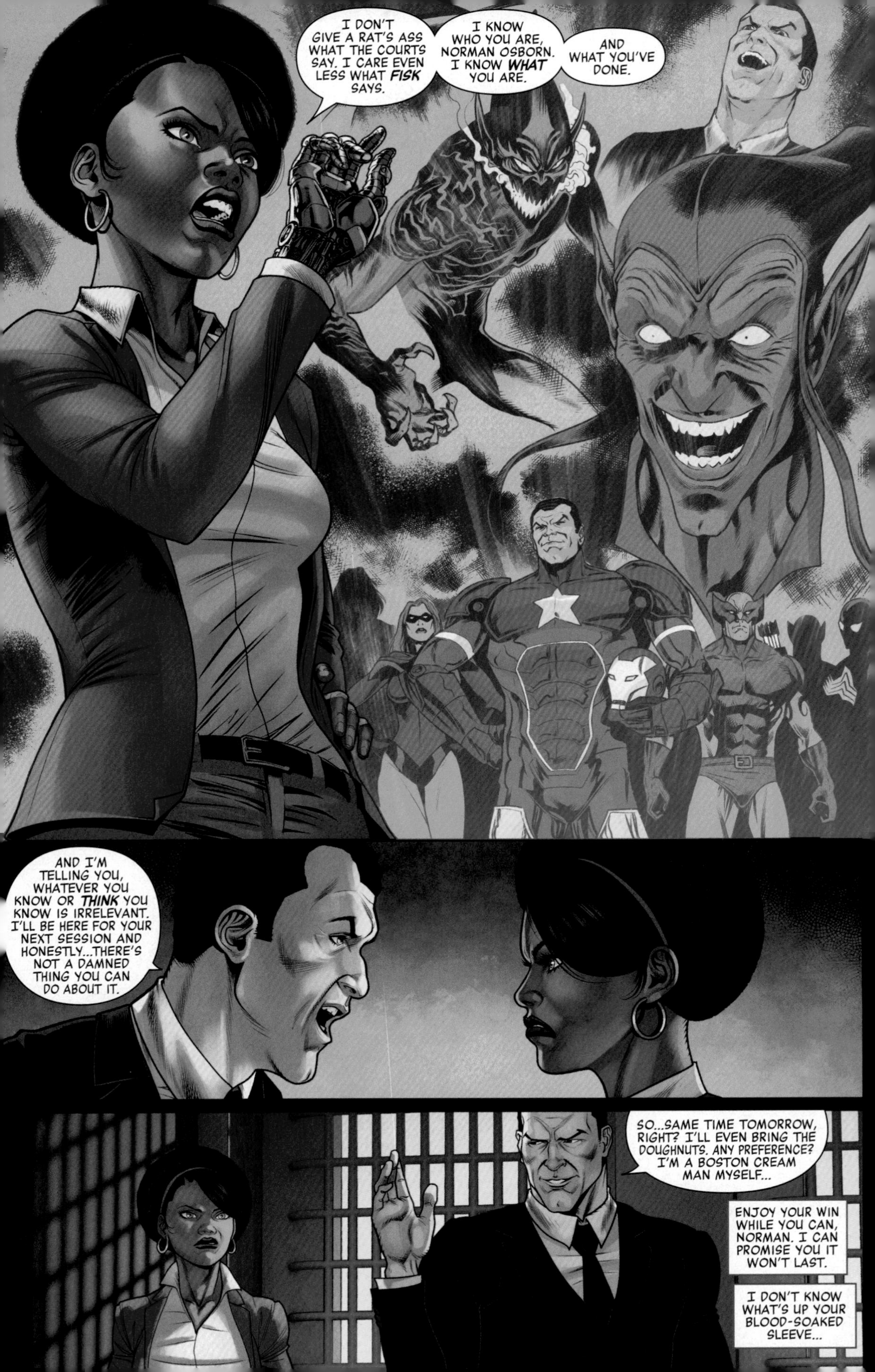
I DON'T GIVE A RAT'S ASS WHAT THE COURTS SAY. I CARE EVEN LESS WHAT FISK SAYS.
I KNOW WHO YOU ARE, NORMAN OSBORN. I KNOW WHAT YOU ARE.
AND WHAT YOU'VE DONE.
AND I'M TELLING YOU, WHATEVER YOU KNOW OR THINK YOU KNOW IS IRRELEVANT. I'LL BE HERE FOR YOUR NEXT SESSION AND HONESTLY...THERE'S NOT A DAMNED THING YOU CAN DO ABOUT IT.
SO...SAME TIME TOMORROW, RIGHT? I'LL EVEN BRING THE DOUGHNUTS. ANY PREFERENCE? I'M A BOSTON CREAM MAN MYSELF...
ENJOY YOUR WIN WHILE YOU CAN, NORMAN. I CAN PROMISE YOU IT WON'T LAST.
I DON'T KNOW WHAT'S UP YOUR BLOOD-SOAKED SLEEVE...

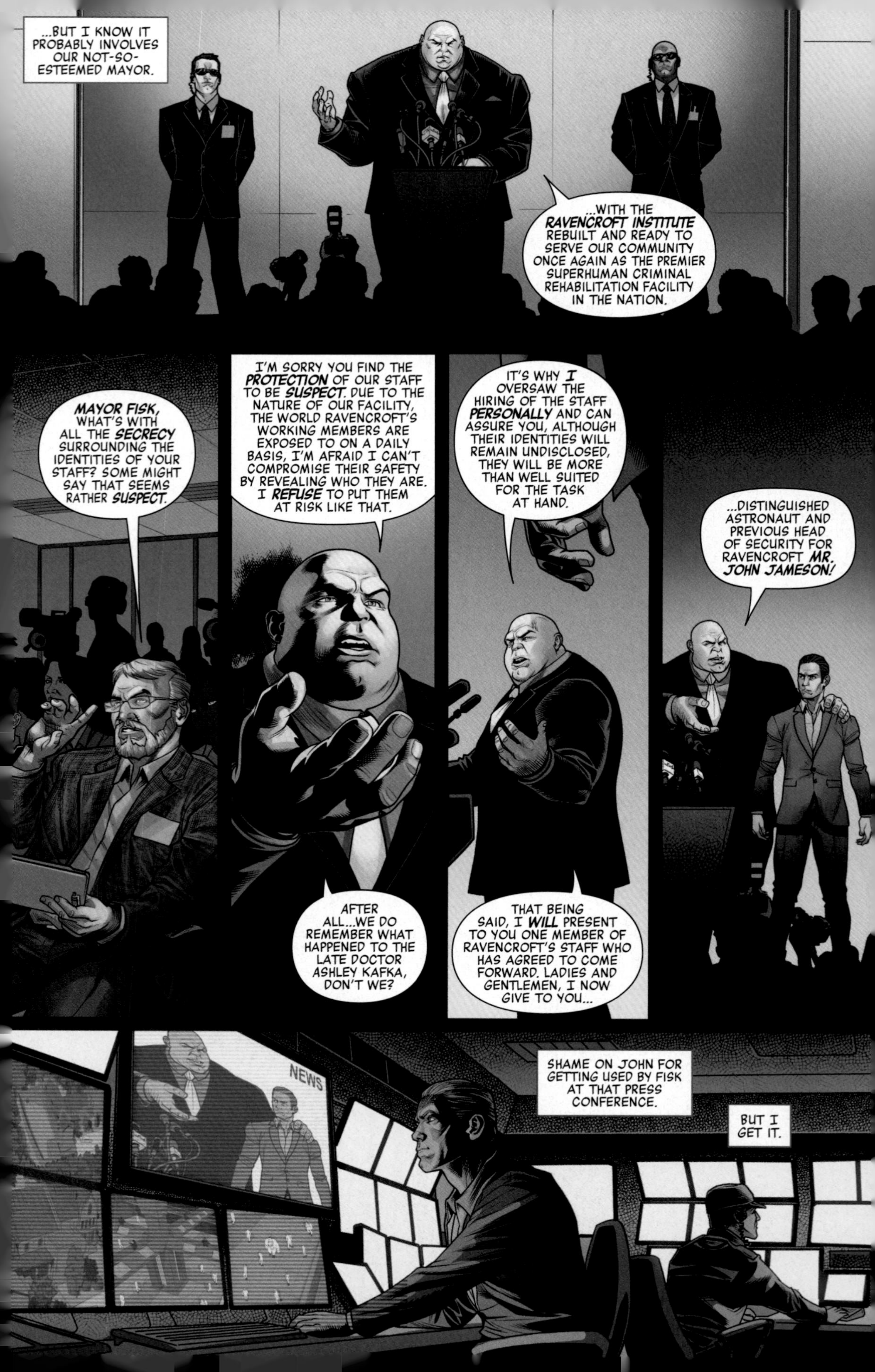
...BUT I KNOW IT PROBABLY INVOLVES OUR NOT-SO-ESTEEMED MAYOR.
...WITH THE RAVENCROFT INSTITUTE REBUILT AND READY TO SERVE OUR COMMUNITY ONCE AGAIN AS THE PREMIER SUPERHUMAN CRIMINAL REHABILITATION FACILITY IN THE NATION.
MAYOR FISK, WHAT'S WITH ALL THE SECRECY SURROUNDING THE IDENTITIES OF YOUR STAFF? SOME MIGHT SAY THAT SEEMS RATHER SUSPECT.
I'M SORRY YOU FIND THE PROTECTION OF OUR STAFF TO BE SUSPECT. DUE TO THE NATURE OF OUR FACILITY, THE WORLD RAVENCROFT'S WORKING MEMBERS ARE EXPOSED TO ON A DAILY BASIS, I'M AFRAID I CAN'T COMPROMISE THEIR SAFETY BY REVEALING WHO THEY ARE. I REFUSE TO PUT THEM AT RISK LIKE THAT.
AFTER ALL...WE DO REMEMBER WHAT HAPPENED TO THE LATE DOCTOR ASHLEY KAFKA, DON'T WE?
IT'S WHY I OVERSAW THE HIRING OF THE STAFF PERSONALLY AND CAN ASSURE YOU, ALTHOUGH THEIR IDENTITIES WILL REMAIN UNDISCLOSED, THEY WILL BE MORE THAN WELL SUITED FOR THE TASK AT HAND.
THAT BEING SAID, I WILL PRESENT TO YOU ONE MEMBER OF RAVENCROFT'S STAFF WHO HAS AGREED TO COME FORWARD. LADIES AND GENTLEMEN, I NOW GIVE TO YOU...
...DISTINGUISHED ASTRONAUT AND PREVIOUS HEAD OF SECURITY FOR RAVENCROFT MR. JOHN JAMESON!
NEWS
SHAME ON JOHN FOR GETTING USED BY FISK AT THAT PRESS CONFERENCE.
BUT I GET IT.

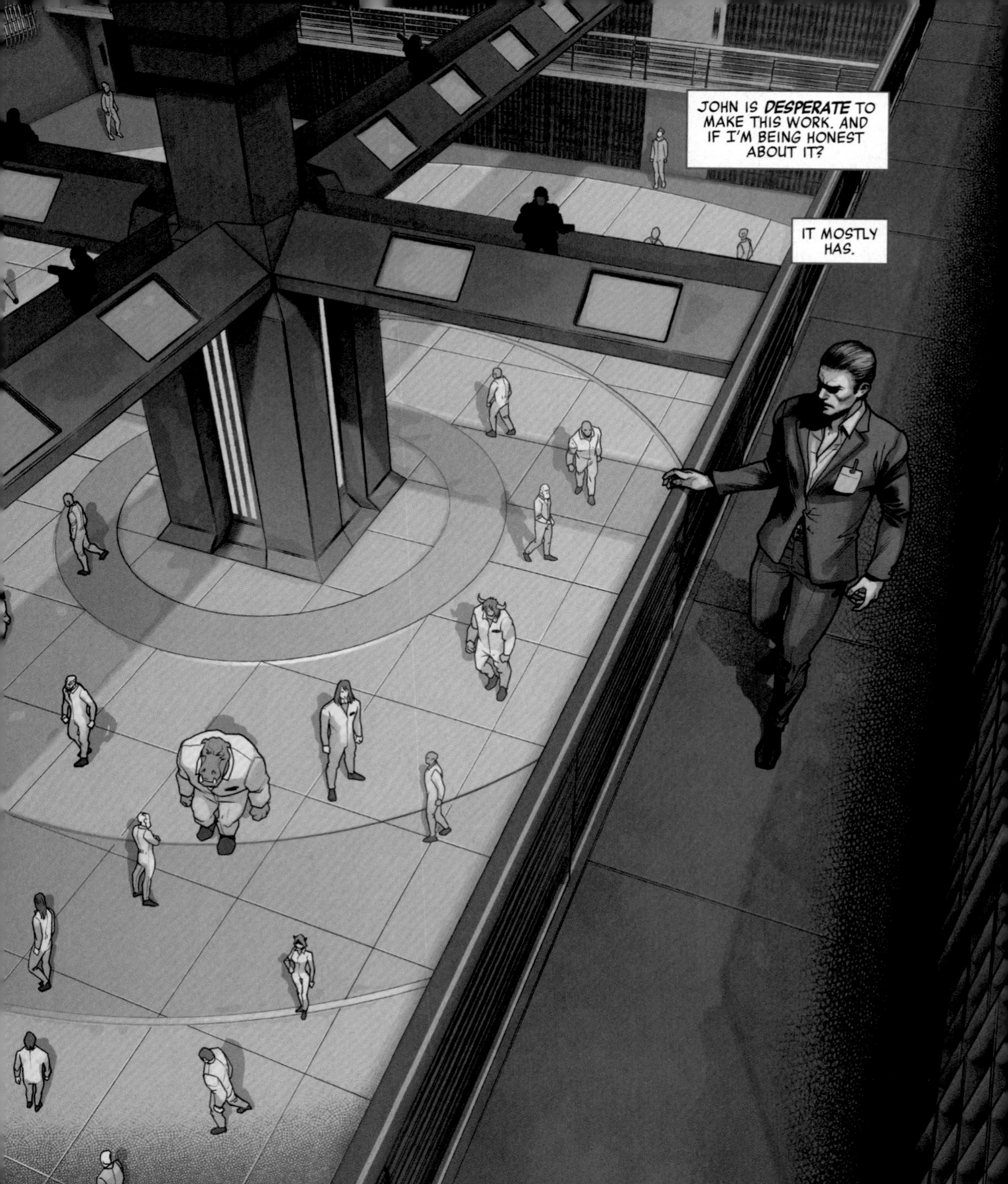
JOHN IS DESPERATE TO MAKE THIS WORK. AND IF I'M BEING HONEST ABOUT IT?
IT MOSTLY HAS.
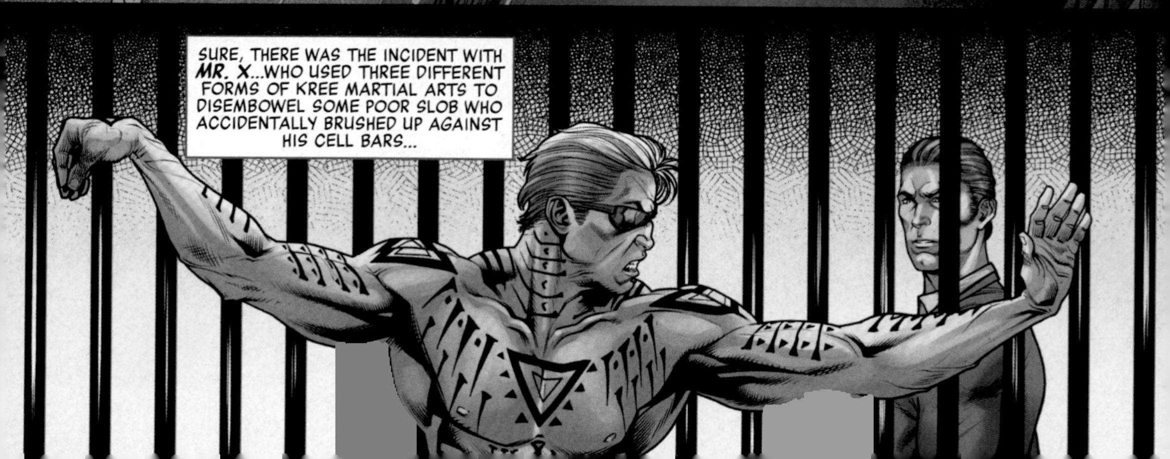
SURE, THERE WAS THE INCIDENT WITH MR. X...WHO USED THREE DIFFERENT FORMS OF KREE MARTIAL ARTS TO DISEMBOWEL SOME POOR SLOB WHO ACCIDENTALLY BRUSHED UP AGAINST HIS CELL BARS...

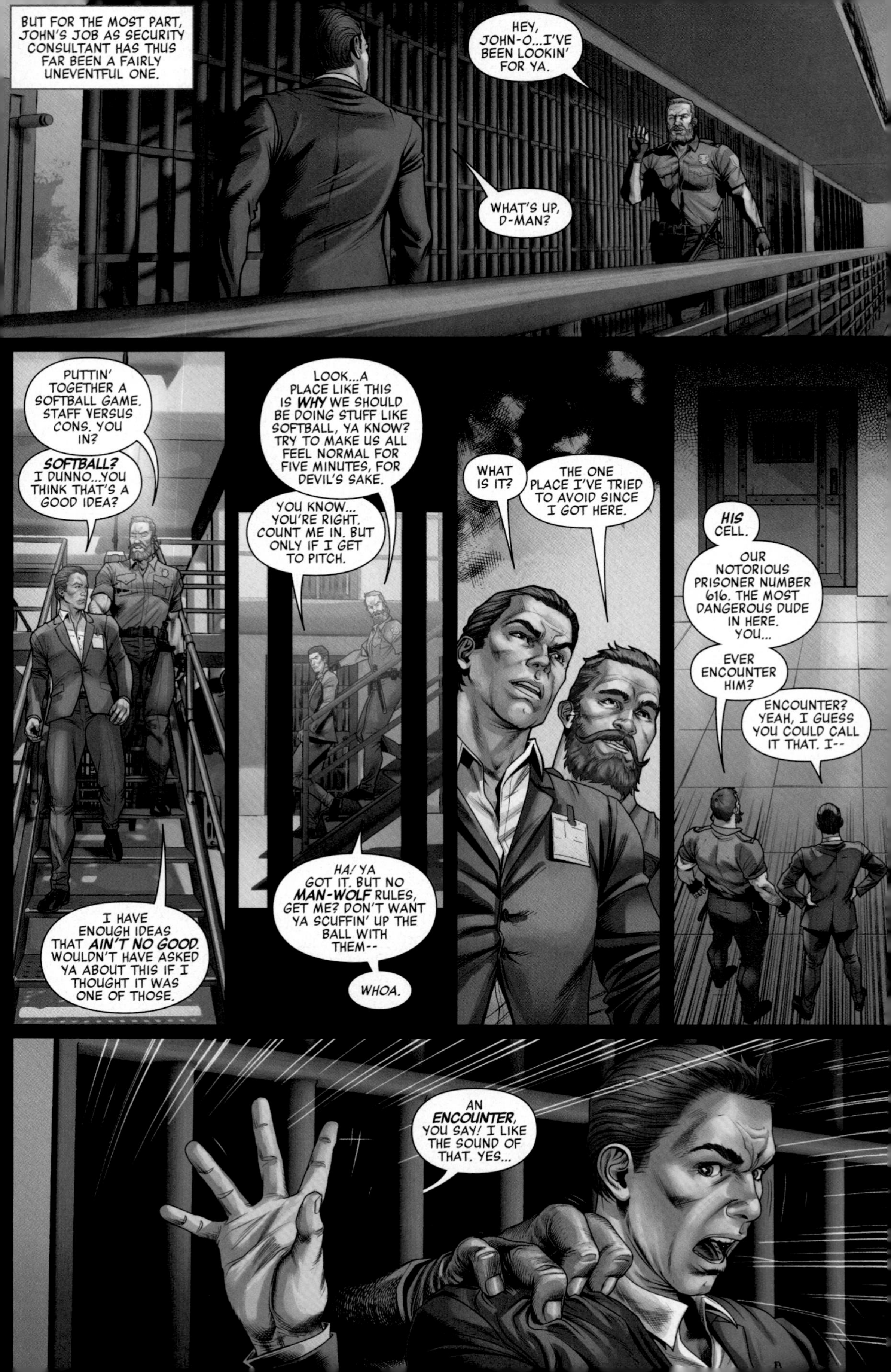
BUT FOR THE MOST PART, JOHN'S JOB AS SECURITY CONSULTANT HAS THUS FAR BEEN A FAIRLY UNEVENTFUL ONE.
HEY, JOHN-O...I'VE BEEN LOOKIN' FOR YA.
WHAT'S UP, D-MAN?
PUTTIN' TOGETHER A SOFTBALL GAME. STAFF VERSUS CONS. YOU IN?
SOFTBALL? I DUNNO...YOU THINK THAT'S A GOOD IDEA?
I HAVE ENOUGH IDEAS THAT AIN'T NO GOOD. WOULDN'T HAVE ASKED YA ABOUT THIS IF I THOUGHT IT WAS ONE OF THOSE.
LOOK...A PLACE LIKE THIS IS WHY WE SHOULD BE DOING STUFF LIKE SOFTBALL, YA KNOW? TRY TO MAKE US ALL FEEL NORMAL FOR FIVE MINUTES, FOR DEVIL'S SAKE.
YOU KNOW... YOU'RE RIGHT. COUNT ME IN. BUT ONLY IF I GET TO PITCH.
HA! YA GOT IT. BUT NO MAN-WOLF RULES, GET ME? DON'T WANT YA SCUFFIN' UP THE BALL WITH THEM--
WHOA.
WHAT IS IT?
THE ONE PLACE I'VE TRIED TO AVOID SINCE I GOT HERE.
HIS CELL.
OUR NOTORIOUS PRISONER NUMBER 616. THE MOST DANGEROUS DUDE IN HERE. YOU...
EVER ENCOUNTER HIM?
ENCOUNTER? YEAH, I GUESS YOU COULD CALL IT THAT. I--
AN ENCOUNTER, YOU SAY! I LIKE THE SOUND OF THAT. YES...

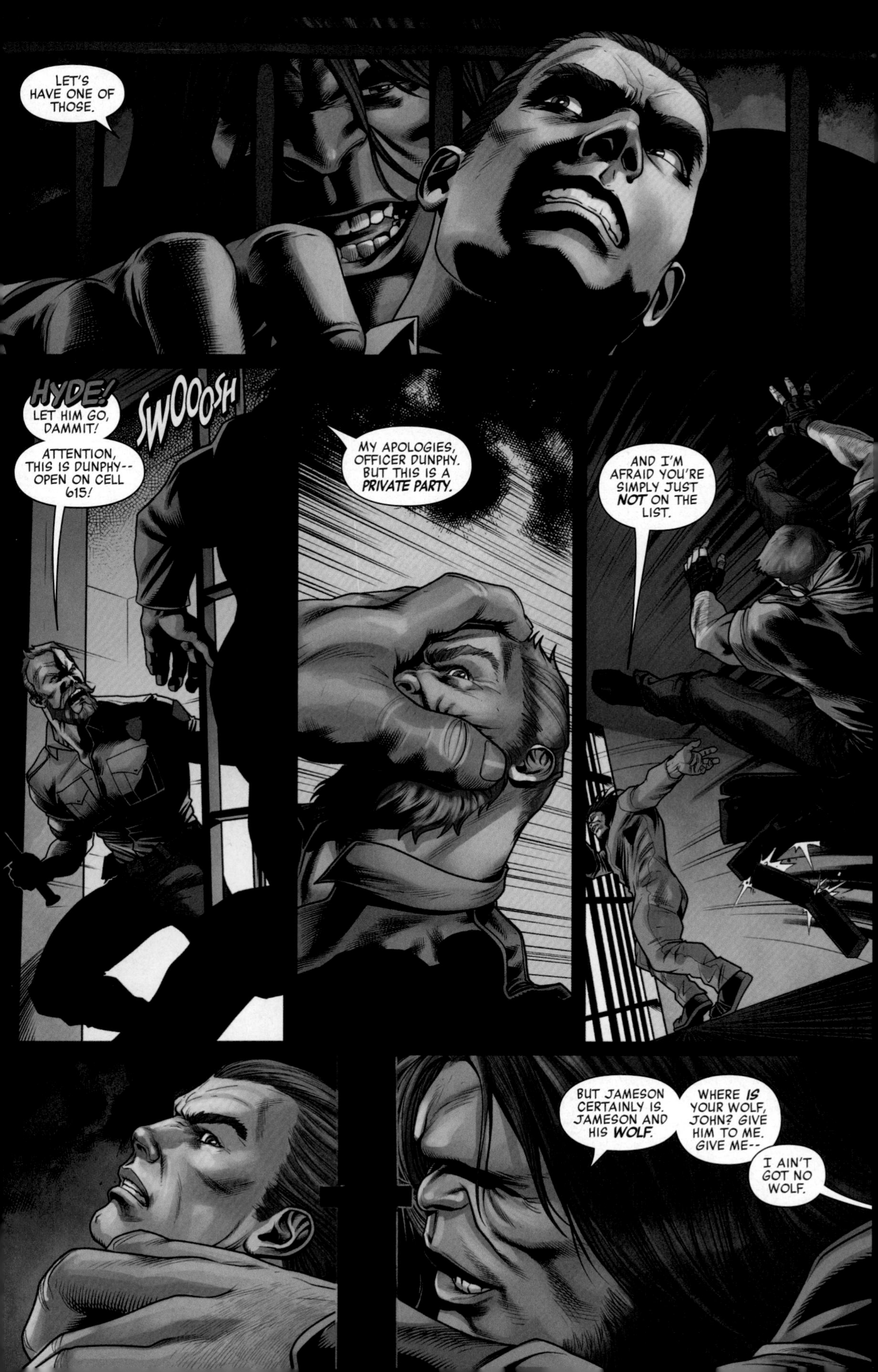
LET'S HAVE ONE OF THOSE.
HYDE!
LET HIM GO, DAMMIT!
ATTENTION, THIS IS DUNPHY-- OPEN ON CELL 615!
SWOOOSH
MY APOLOGIES, OFFICER DUNPHY. BUT THIS IS A PRIVATE PARTY.
AND I'M AFRAID YOU'RE SIMPLY JUST NOT ON THE LIST.
BUT JAMESON CERTAINLY IS. JAMESON AND HIS WOLF.
WHERE IS YOUR WOLF, JOHN? GIVE HIM TO ME. GIVE ME--
I AIN'T GOT NO WOLF.

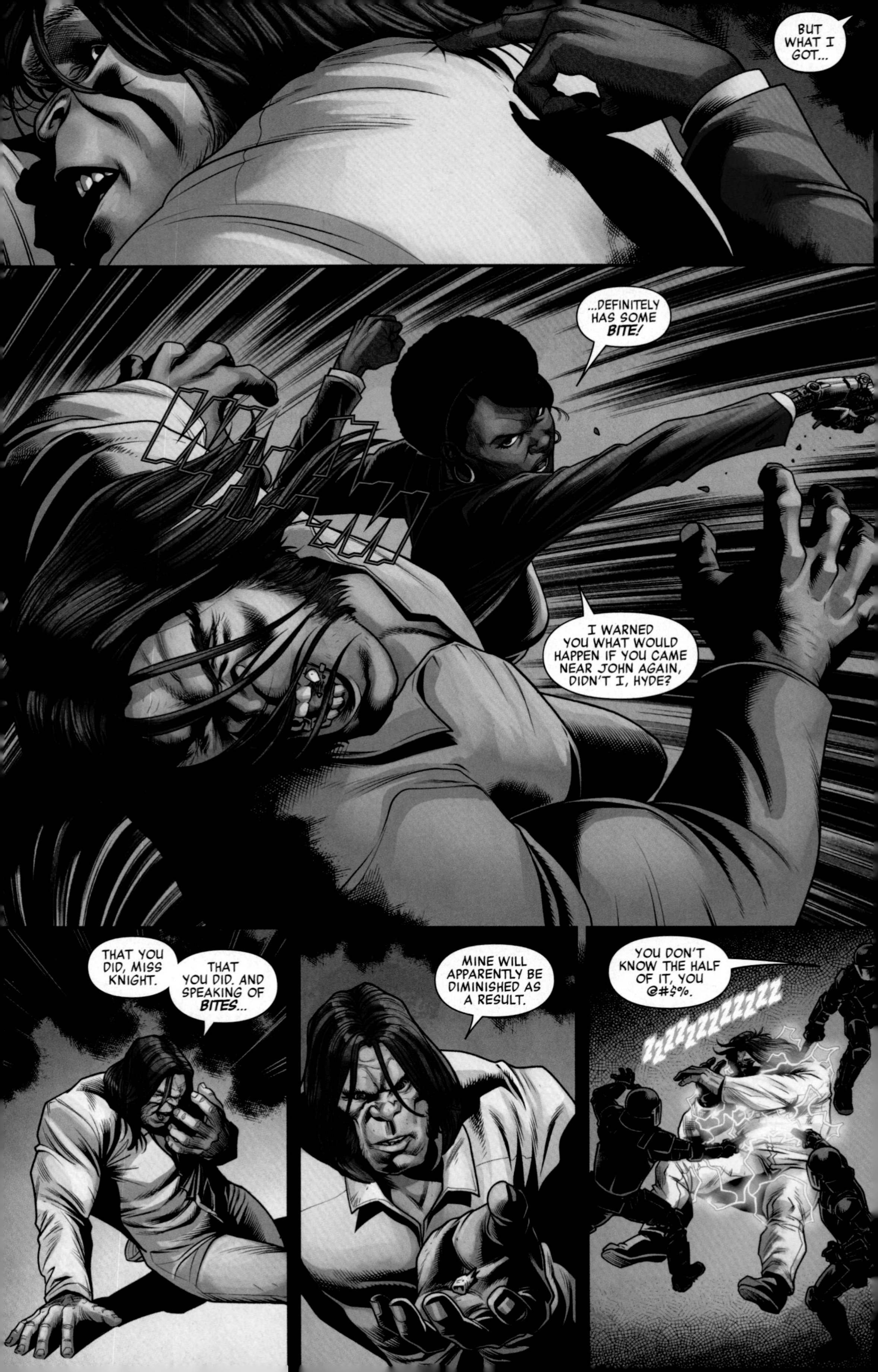
BUT WHAT I GOT...
...DEFINITELY HAS SOME BITE!
I WARNED YOU WHAT WOULD HAPPEN IF YOU CAME NEAR JOHN AGAIN, DIDN'T I, HYDE?
THAT YOU DID, MISS KNIGHT.
THAT YOU DID. AND SPEAKING OF BITES...
MINE WILL APPARENTLY BE DIMINISHED AS A RESULT.
YOU DON'T KNOW THE HALF OF IT, YOU @#$%.
ZZZZZZZZZZZZ

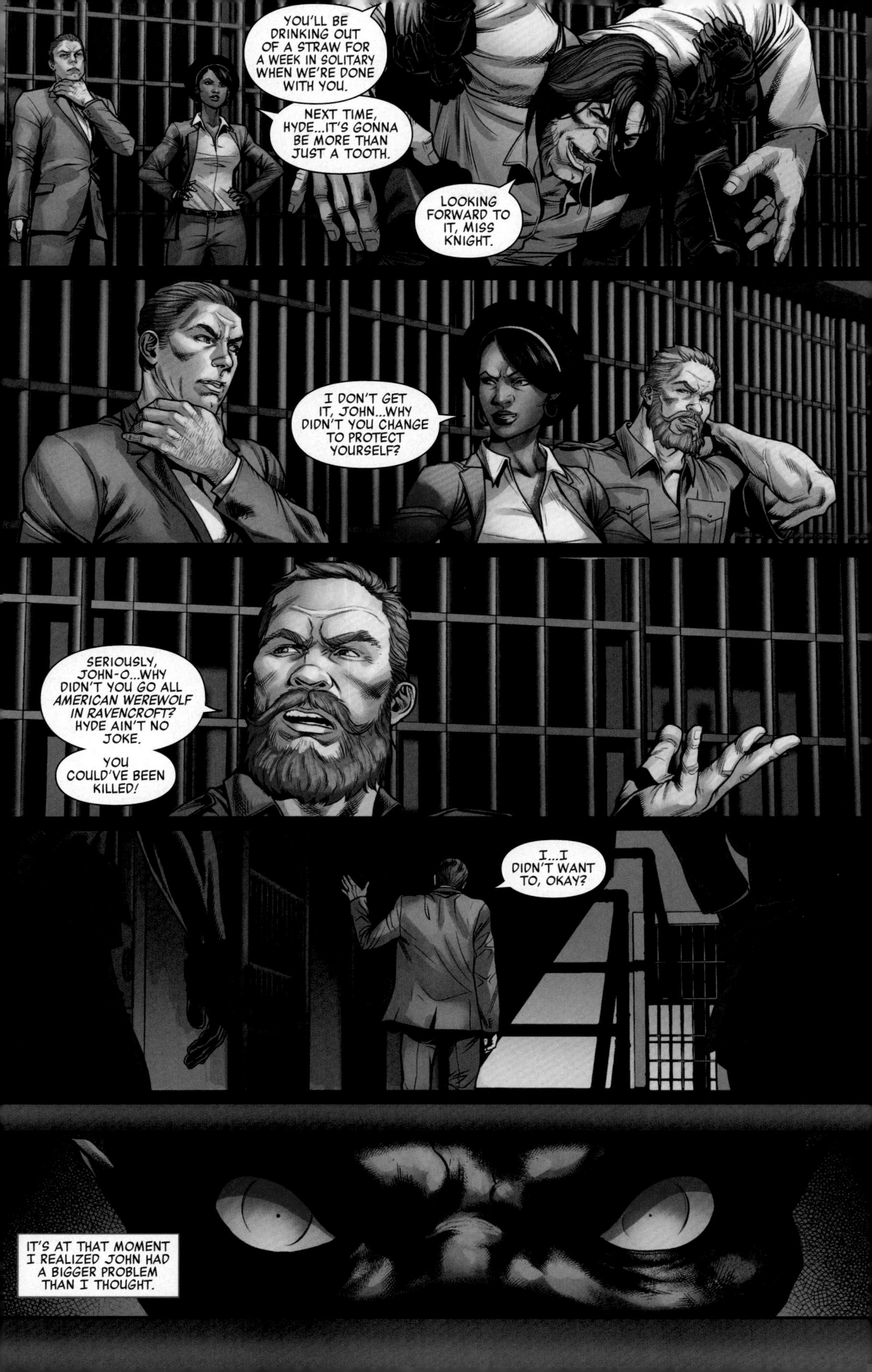
YOU'LL BE DRINKING OUT OF A STRAW FOR A WEEK IN SOLITARY WHEN WE'RE DONE WITH YOU.
NEXT TIME, HYDE...IT'S GONNA BE MORE THAN JUST A TOOTH.
LOOKING FORWARD TO IT, MISS KNIGHT.
I DON'T GET IT, JOHN...WHY DIDN'T YOU CHANGE TO PROTECT YOURSELF?
SERIOUSLY, JOHN-O...WHY DIDN'T YOU GO ALL *AMERICAN WEREWOLF IN RAVENCROFT?* HYDE AIN'T NO JOKE.
YOU COULD'VE BEEN KILLED!
I...I DIDN'T WANT TO, OKAY?
IT'S AT THAT MOMENT I REALIZED JOHN HAD A BIGGER PROBLEM THAN I THOUGHT.

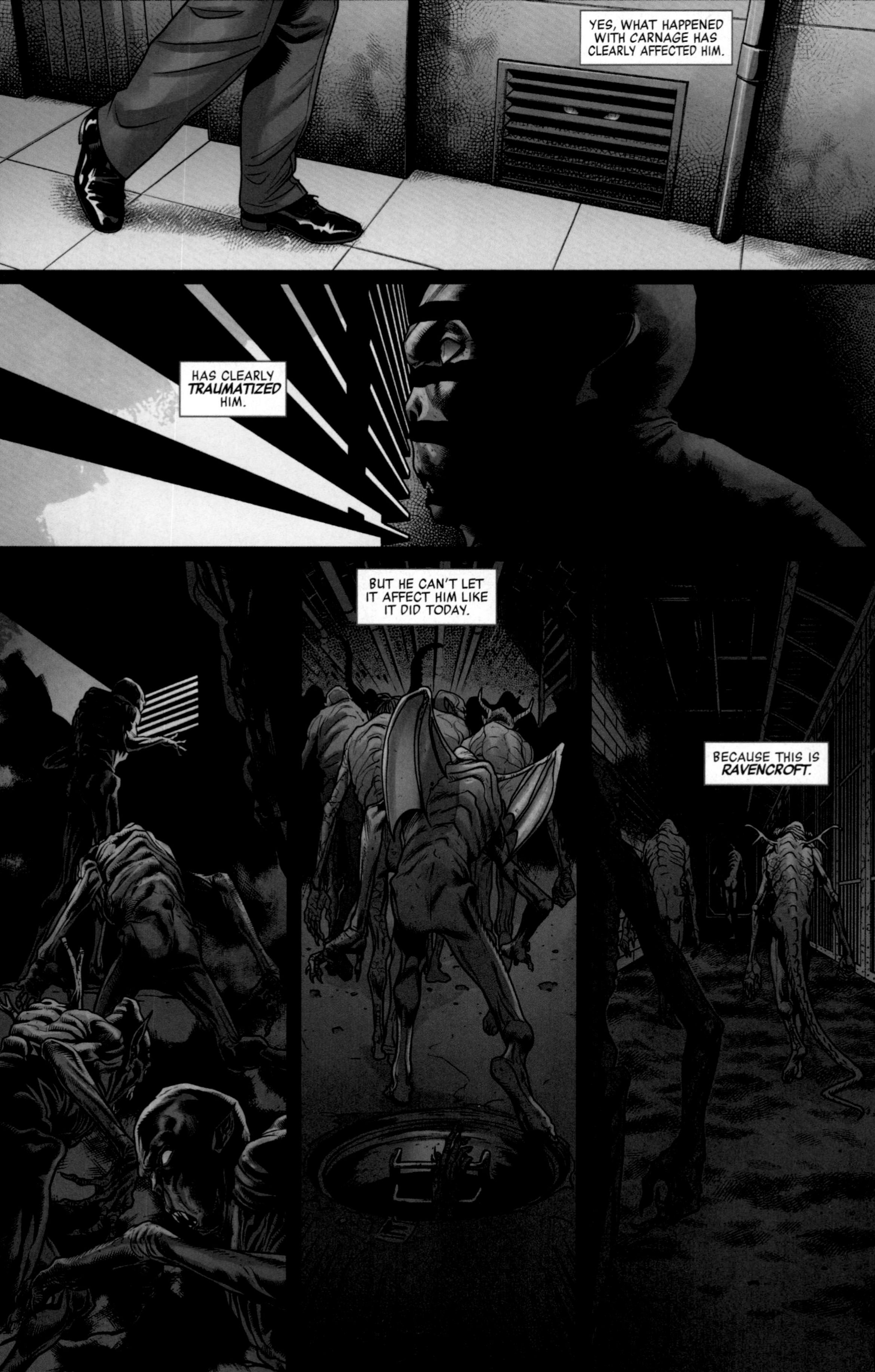
YES, WHAT HAPPENED WITH CARNAGE HAS CLEARLY AFFECTED HIM.
HAS CLEARLY *TRAUMATIZED* HIM.
BUT HE CAN'T LET IT AFFECT HIM LIKE IT DID TODAY.
BECAUSE THIS IS *RAVENCROFT.*

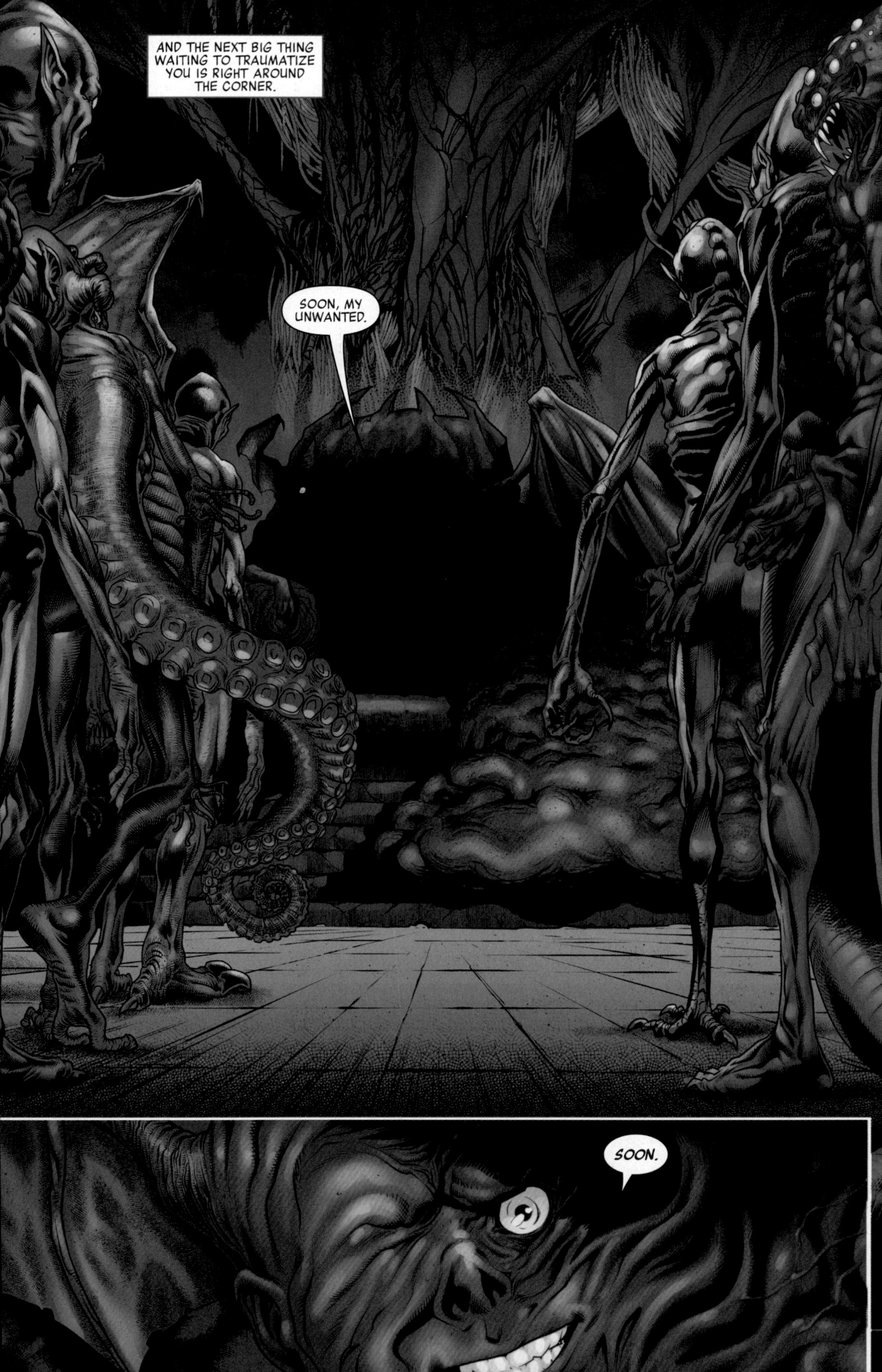
AND THE NEXT BIG THING WAITING TO TRAUMATIZE YOU IS RIGHT AROUND THE CORNER.
SOON, MY UNWANTED.
SOON.

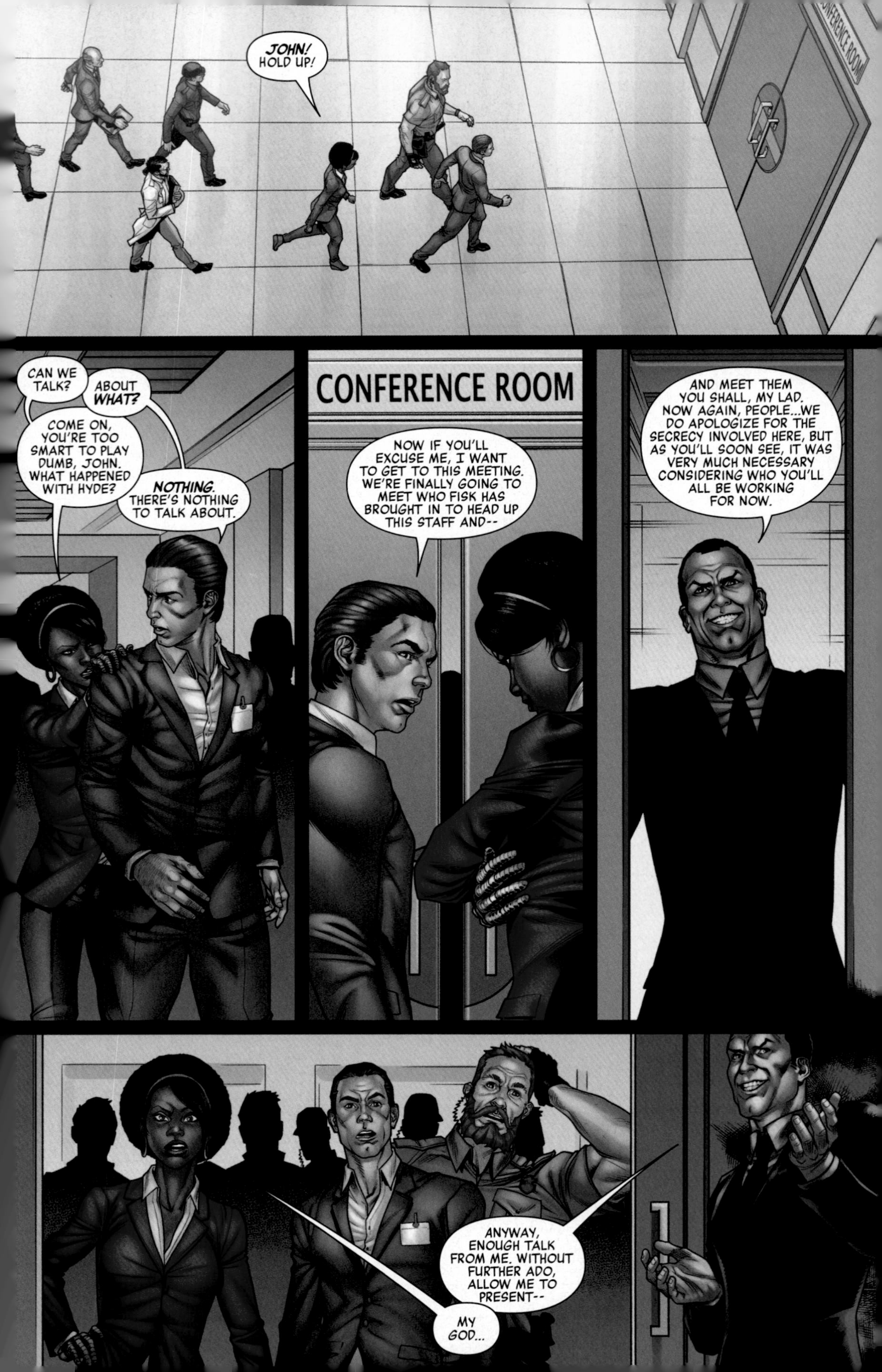
JOHN! HOLD UP!
CONFERENCE ROOM
CAN WE TALK?
ABOUT WHAT?
COME ON, YOU'RE TOO SMART TO PLAY DUMB, JOHN. WHAT HAPPENED WITH HYDE?
NOTHING. THERE'S NOTHING TO TALK ABOUT.
CONFERENCE ROOM
NOW IF YOU'LL EXCUSE ME, I WANT TO GET TO THIS MEETING. WE'RE FINALLY GOING TO MEET WHO FISK HAS BROUGHT IN TO HEAD UP THIS STAFF AND--
AND MEET THEM YOU SHALL, MY LAD. NOW AGAIN, PEOPLE...WE DO APOLOGIZE FOR THE SECRECY INVOLVED HERE, BUT AS YOU'LL SOON SEE, IT WAS VERY MUCH NECESSARY CONSIDERING WHO YOU'LL ALL BE WORKING FOR NOW.
ANYWAY, ENOUGH TALK FROM ME. WITHOUT FURTHER ADO, ALLOW ME TO PRESENT--
MY GOD...

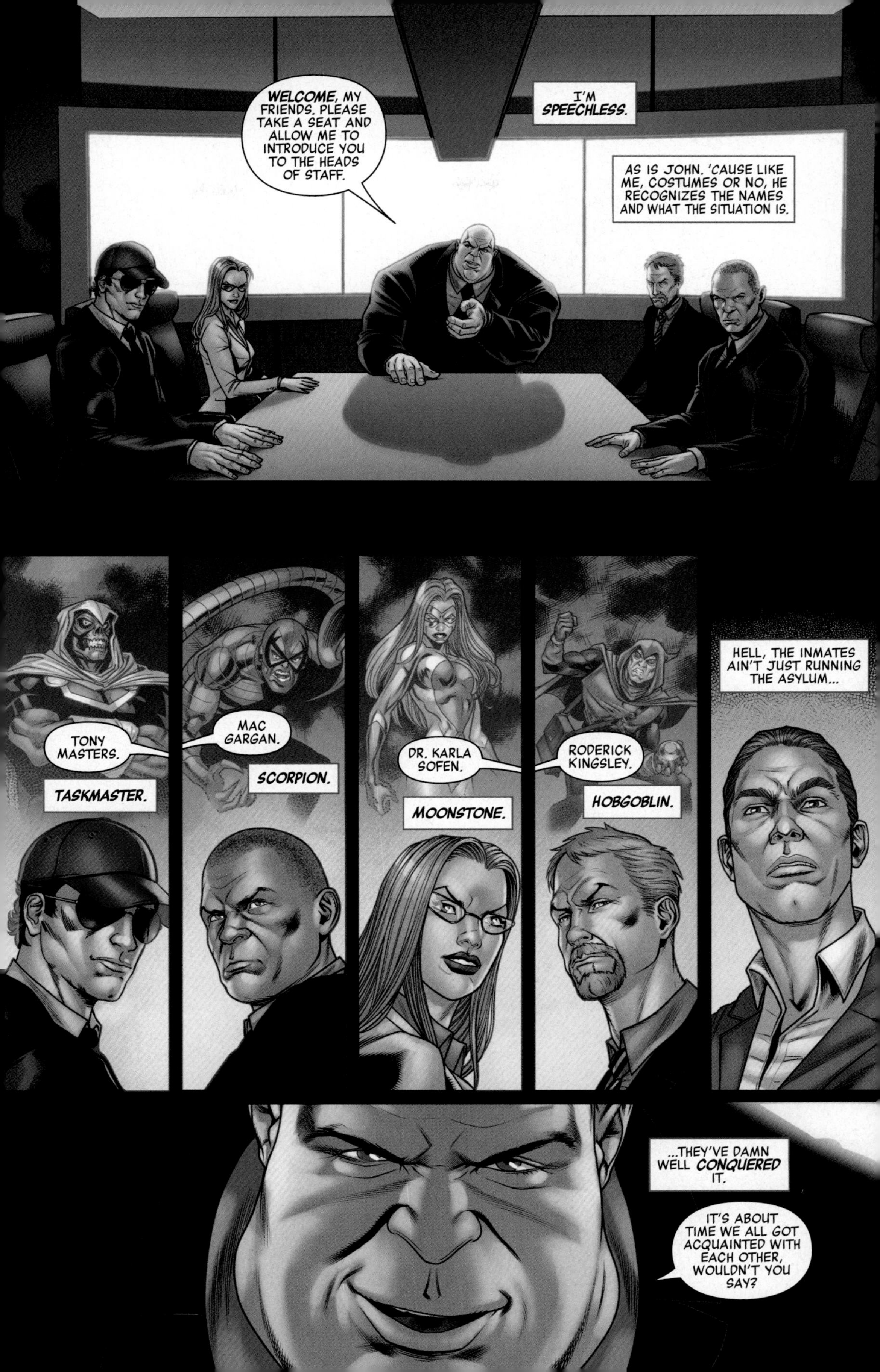
WELCOME, MY FRIENDS. PLEASE TAKE A SEAT AND ALLOW ME TO INTRODUCE YOU TO THE HEADS OF STAFF.
I'M SPEECHLESS.
AS IS JOHN. 'CAUSE LIKE ME, COSTUMES OR NO, HE RECOGNIZES THE NAMES AND WHAT THE SITUATION IS.
TONY MASTERS.
TASKMASTER.
MAC GARGAN.
SCORPION.
DR. KARLA SOFEN.
MOONSTONE.
RODERICK KINGSLEY.
HOBGOBLIN.
HELL, THE INMATES AIN'T JUST RUNNING THE ASYLUM...
...THEY'VE DAMN WELL CONQUERED IT.
IT'S ABOUT TIME WE ALL GOT ACQUAINTED WITH EACH OTHER, WOULDN'T YOU SAY?

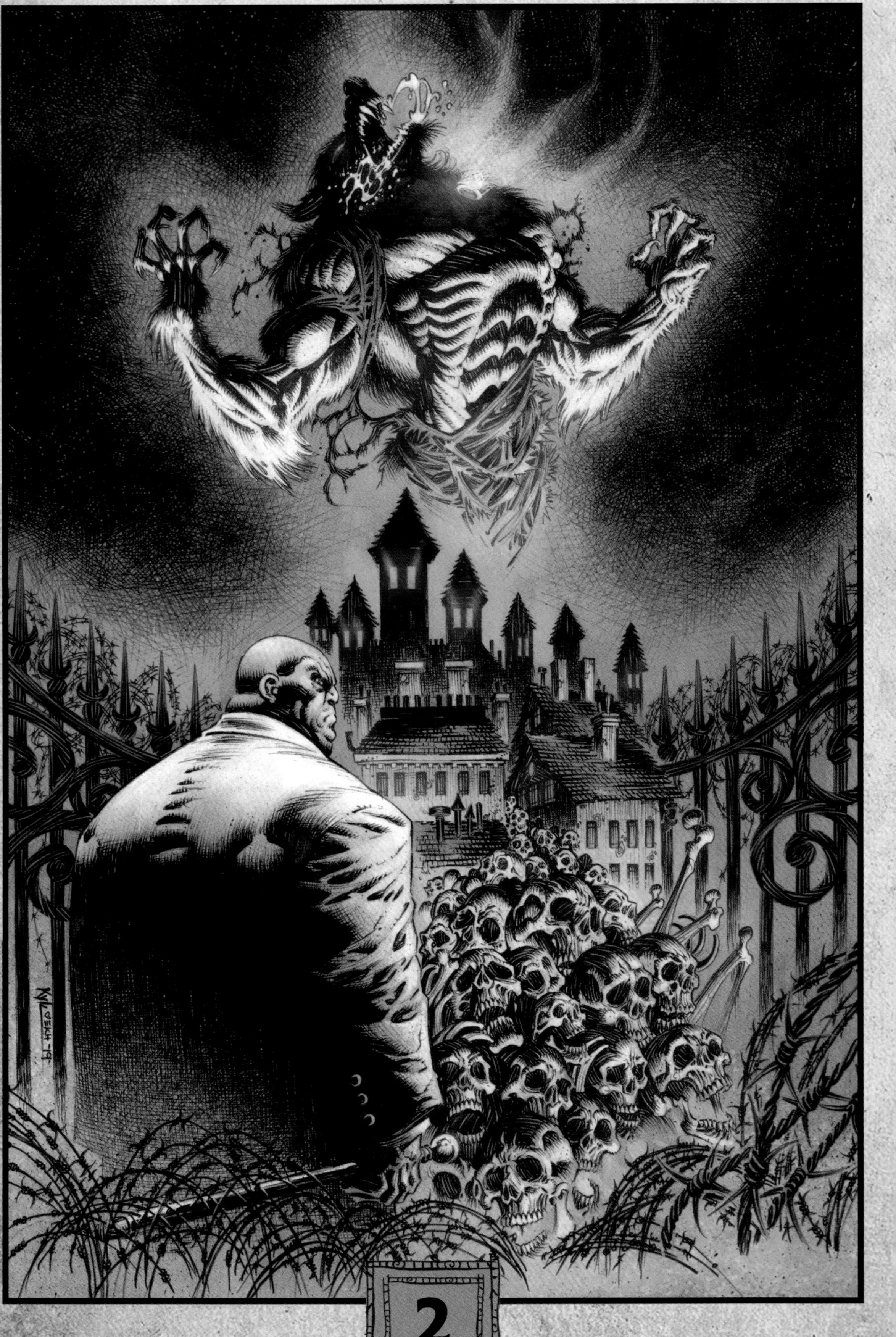

2

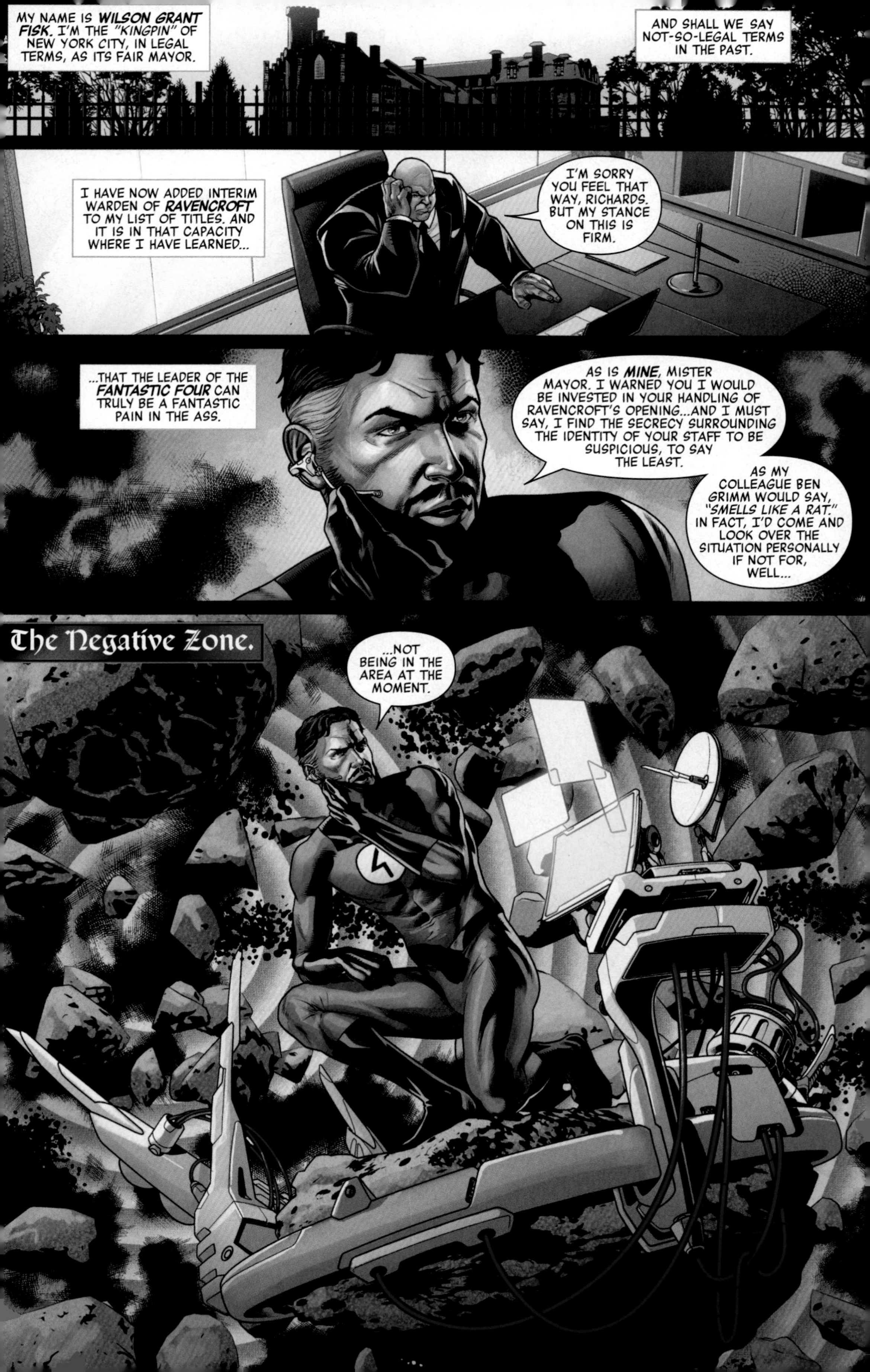

MY NAME IS WILSON GRANT FISK. I'M THE "KINGPIN" OF NEW YORK CITY, IN LEGAL TERMS, AS ITS FAIR MAYOR.
AND SHALL WE SAY NOT-SO-LEGAL TERMS IN THE PAST.
I HAVE NOW ADDED INTERIM WARDEN OF RAVENCROFT TO MY LIST OF TITLES. AND IT IS IN THAT CAPACITY WHERE I HAVE LEARNED...
I'M SORRY YOU FEEL THAT WAY, RICHARDS. BUT MY STANCE ON THIS IS FIRM.
...THAT THE LEADER OF THE FANTASTIC FOUR CAN TRULY BE A FANTASTIC PAIN IN THE ASS.
AS IS MINE, MISTER MAYOR. I WARNED YOU I WOULD BE INVESTED IN YOUR HANDLING OF RAVENCROFT'S OPENING...AND I MUST SAY, I FIND THE SECRECY SURROUNDING THE IDENTITY OF YOUR STAFF TO BE SUSPICIOUS, TO SAY THE LEAST.
AS MY COLLEAGUE BEN GRIMM WOULD SAY, "SMELLS LIKE A RAT." IN FACT, I'D COME AND LOOK OVER THE SITUATION PERSONALLY IF NOT FOR, WELL...
The Negative Zone.
...NOT BEING IN THE AREA AT THE MOMENT.

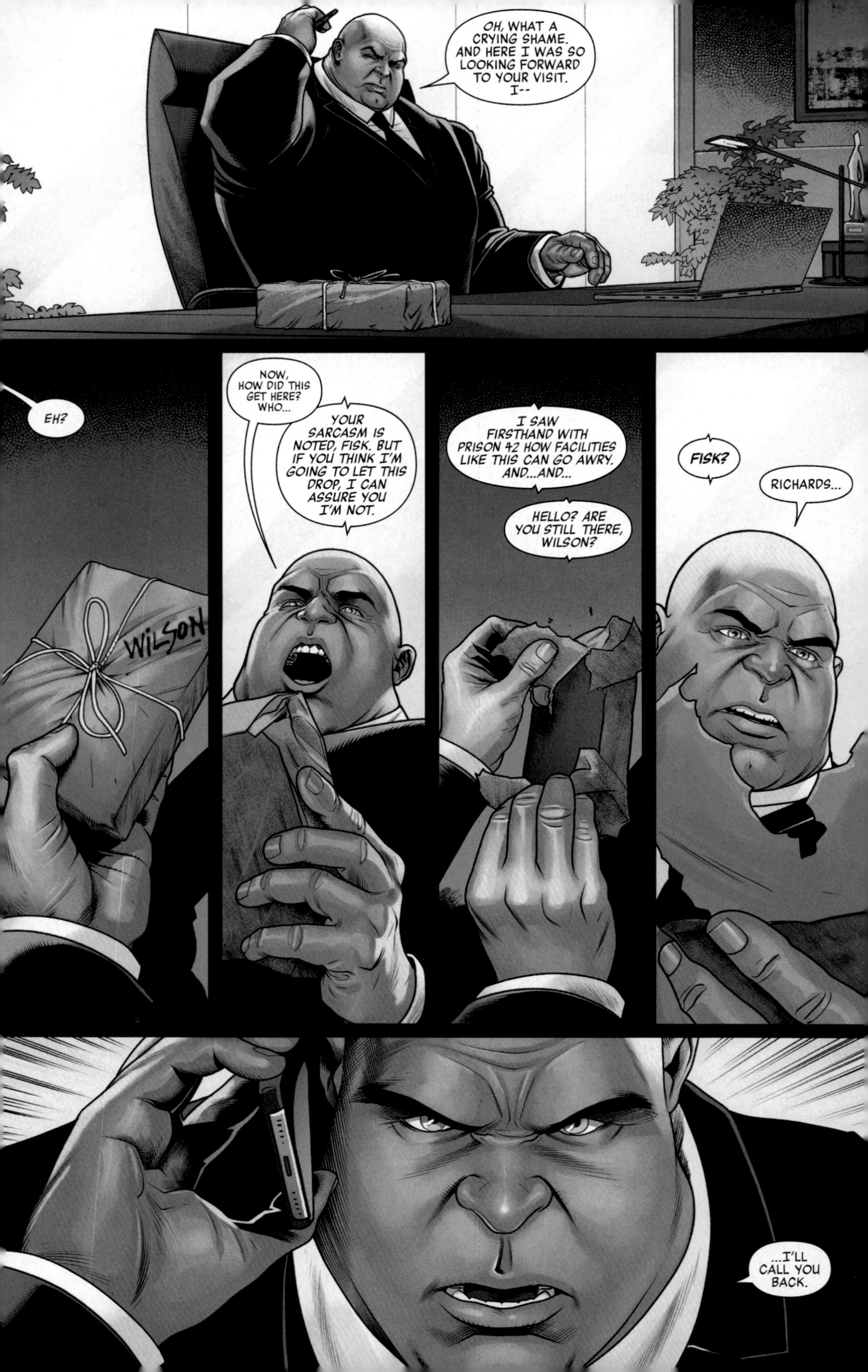
OH, WHAT A CRYING SHAME. AND HERE I WAS SO LOOKING FORWARD TO YOUR VISIT. I--
EH?
NOW, HOW DID THIS GET HERE? WHO...
YOUR SARCASM IS NOTED, FISK. BUT IF YOU THINK I'M GOING TO LET THIS DROP, I CAN ASSURE YOU I'M NOT.
WILSON
I SAW FIRSTHAND WITH PRISON 42 HOW FACILITIES LIKE THIS CAN GO AWRY. AND...AND...
HELLO? ARE YOU STILL THERE, WILSON?
FISK?
RICHARDS...
...I'LL CALL YOU BACK.

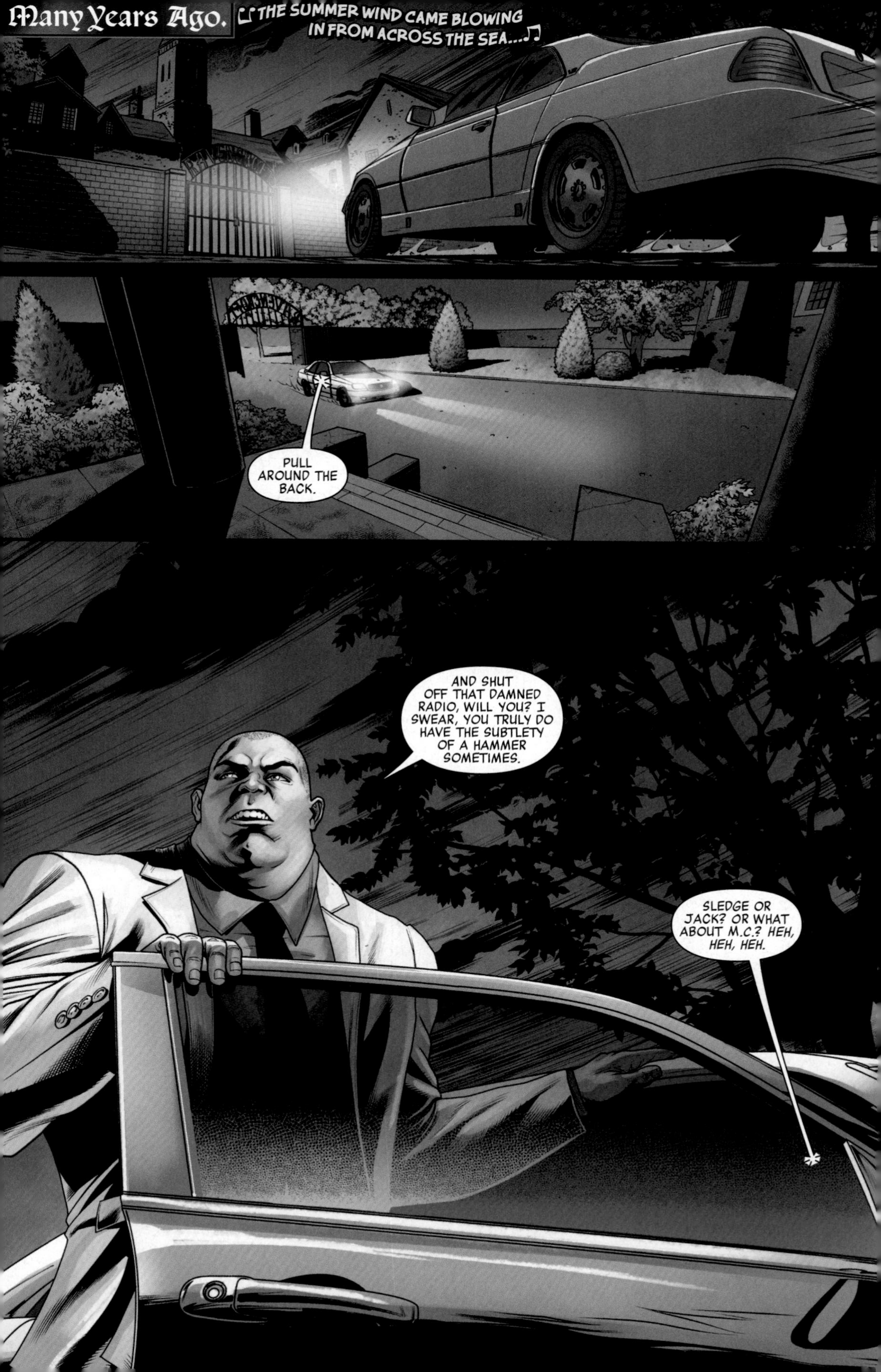
Many Years Ago.
♫THE SUMMER WIND CAME BLOWING IN FROM ACROSS THE SEA...♫
PULL AROUND THE BACK.
AND SHUT OFF THAT DAMNED RADIO, WILL YOU? I SWEAR, YOU TRULY DO HAVE THE SUBTLETY OF A HAMMER SOMETIMES.
SLEDGE OR JACK? OR WHAT ABOUT M.C.? HEH, HEH, HEH.

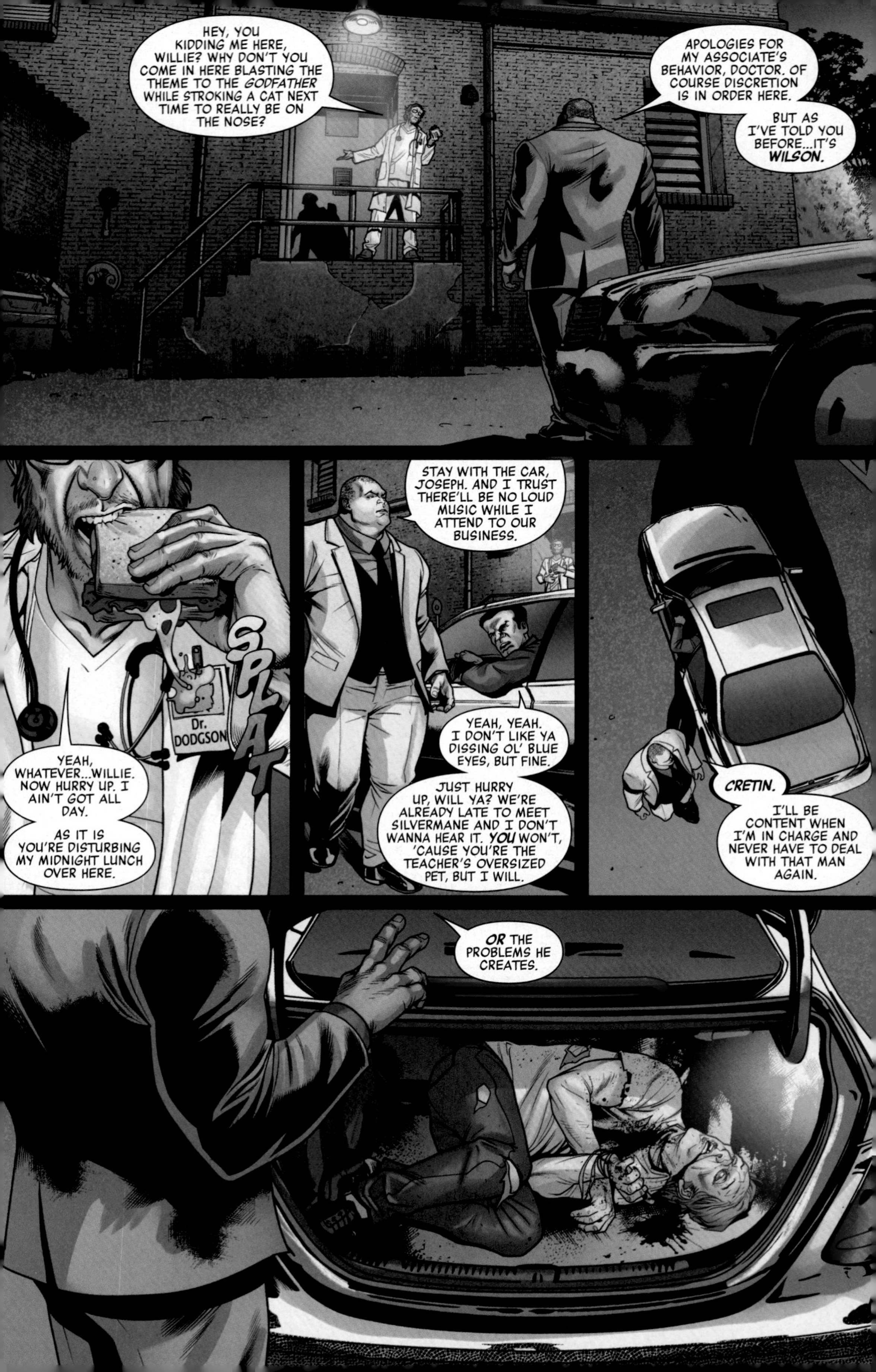
HEY, YOU KIDDING ME HERE, WILLIE? WHY DON'T YOU COME IN HERE BLASTING THE THEME TO THE *GODFATHER* WHILE STROKING A CAT NEXT TIME TO REALLY BE ON THE NOSE?
APOLOGIES FOR MY ASSOCIATE'S BEHAVIOR, DOCTOR. OF COURSE DISCRETION IS IN ORDER HERE.
BUT AS I'VE TOLD YOU BEFORE...IT'S *WILSON.*
SPLAT
Dr. DODGSON
YEAH, WHATEVER...WILLIE. NOW HURRY UP. I AIN'T GOT ALL DAY.
AS IT IS YOU'RE DISTURBING MY MIDNIGHT LUNCH OVER HERE.
STAY WITH THE CAR, JOSEPH. AND I TRUST THERE'LL BE NO LOUD MUSIC WHILE I ATTEND TO OUR BUSINESS.
YEAH, YEAH. I DON'T LIKE YA DISSING OL' BLUE EYES, BUT FINE.
JUST HURRY UP, WILL YA? WE'RE ALREADY LATE TO MEET SILVERMANE AND I DON'T WANNA HEAR IT. *YOU* WON'T, 'CAUSE YOU'RE THE TEACHER'S OVERSIZED PET, BUT I WILL.
CRETIN.
I'LL BE CONTENT WHEN I'M IN CHARGE AND NEVER HAVE TO DEAL WITH THAT MAN AGAIN.
OR THE PROBLEMS HE CREATES.

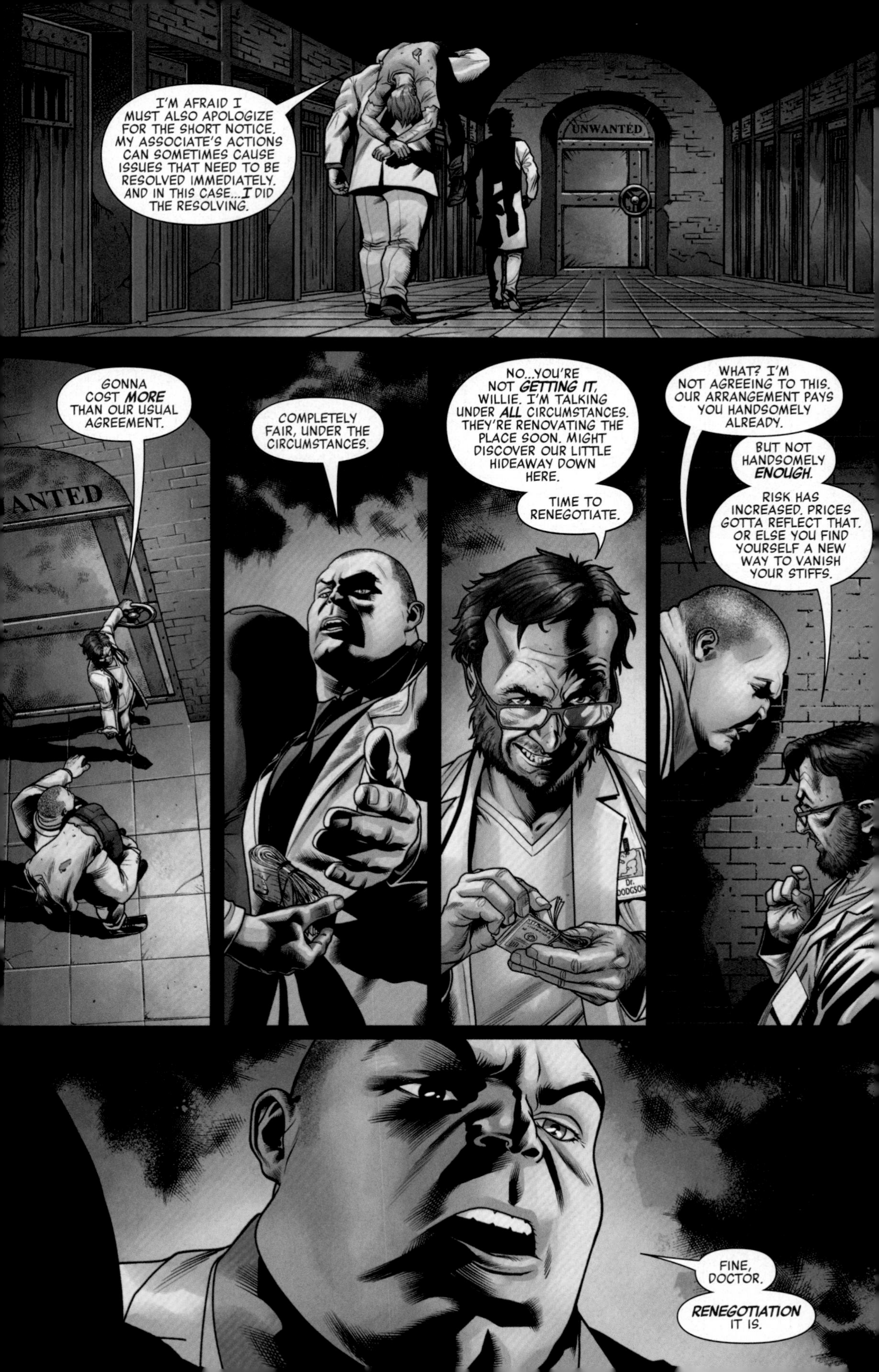
I'M AFRAID I MUST ALSO APOLOGIZE FOR THE SHORT NOTICE. MY ASSOCIATE'S ACTIONS CAN SOMETIMES CAUSE ISSUES THAT NEED TO BE RESOLVED IMMEDIATELY. AND IN THIS CASE...I DID THE RESOLVING.
UNWANTED
GONNA COST MORE THAN OUR USUAL AGREEMENT.
ANTED
COMPLETELY FAIR, UNDER THE CIRCUMSTANCES.
NO...YOU'RE NOT GETTING IT, WILLIE. I'M TALKING UNDER ALL CIRCUMSTANCES. THEY'RE RENOVATING THE PLACE SOON. MIGHT DISCOVER OUR LITTLE HIDEAWAY DOWN HERE.
TIME TO RENEGOTIATE.
WHAT? I'M NOT AGREEING TO THIS. OUR ARRANGEMENT PAYS YOU HANDSOMELY ALREADY.
BUT NOT HANDSOMELY ENOUGH.
RISK HAS INCREASED. PRICES GOTTA REFLECT THAT. OR ELSE YOU FIND YOURSELF A NEW WAY TO VANISH YOUR STIFFS.
FINE, DOCTOR.
RENEGOTIATION IT IS.

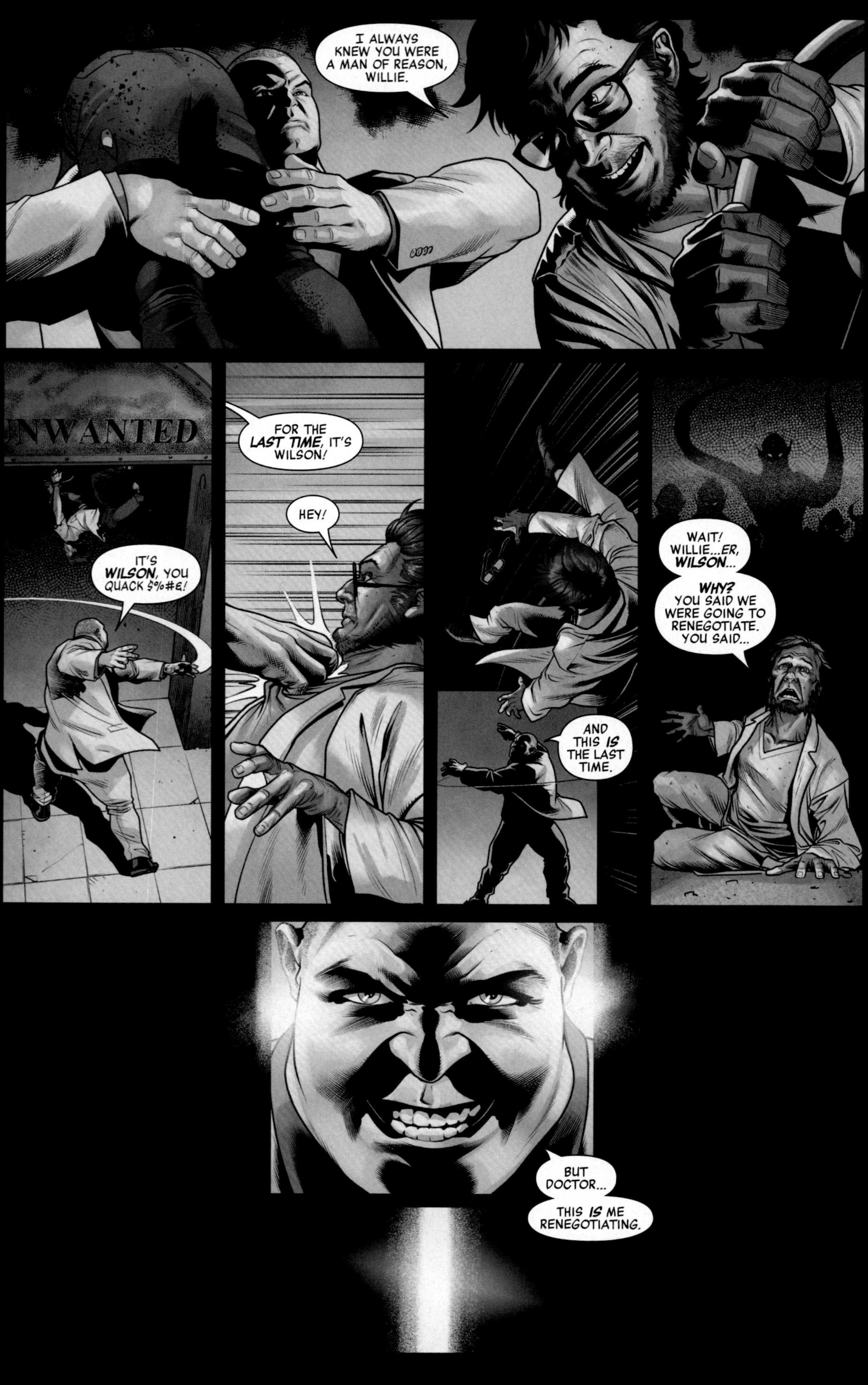

I ALWAYS KNEW YOU WERE A MAN OF REASON, WILLIE.
UNWANTED
IT'S WILSON, YOU QUACK $%#&!
FOR THE LAST TIME, IT'S WILSON!
HEY!
AND THIS IS THE LAST TIME.
WAIT! WILLIE...ER, WILSON...
WHY? YOU SAID WE WERE GOING TO RENEGOTIATE. YOU SAID...
BUT DOCTOR...
THIS IS ME RENEGOTIATING.

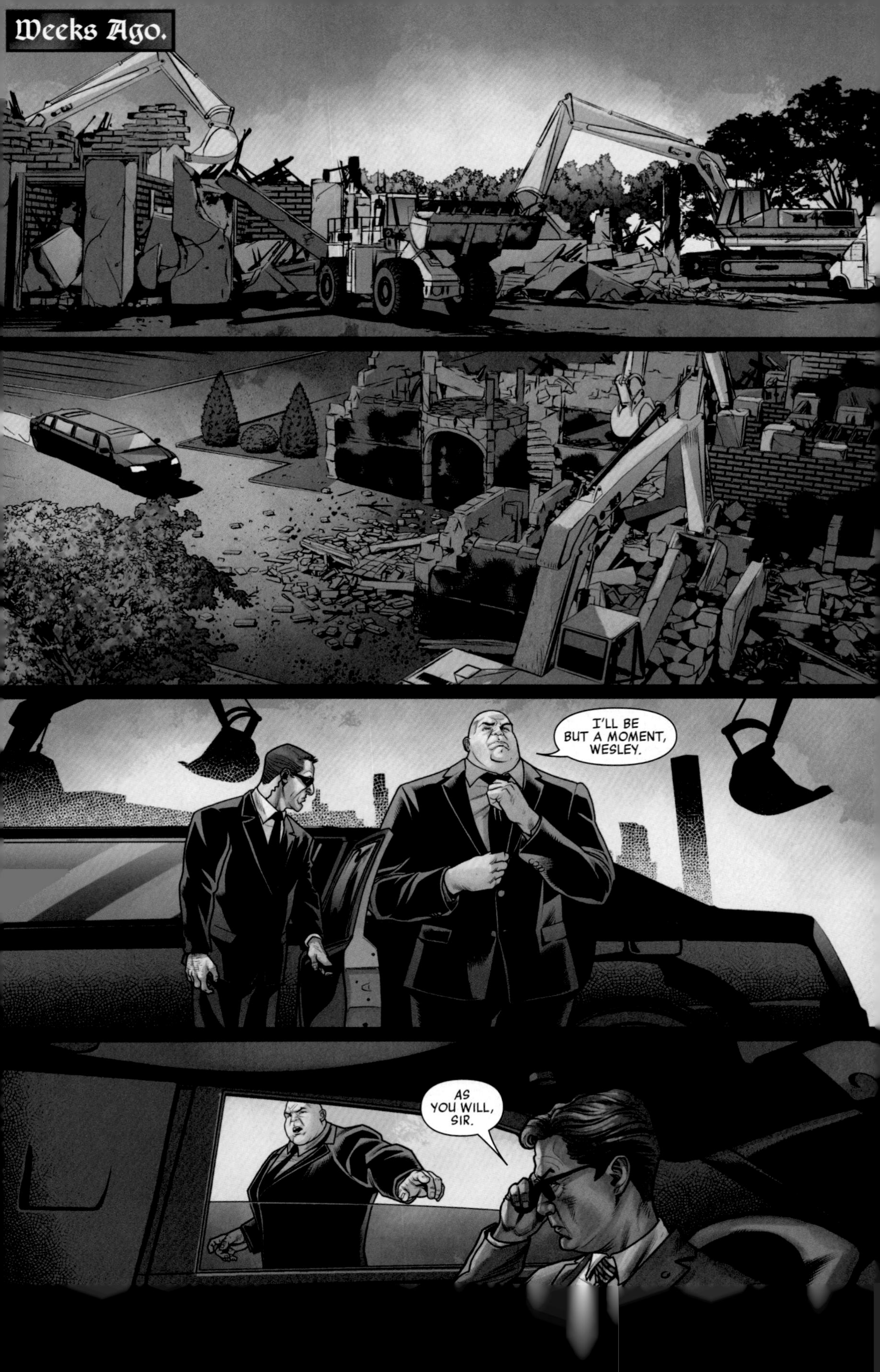
Weeks Ago.
I'LL BE BUT A MOMENT, WESLEY.
AS YOU WILL, SIR.

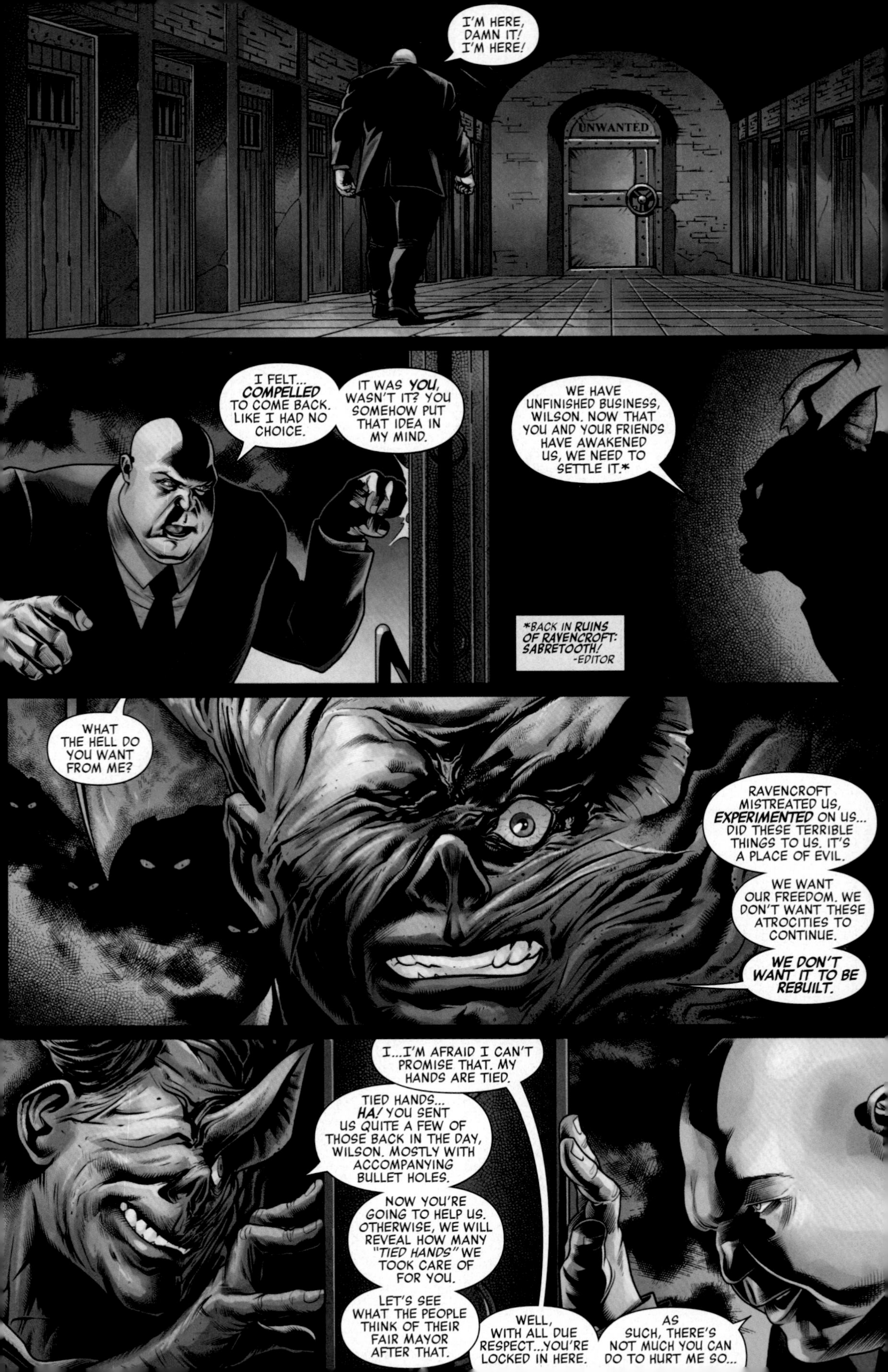
I'M HERE, DAMN IT! I'M HERE!
UNWANTED
I FELT... COMPELLED TO COME BACK. LIKE I HAD NO CHOICE.
IT WAS YOU, WASN'T IT? YOU SOMEHOW PUT THAT IDEA IN MY MIND.
WE HAVE UNFINISHED BUSINESS, WILSON. NOW THAT YOU AND YOUR FRIENDS HAVE AWAKENED US, WE NEED TO SETTLE IT.*
*BACK IN RUINS OF RAVENCROFT: SABRETOOTH! -EDITOR
WHAT THE HELL DO YOU WANT FROM ME?
RAVENCROFT MISTREATED US, EXPERIMENTED ON US... DID THESE TERRIBLE THINGS TO US. IT'S A PLACE OF EVIL.
WE WANT OUR FREEDOM. WE DON'T WANT THESE ATROCITIES TO CONTINUE.
WE DON'T WANT IT TO BE REBUILT.
I...I'M AFRAID I CAN'T PROMISE THAT. MY HANDS ARE TIED.
TIED HANDS... HA! YOU SENT US QUITE A FEW OF THOSE BACK IN THE DAY, WILSON. MOSTLY WITH ACCOMPANYING BULLET HOLES.
NOW YOU'RE GOING TO HELP US. OTHERWISE, WE WILL REVEAL HOW MANY "TIED HANDS" WE TOOK CARE OF FOR YOU.
LET'S SEE WHAT THE PEOPLE THINK OF THEIR FAIR MAYOR AFTER THAT.
WELL, WITH ALL DUE RESPECT...YOU'RE LOCKED IN HERE.
AS SUCH, THERE'S NOT MUCH YOU CAN DO TO HURT ME SO...

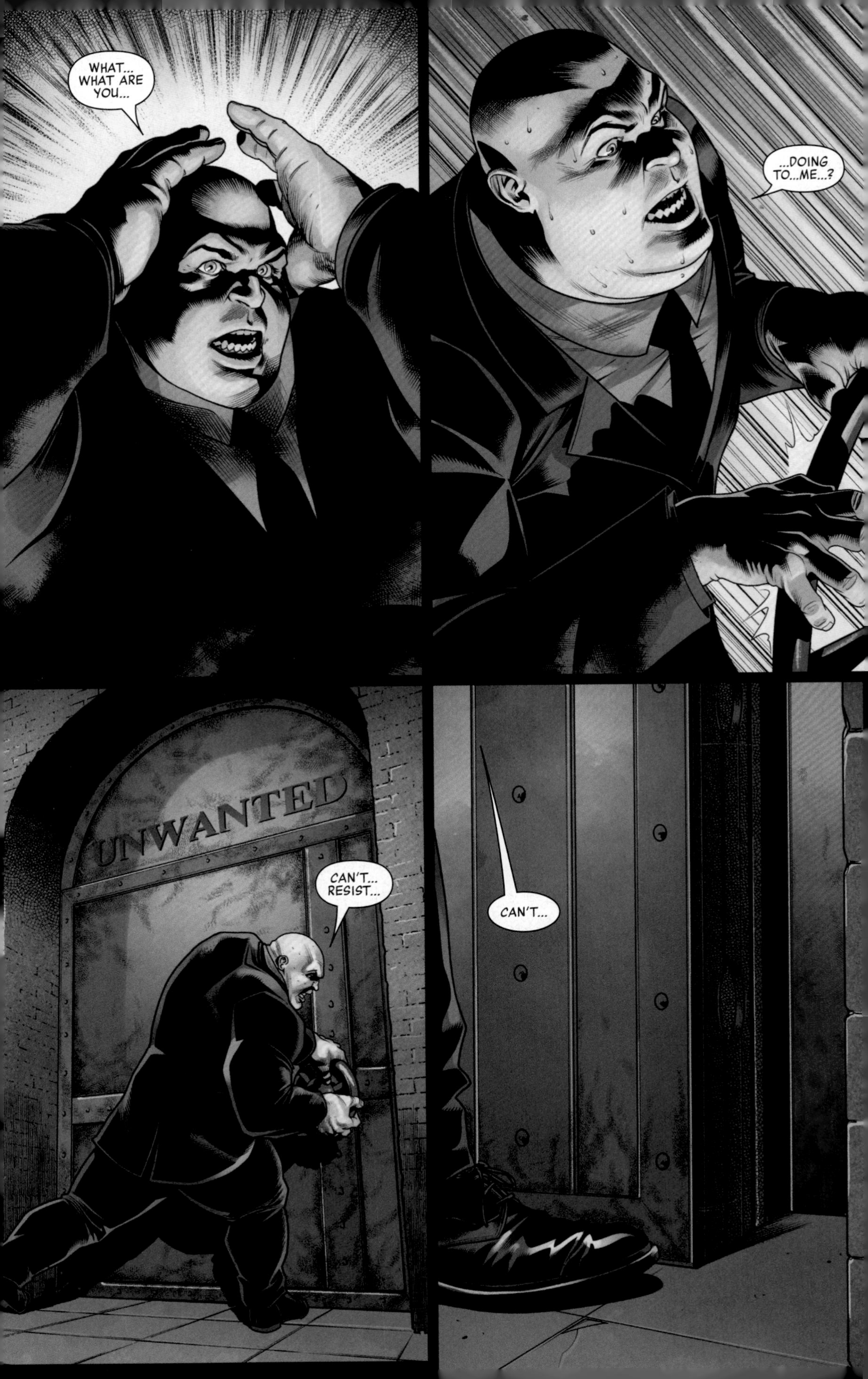
WHAT... WHAT ARE YOU...
...DOING TO...ME...?
UNWANTED
CAN'T... RESIST...
CAN'T...

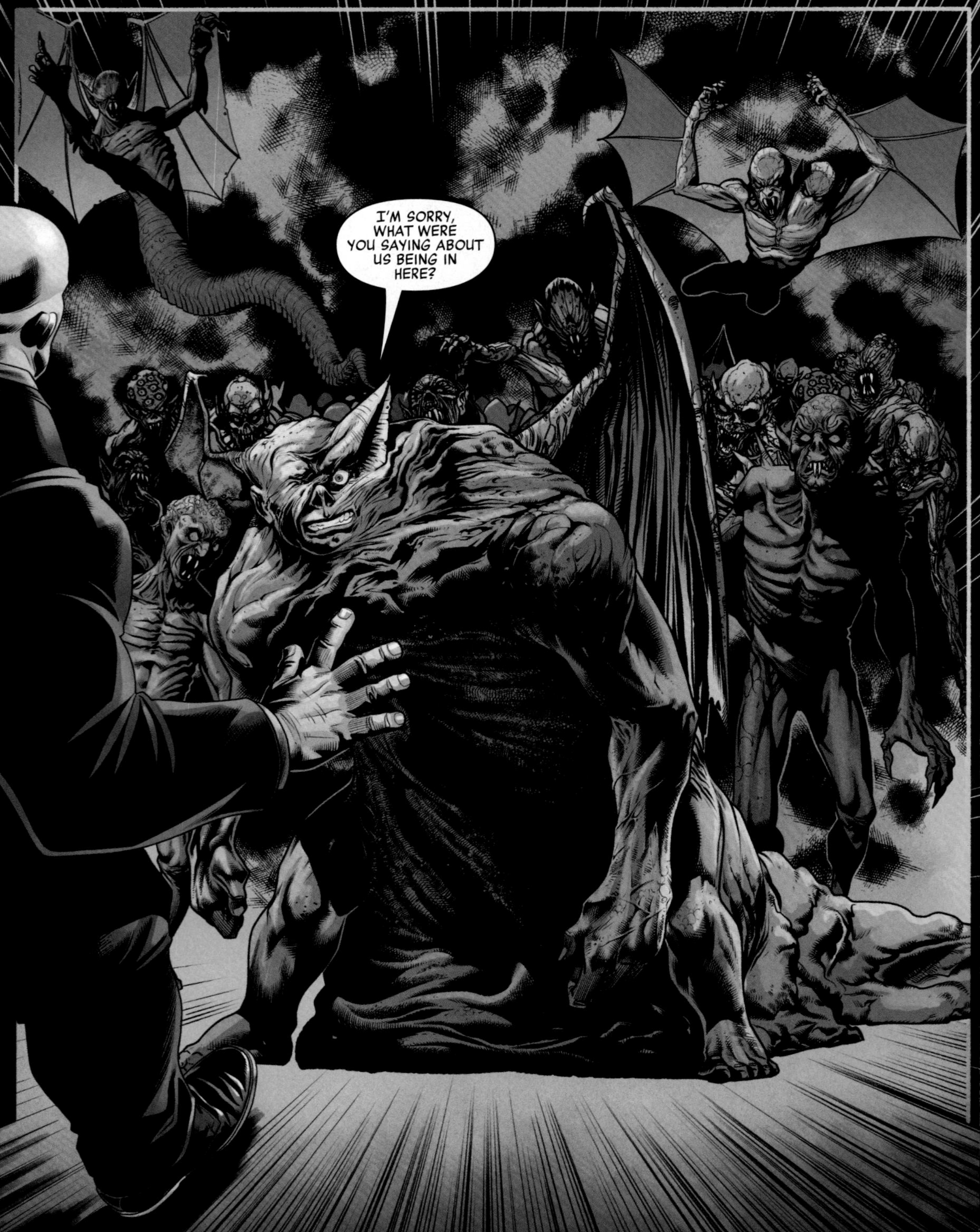
I'M SORRY, WHAT WERE YOU SAYING ABOUT US BEING IN HERE?

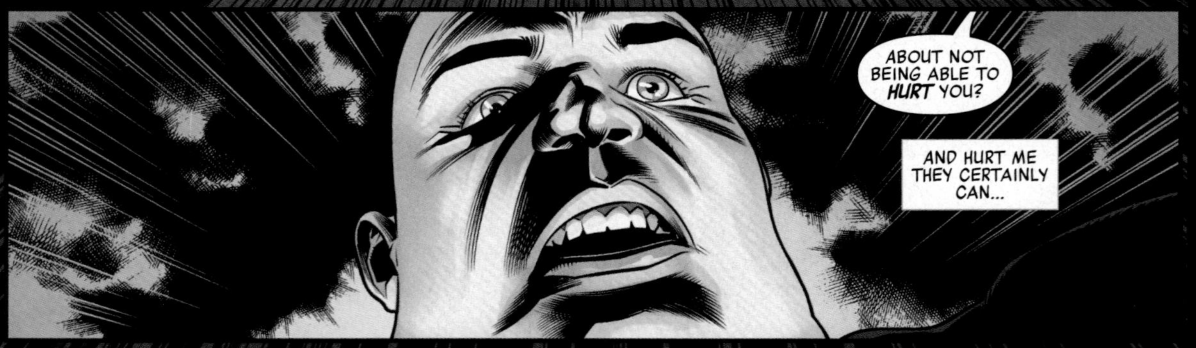
ABOUT NOT BEING ABLE TO *HURT* YOU?
AND HURT ME THEY CERTAINLY CAN...

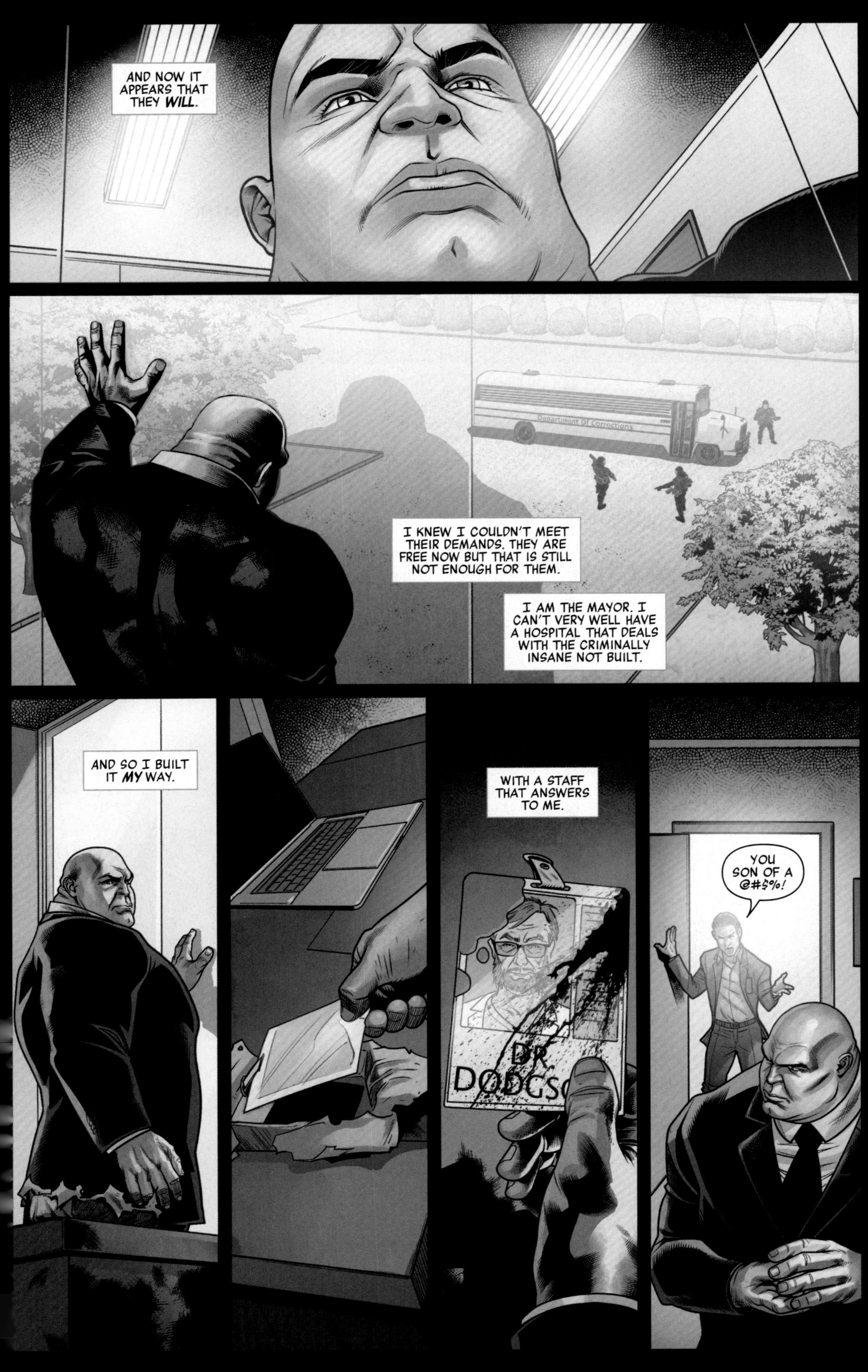
AND NOW IT APPEARS THAT THEY WILL.
Department Of Corrections
I KNEW I COULDN'T MEET THEIR DEMANDS. THEY ARE FREE NOW BUT THAT IS STILL NOT ENOUGH FOR THEM.
I AM THE MAYOR. I CAN'T VERY WELL HAVE A HOSPITAL THAT DEALS WITH THE CRIMINALLY INSANE NOT BUILT.
AND SO I BUILT IT MY WAY.
WITH A STAFF THAT ANSWERS TO ME.
DR. DODGSO
YOU SON OF A @#$%!

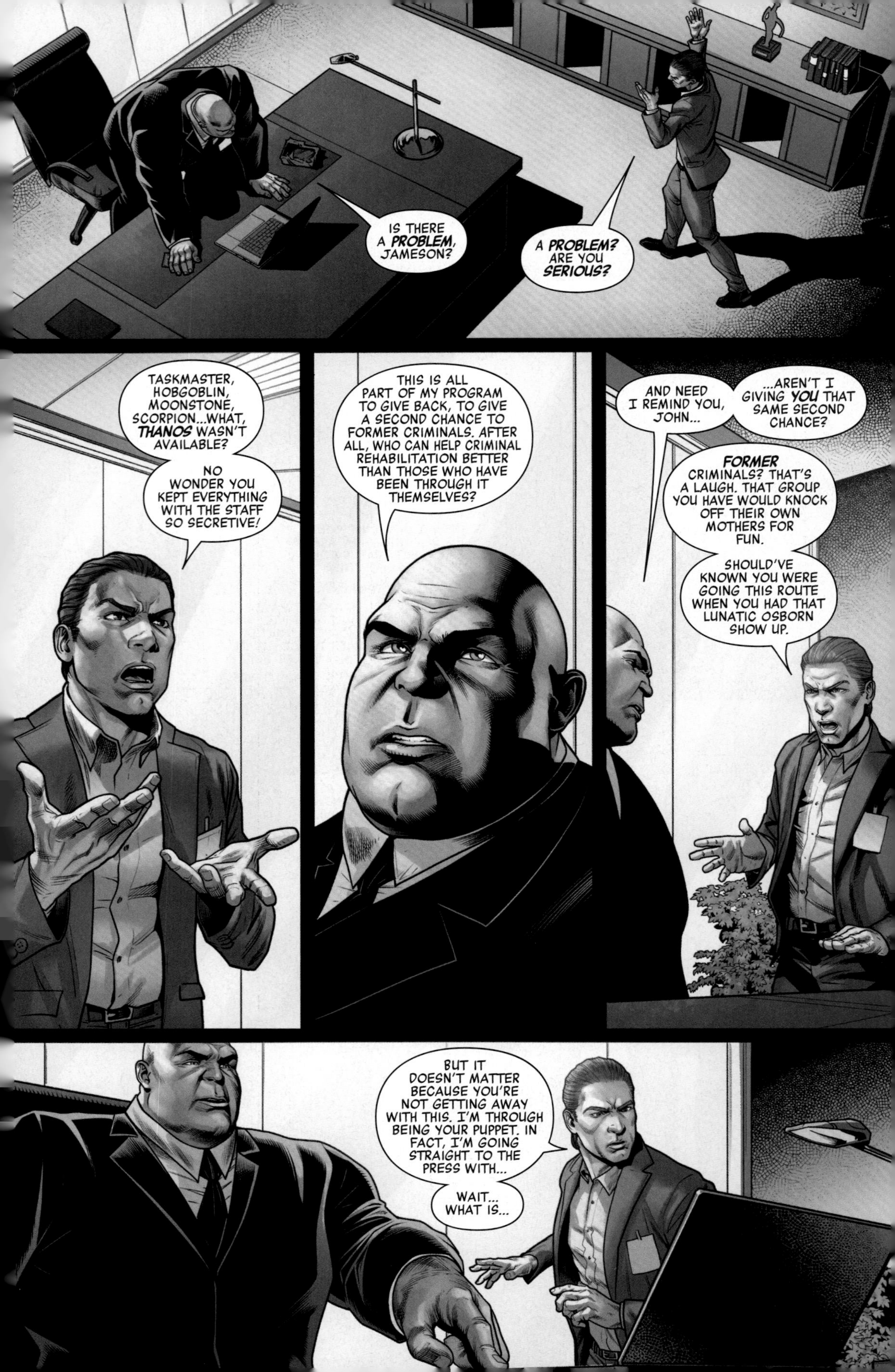
IS THERE A PROBLEM, JAMESON?
A PROBLEM? ARE YOU SERIOUS?
TASKMASTER, HOBGOBLIN, MOONSTONE, SCORPION...WHAT, THANOS WASN'T AVAILABLE?
NO WONDER YOU KEPT EVERYTHING WITH THE STAFF SO SECRETIVE!
THIS IS ALL PART OF MY PROGRAM TO GIVE BACK, TO GIVE A SECOND CHANCE TO FORMER CRIMINALS. AFTER ALL, WHO CAN HELP CRIMINAL REHABILITATION BETTER THAN THOSE WHO HAVE BEEN THROUGH IT THEMSELVES?
AND NEED I REMIND YOU, JOHN...
...AREN'T I GIVING YOU THAT SAME SECOND CHANCE?
FORMER CRIMINALS? THAT'S A LAUGH. THAT GROUP YOU HAVE WOULD KNOCK OFF THEIR OWN MOTHERS FOR FUN.
SHOULD'VE KNOWN YOU WERE GOING THIS ROUTE WHEN YOU HAD THAT LUNATIC OSBORN SHOW UP.
BUT IT DOESN'T MATTER BECAUSE YOU'RE NOT GETTING AWAY WITH THIS. I'M THROUGH BEING YOUR PUPPET. IN FACT, I'M GOING STRAIGHT TO THE PRESS WITH...
WAIT... WHAT IS...

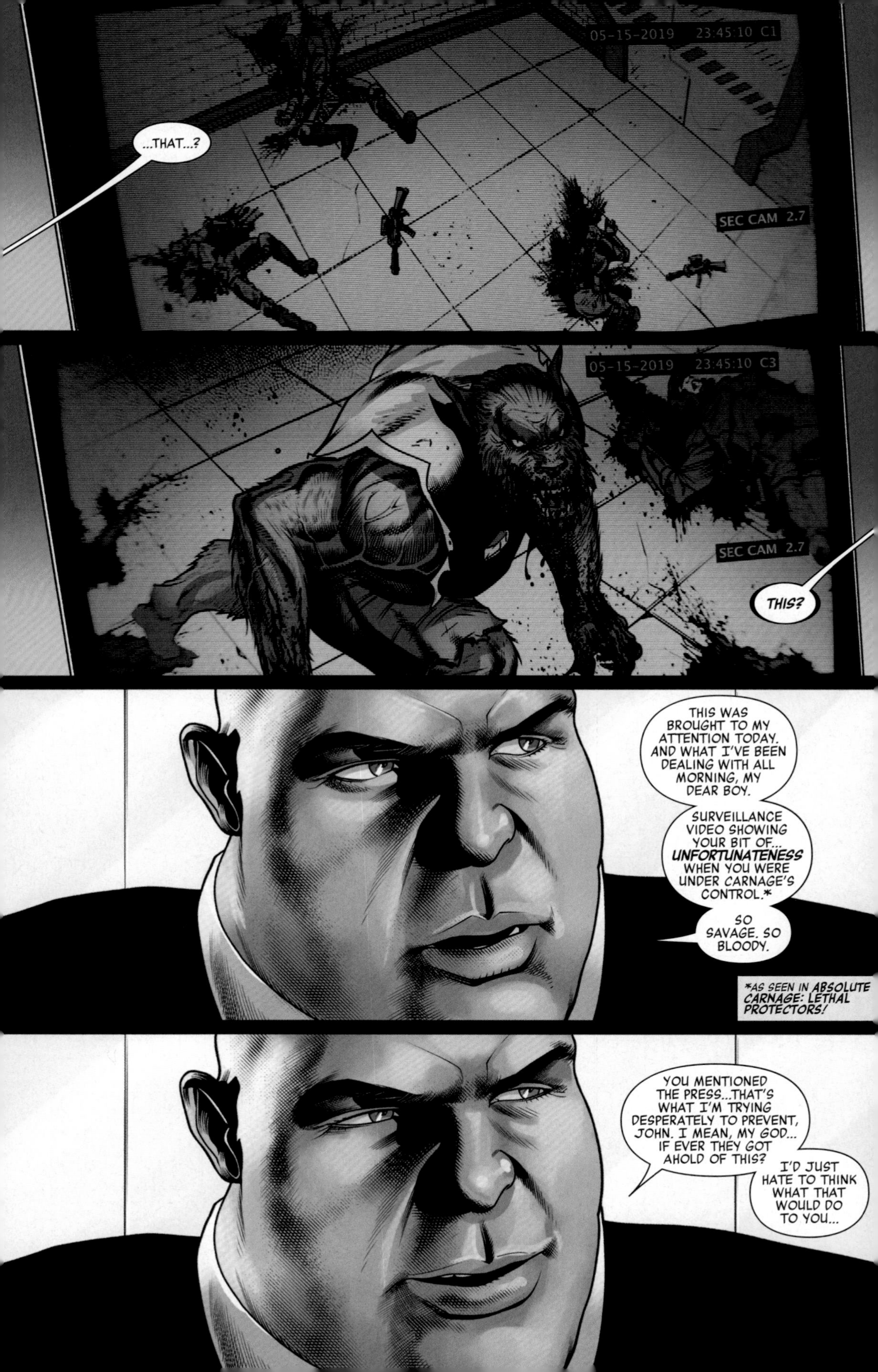

05-15-2019 23:45:10 C1
...THAT...?
SEC CAM 2.7
05-15-2019 23:45:10 C3
SEC CAM 2.7
THIS?
THIS WAS BROUGHT TO MY ATTENTION TODAY. AND WHAT I'VE BEEN DEALING WITH ALL MORNING, MY DEAR BOY.
SURVEILLANCE VIDEO SHOWING YOUR BIT OF... UNFORTUNATENESS WHEN YOU WERE UNDER CARNAGE'S CONTROL.*
SO SAVAGE. SO BLOODY.
*AS SEEN IN ABSOLUTE CARNAGE: LETHAL PROTECTORS!
YOU MENTIONED THE PRESS...THAT'S WHAT I'M TRYING DESPERATELY TO PREVENT, JOHN. I MEAN, MY GOD... IF EVER THEY GOT AHOLD OF THIS?
I'D JUST HATE TO THINK WHAT THAT WOULD DO TO YOU...

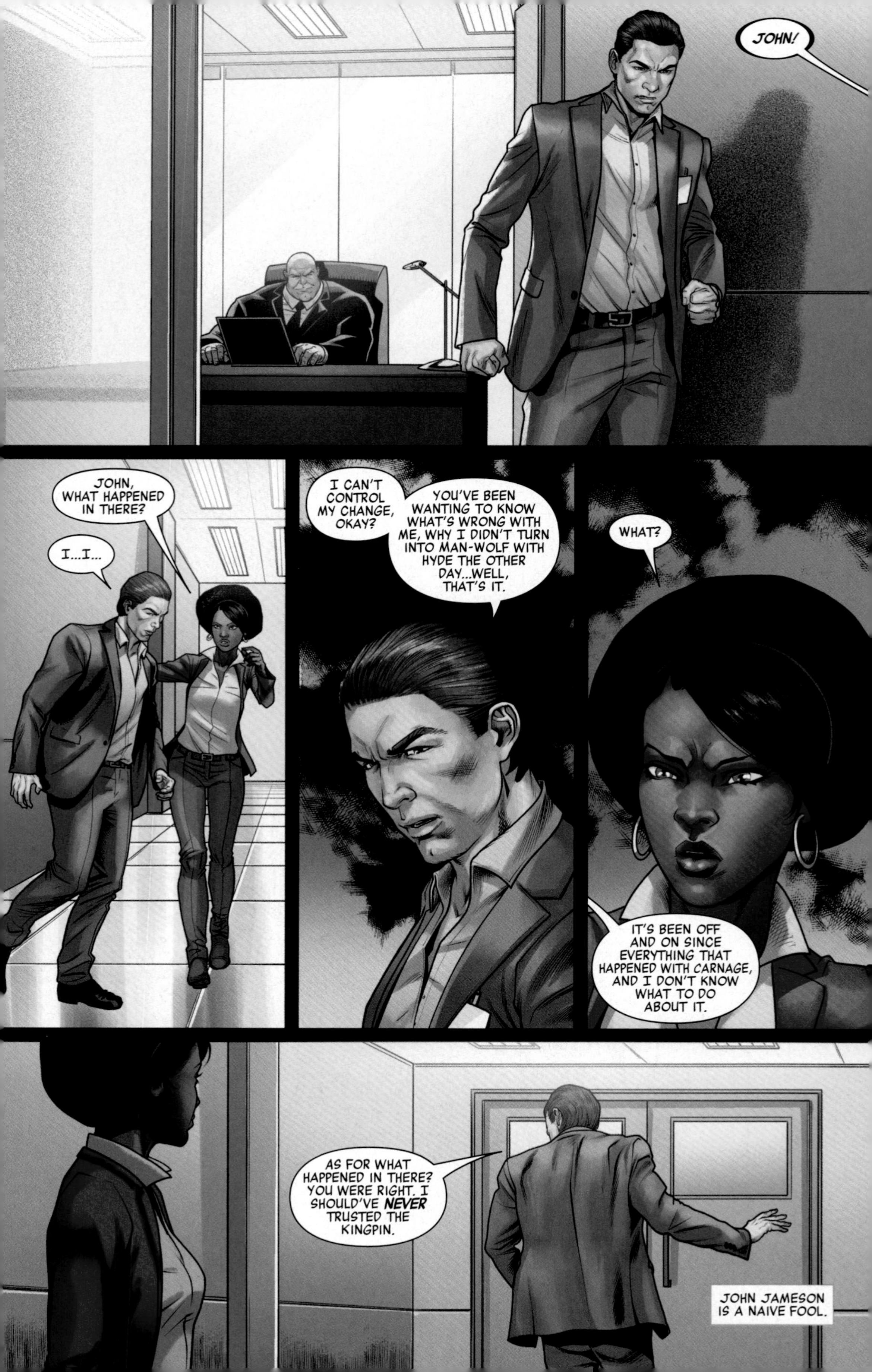
JOHN!
JOHN, WHAT HAPPENED IN THERE?
I...I...
I CAN'T CONTROL MY CHANGE, OKAY?
YOU'VE BEEN WANTING TO KNOW WHAT'S WRONG WITH ME, WHY I DIDN'T TURN INTO MAN-WOLF WITH HYDE THE OTHER DAY...WELL, THAT'S IT.
WHAT?
IT'S BEEN OFF AND ON SINCE EVERYTHING THAT HAPPENED WITH CARNAGE, AND I DON'T KNOW WHAT TO DO ABOUT IT.
AS FOR WHAT HAPPENED IN THERE? YOU WERE RIGHT. I SHOULD'VE NEVER TRUSTED THE KINGPIN.
JOHN JAMESON IS A NAIVE FOOL.

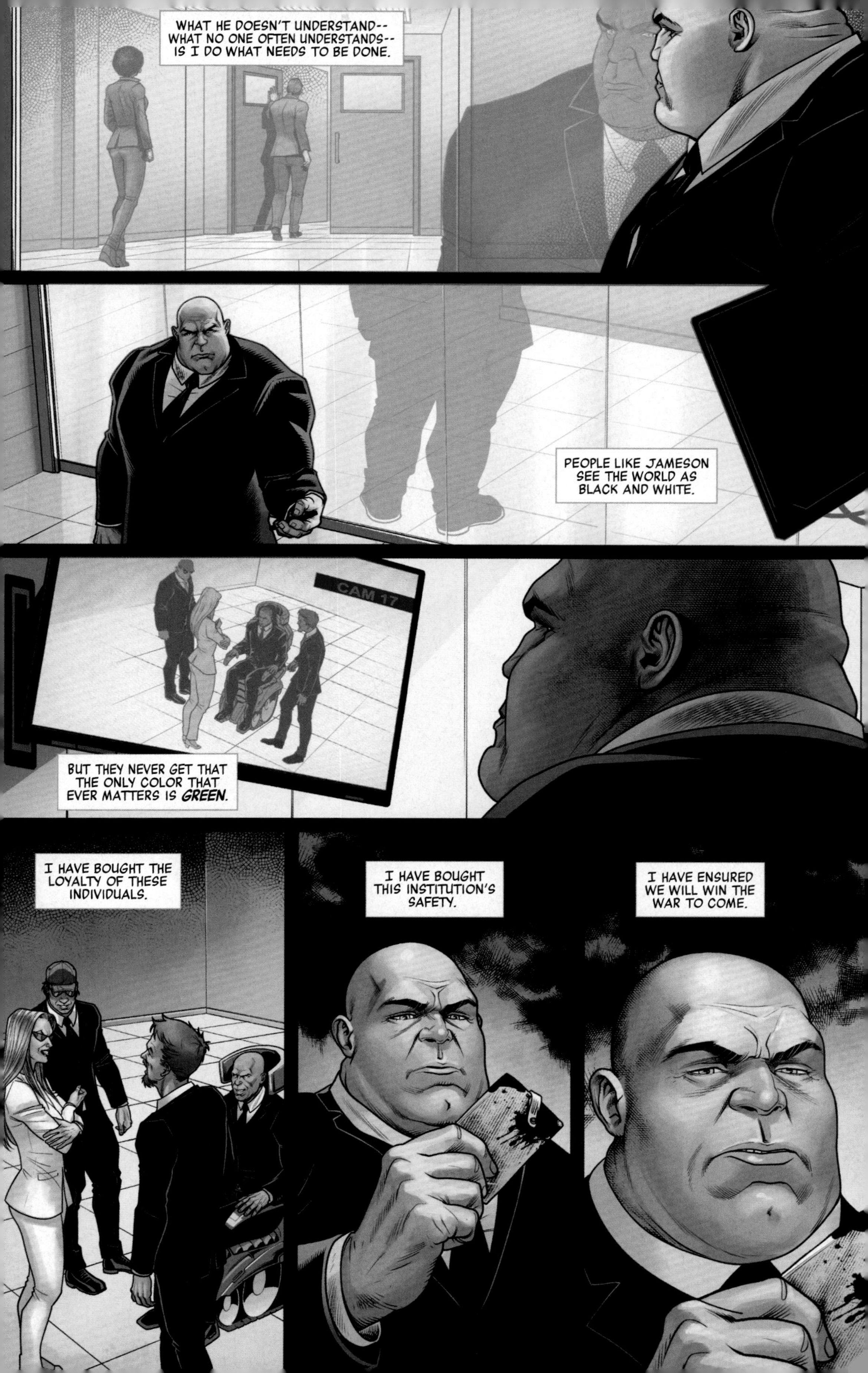
WHAT HE DOESN'T UNDERSTAND--
WHAT NO ONE OFTEN UNDERSTANDS--
IS I DO WHAT NEEDS TO BE DONE.
PEOPLE LIKE JAMESON SEE THE WORLD AS BLACK AND WHITE.
CAM 17
BUT THEY NEVER GET THAT THE ONLY COLOR THAT EVER MATTERS IS *GREEN.*
I HAVE BOUGHT THE LOYALTY OF THESE INDIVIDUALS.
I HAVE BOUGHT THIS INSTITUTION'S SAFETY.
I HAVE ENSURED WE WILL WIN THE WAR TO COME.

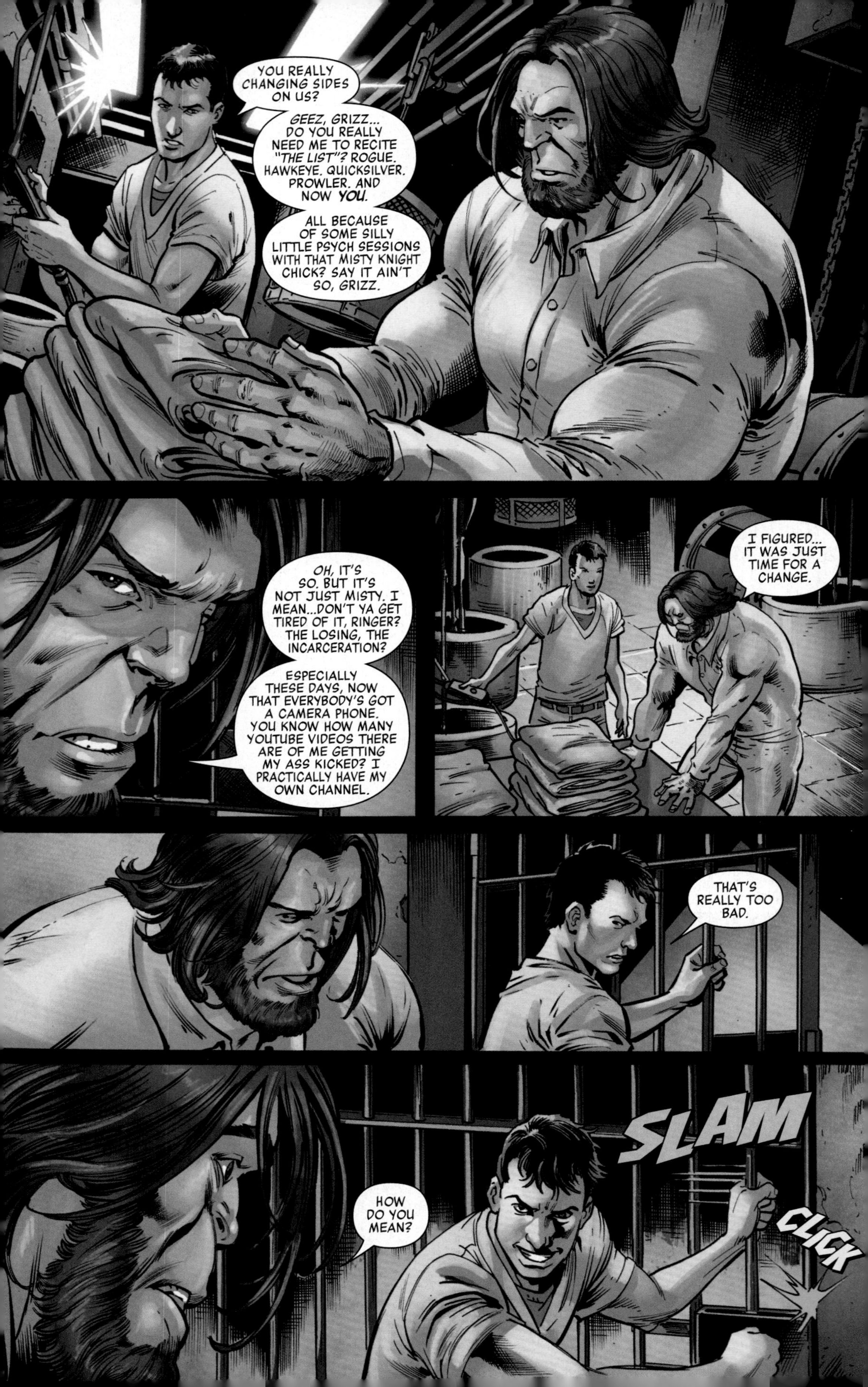
YOU REALLY CHANGING SIDES ON US?
GEEZ, GRIZZ... DO YOU REALLY NEED ME TO RECITE "THE LIST"? ROGUE. HAWKEYE. QUICKSILVER. PROWLER. AND NOW *YOU*.
ALL BECAUSE OF SOME SILLY LITTLE PSYCH SESSIONS WITH THAT MISTY KNIGHT CHICK? SAY IT AIN'T SO, GRIZZ.
OH, IT'S SO. BUT IT'S NOT JUST MISTY. I MEAN...DON'T YA GET TIRED OF IT, RINGER? THE LOSING, THE INCARCERATION?
ESPECIALLY THESE DAYS, NOW THAT EVERYBODY'S GOT A CAMERA PHONE. YOU KNOW HOW MANY YOUTUBE VIDEOS THERE ARE OF ME GETTING MY ASS KICKED? I PRACTICALLY HAVE MY OWN CHANNEL.
I FIGURED... IT WAS JUST TIME FOR A CHANGE.
THAT'S REALLY TOO BAD.
HOW DO YOU MEAN?
SLAM
CLICK

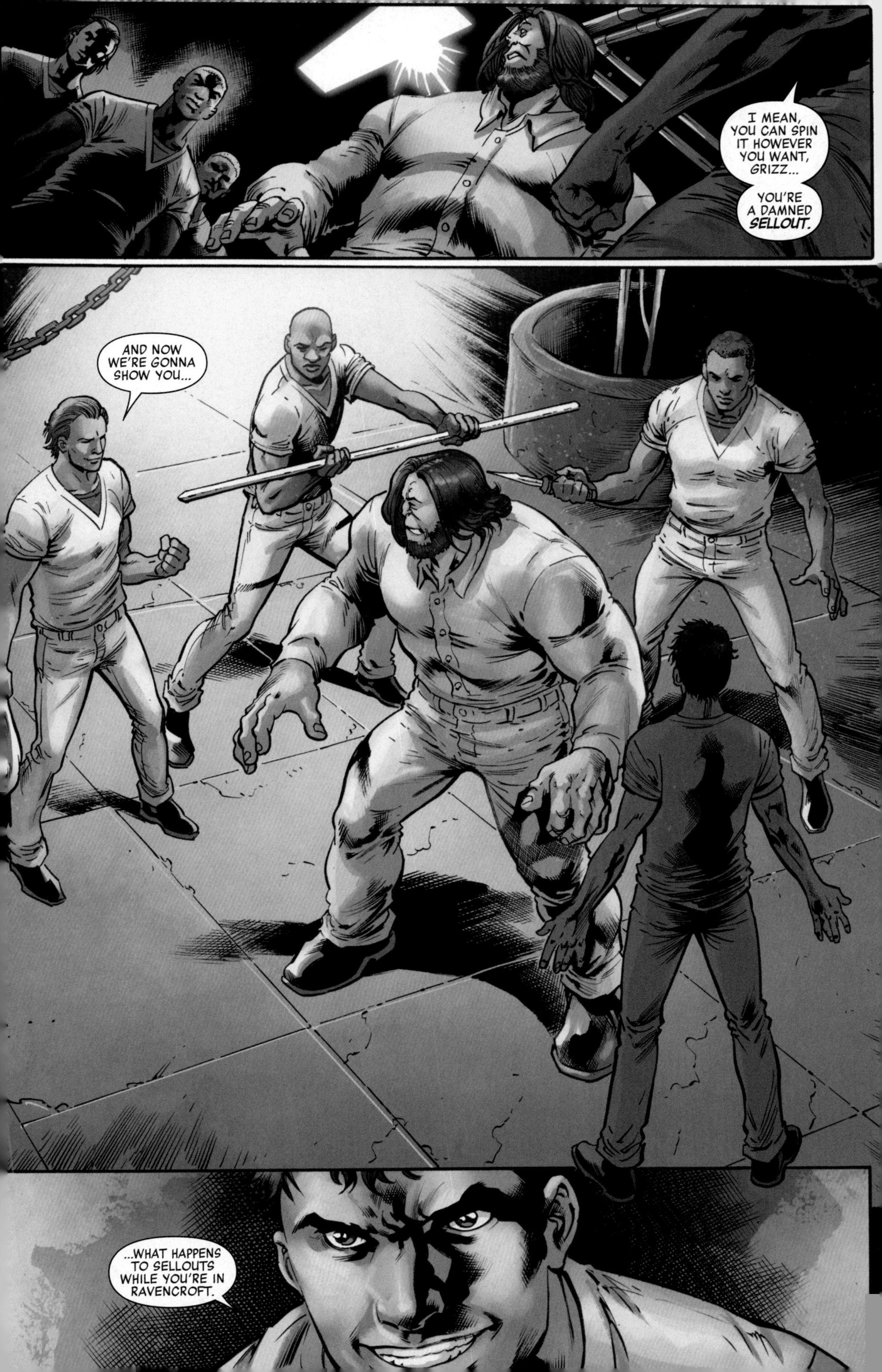
I MEAN, YOU CAN SPIN IT HOWEVER YOU WANT, GRIZZ...
YOU'RE A DAMNED SELLOUT.
AND NOW WE'RE GONNA SHOW YOU...
...WHAT HAPPENS TO SELLOUTS WHILE YOU'RE IN RAVENCROFT.

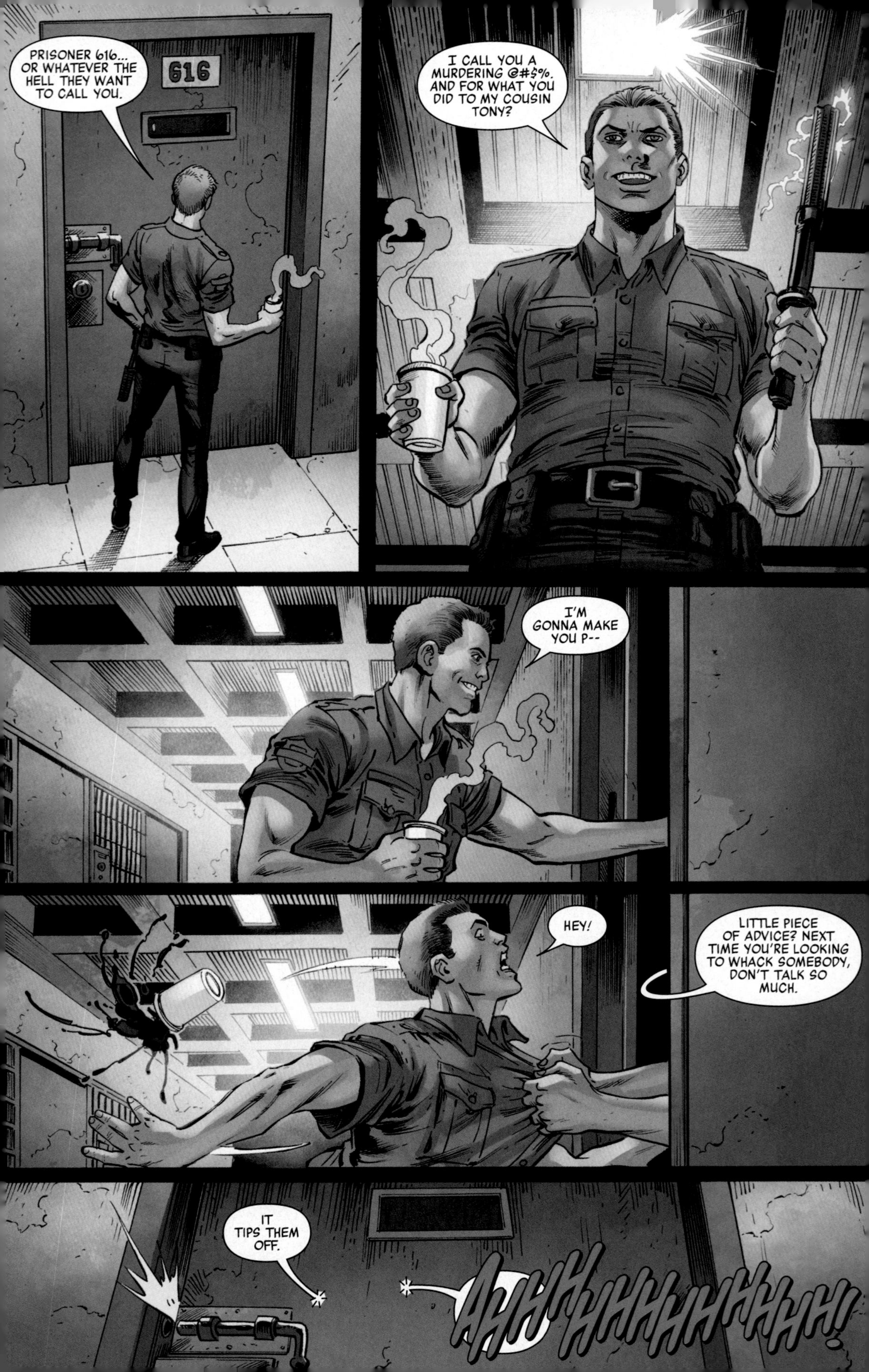

PRISONER 616... OR WHATEVER THE HELL THEY WANT TO CALL YOU.
616
I CALL YOU A MURDERING @#$%. AND FOR WHAT YOU DID TO MY COUSIN TONY?
I'M GONNA MAKE YOU P--
HEY!
LITTLE PIECE OF ADVICE? NEXT TIME YOU'RE LOOKING TO WHACK SOMEBODY, DON'T TALK SO MUCH.
IT TIPS THEM OFF.
AHHHHHHHHHH!

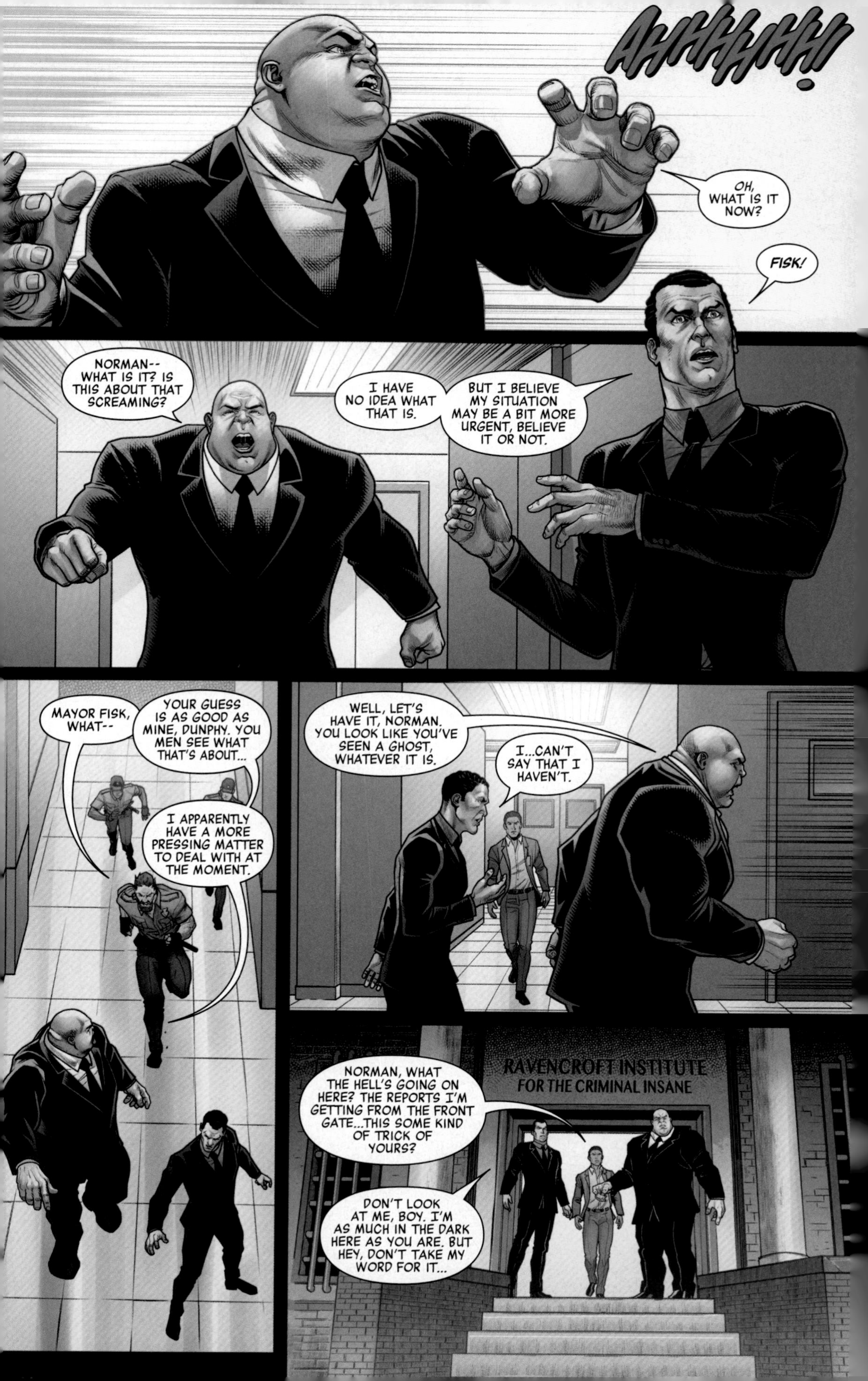
AHHHHHH!
OH, WHAT IS IT NOW?
FISK!
NORMAN-- WHAT IS IT? IS THIS ABOUT THAT SCREAMING?
I HAVE NO IDEA WHAT THAT IS.
BUT I BELIEVE MY SITUATION MAY BE A BIT MORE URGENT, BELIEVE IT OR NOT.
MAYOR FISK, WHAT--
YOUR GUESS IS AS GOOD AS MINE, DUNPHY. YOU MEN SEE WHAT THAT'S ABOUT...
I APPARENTLY HAVE A MORE PRESSING MATTER TO DEAL WITH AT THE MOMENT.
WELL, LET'S HAVE IT, NORMAN. YOU LOOK LIKE YOU'VE SEEN A GHOST, WHATEVER IT IS.
I...CAN'T SAY THAT I HAVEN'T.
RAVENCROFT INSTITUTE FOR THE CRIMINAL INSANE
NORMAN, WHAT THE HELL'S GOING ON HERE? THE REPORTS I'M GETTING FROM THE FRONT GATE...THIS SOME KIND OF TRICK OF YOURS?
DON'T LOOK AT ME, BOY. I'M AS MUCH IN THE DARK HERE AS YOU ARE. BUT HEY, DON'T TAKE MY WORD FOR IT...

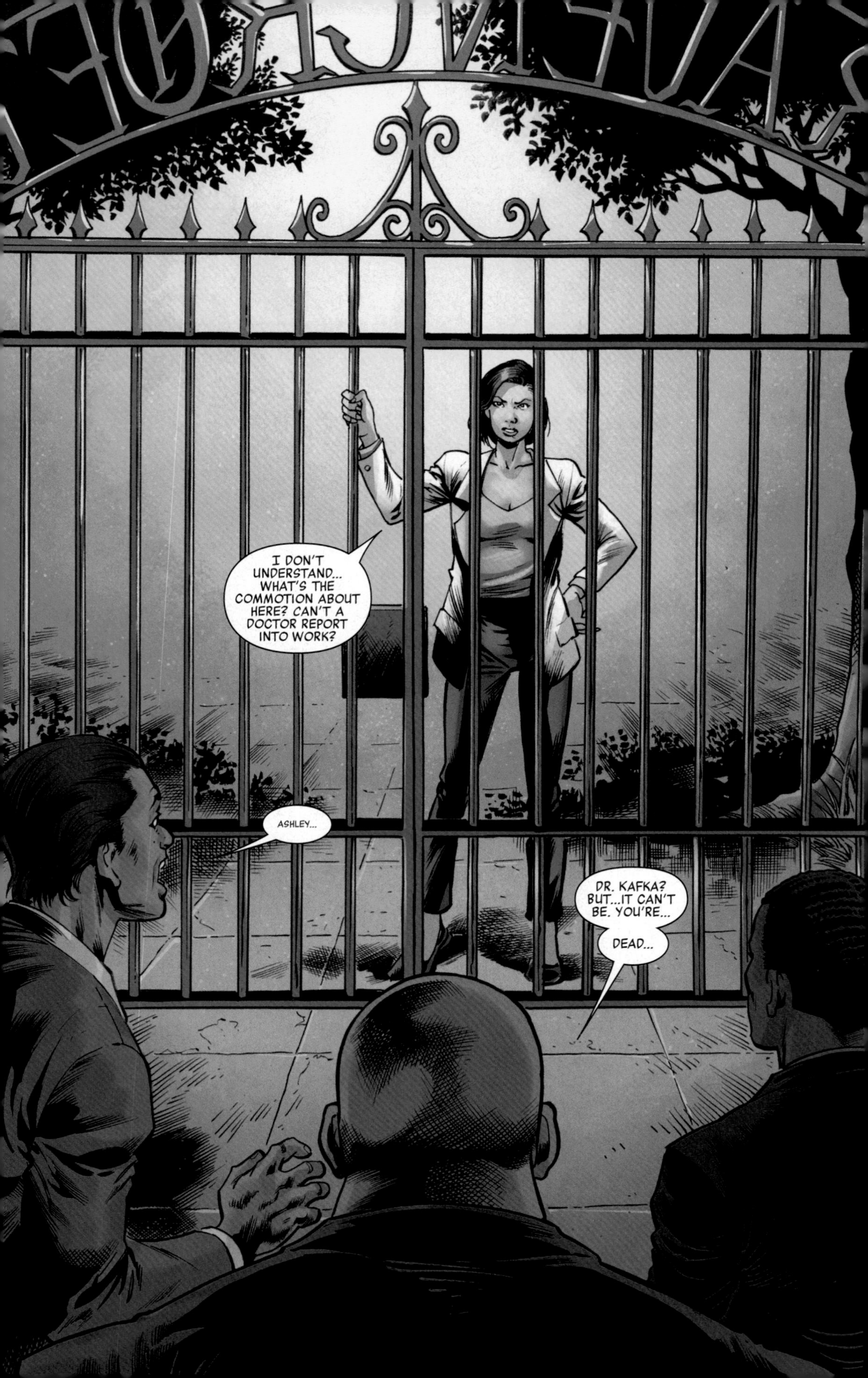
I DON'T UNDERSTAND... WHAT'S THE COMMOTION ABOUT HERE? CAN'T A DOCTOR REPORT INTO WORK?
ASHLEY...
DR. KAFKA? BUT...IT CAN'T BE. YOU'RE...
DEAD...

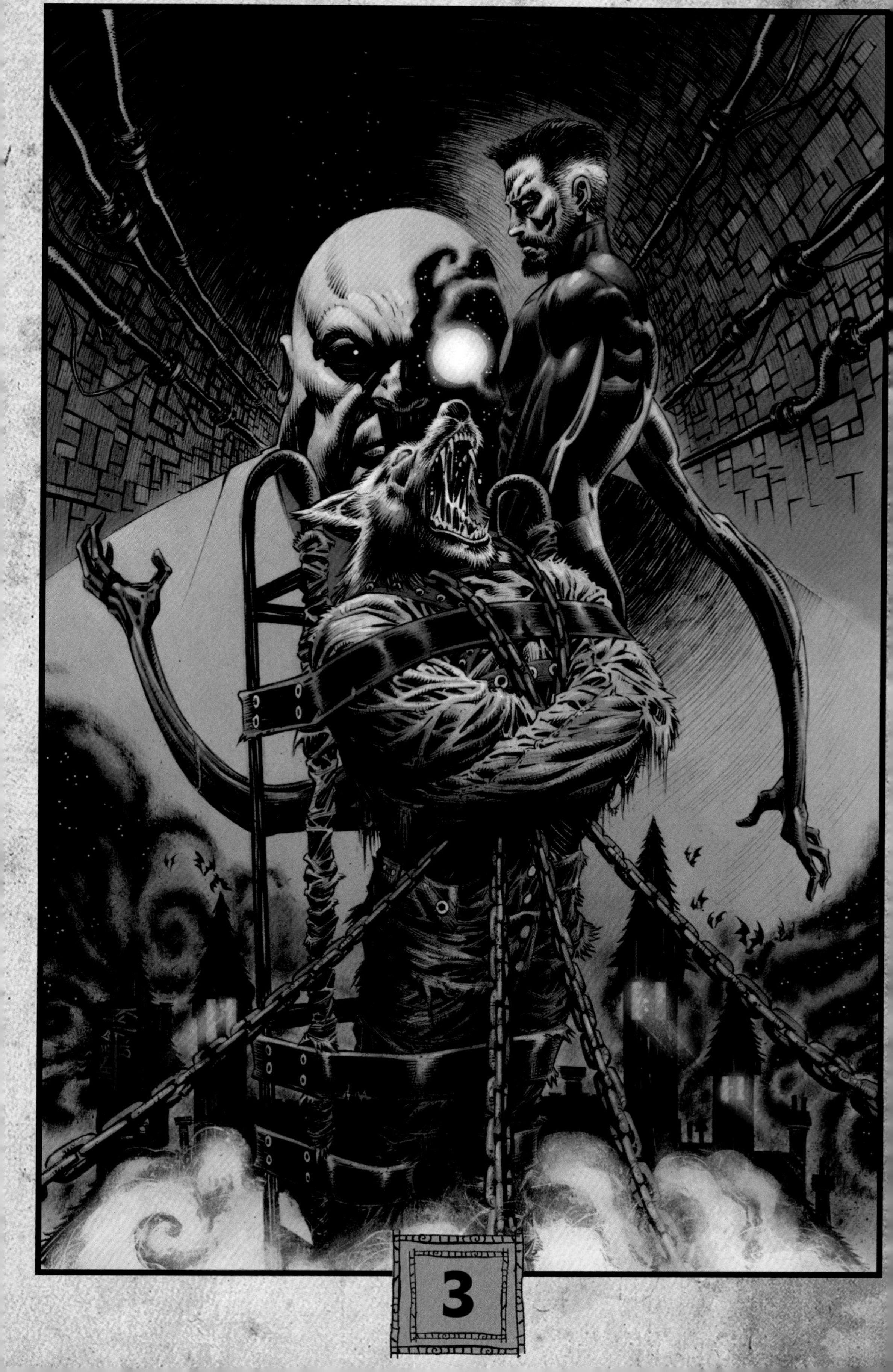

3

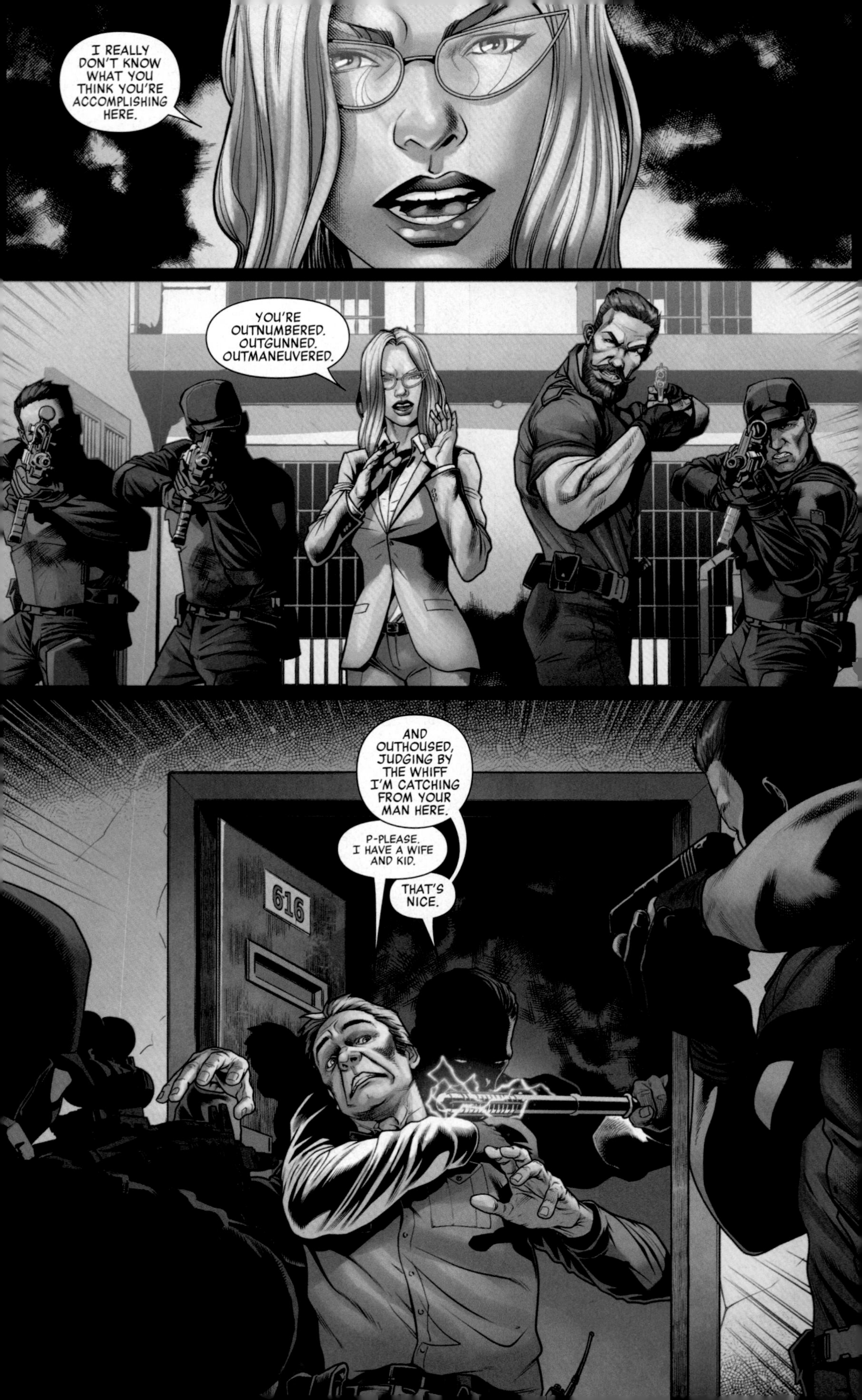
I REALLY DON'T KNOW WHAT YOU THINK YOU'RE ACCOMPLISHING HERE.
YOU'RE OUTNUMBERED. OUTGUNNED. OUTMANEUVERED.
AND OUTHOUSED, JUDGING BY THE WHIFF I'M CATCHING FROM YOUR MAN HERE.
P-PLEASE. I HAVE A WIFE AND KID.
THAT'S NICE.
616

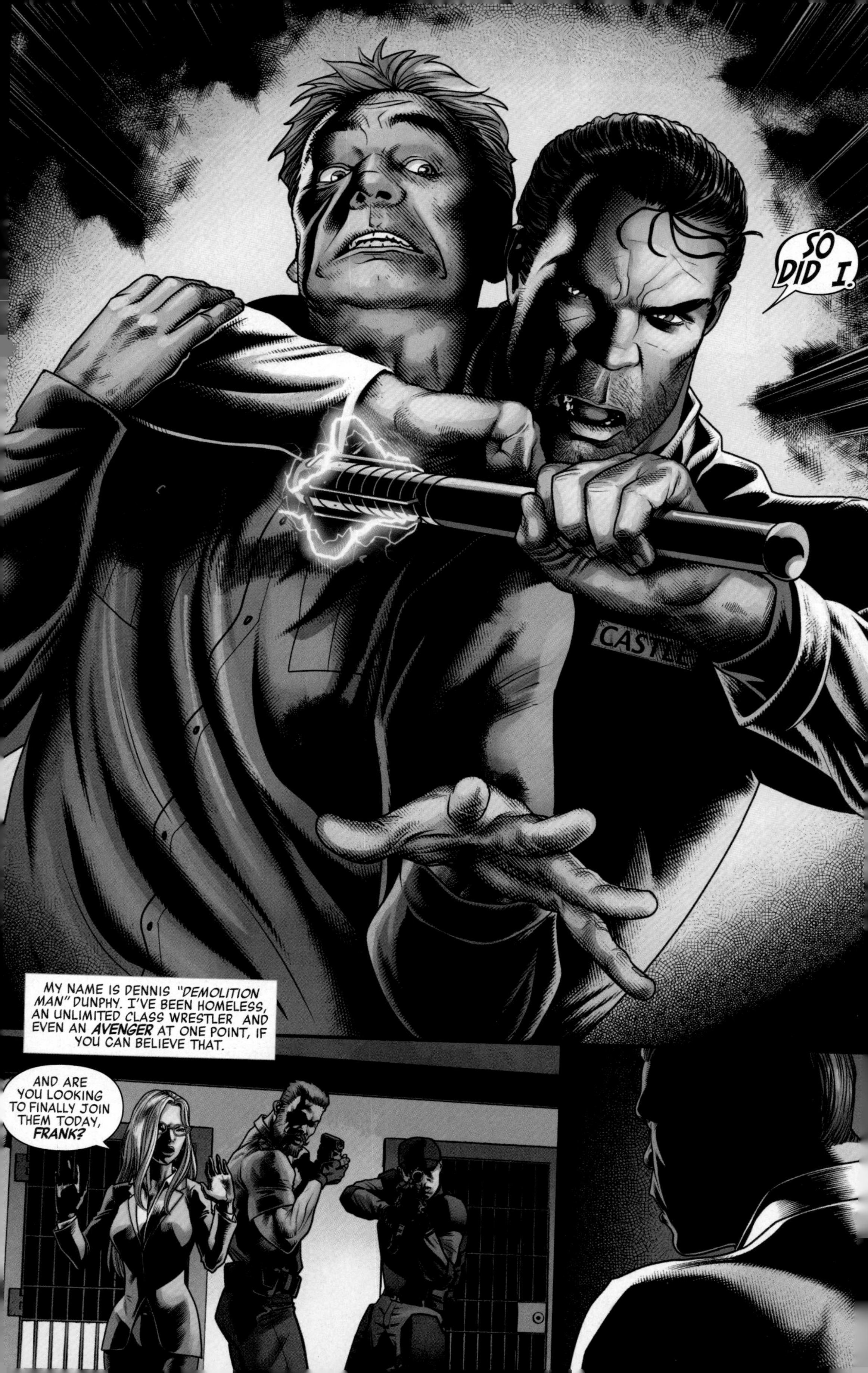
SO DID I.
MY NAME IS DENNIS "DEMOLITION MAN" DUNPHY. I'VE BEEN HOMELESS, AN UNLIMITED CLASS WRESTLER AND EVEN AN AVENGER AT ONE POINT, IF YOU CAN BELIEVE THAT.
AND ARE YOU LOOKING TO FINALLY JOIN THEM TODAY, FRANK?

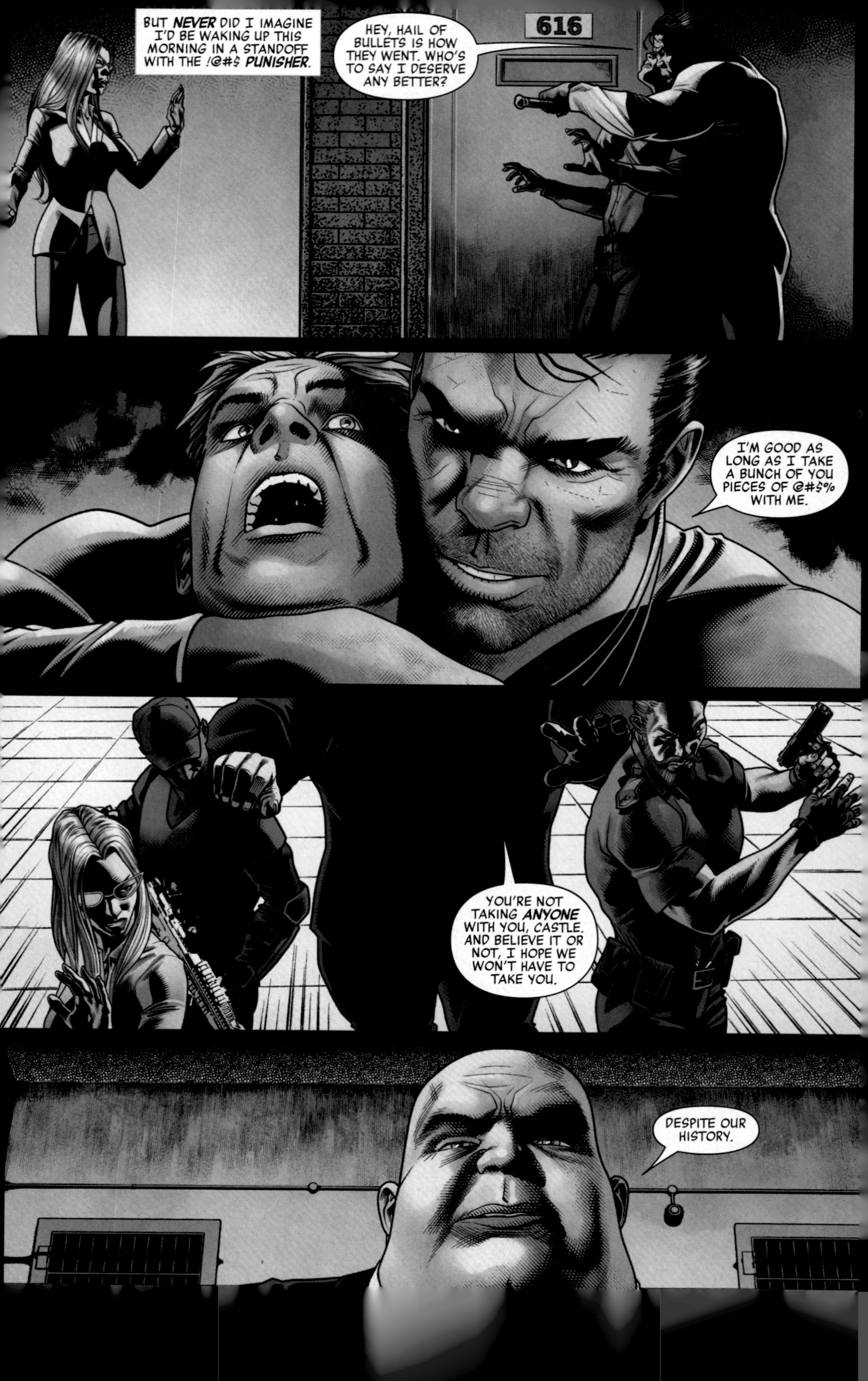
BUT NEVER DID I IMAGINE I'D BE WAKING UP THIS MORNING IN A STANDOFF WITH THE !@#$ PUNISHER.
616
HEY, HAIL OF BULLETS IS HOW THEY WENT. WHO'S TO SAY I DESERVE ANY BETTER?
I'M GOOD AS LONG AS I TAKE A BUNCH OF YOU PIECES OF @#$% WITH ME.
YOU'RE NOT TAKING ANYONE WITH YOU, CASTLE. AND BELIEVE IT OR NOT, I HOPE WE WON'T HAVE TO TAKE YOU.
DESPITE OUR HISTORY.

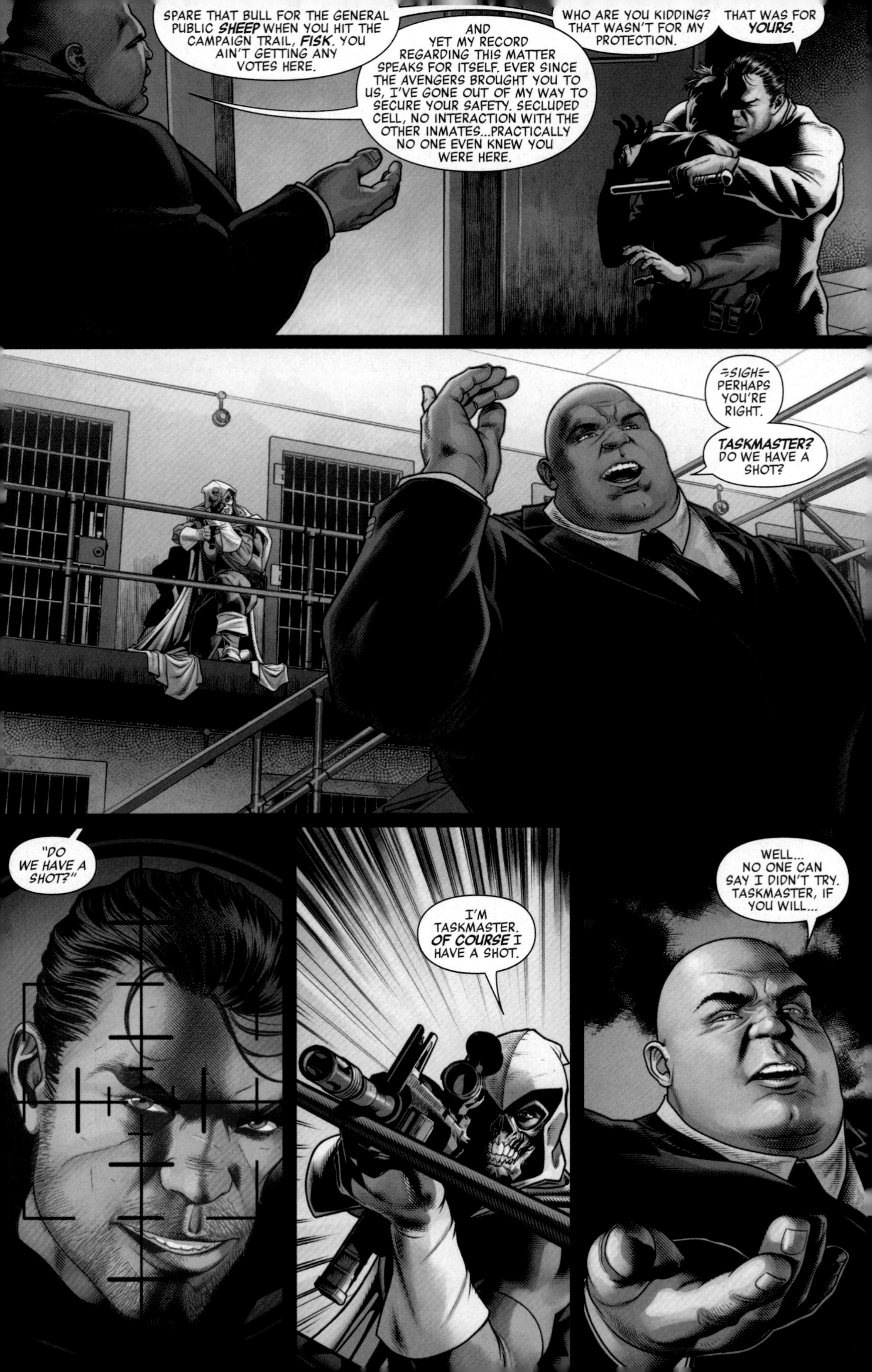
SPARE THAT BULL FOR THE GENERAL PUBLIC SHEEP WHEN YOU HIT THE CAMPAIGN TRAIL, FISK. YOU AIN'T GETTING ANY VOTES HERE.
AND YET MY RECORD REGARDING THIS MATTER SPEAKS FOR ITSELF. EVER SINCE THE AVENGERS BROUGHT YOU TO US, I'VE GONE OUT OF MY WAY TO SECURE YOUR SAFETY. SECLUDED CELL, NO INTERACTION WITH THE OTHER INMATES...PRACTICALLY NO ONE EVEN KNEW YOU WERE HERE.
WHO ARE YOU KIDDING? THAT WASN'T FOR MY PROTECTION.
THAT WAS FOR YOURS.
=SIGH= PERHAPS YOU'RE RIGHT.
TASKMASTER? DO WE HAVE A SHOT?
"DO WE HAVE A SHOT?"
I'M TASKMASTER. OF COURSE I HAVE A SHOT.
WELL... NO ONE CAN SAY I DIDN'T TRY. TASKMASTER, IF YOU WILL...

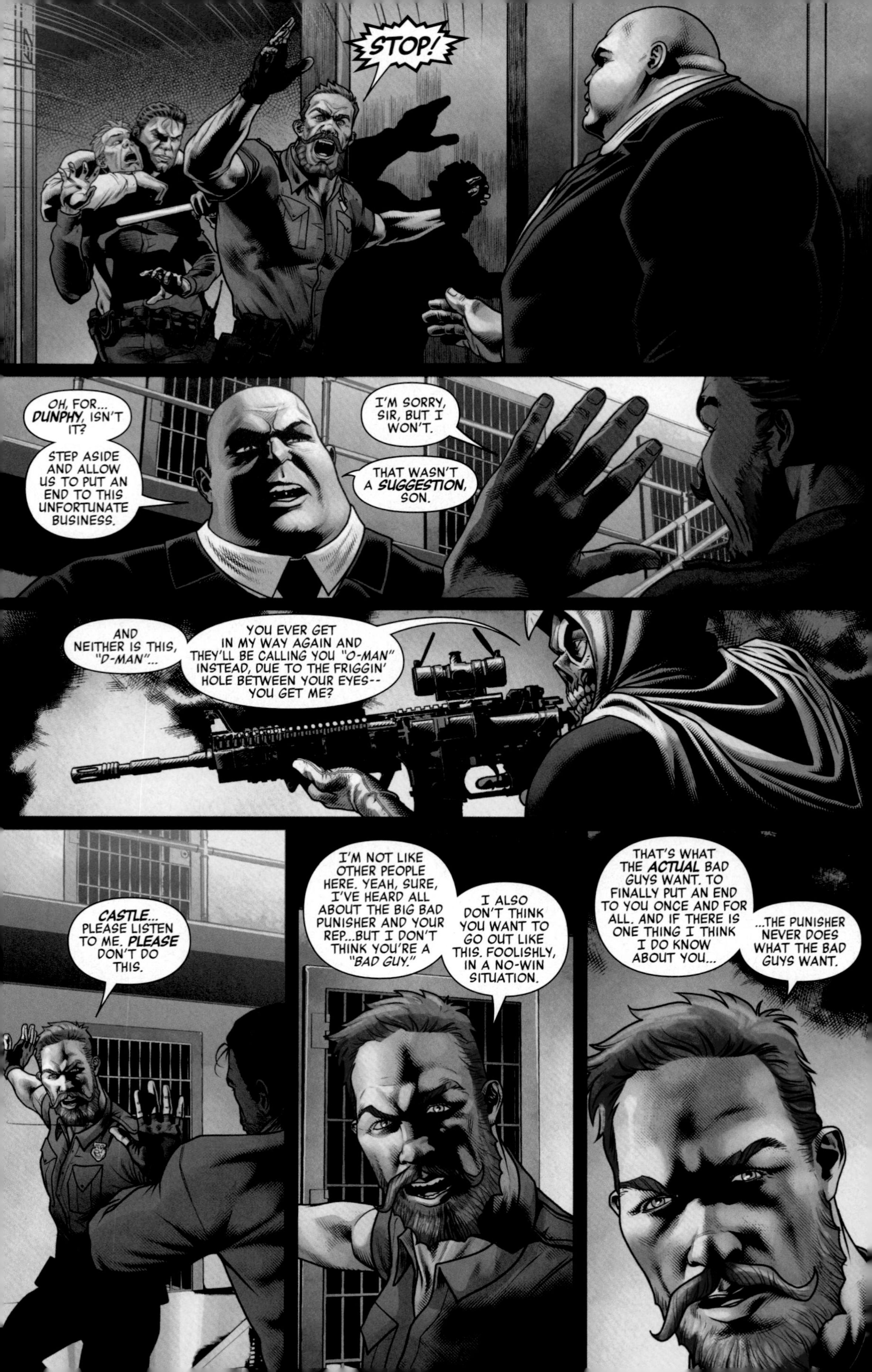
STOP!
OH, FOR... DUNPHY, ISN'T IT?
STEP ASIDE AND ALLOW US TO PUT AN END TO THIS UNFORTUNATE BUSINESS.
I'M SORRY, SIR, BUT I WON'T.
THAT WASN'T A SUGGESTION, SON.
AND NEITHER IS THIS, "D-MAN"...
YOU EVER GET IN MY WAY AGAIN AND THEY'LL BE CALLING YOU "O-MAN" INSTEAD, DUE TO THE FRIGGIN' HOLE BETWEEN YOUR EYES-- YOU GET ME?
CASTLE... PLEASE LISTEN TO ME. PLEASE DON'T DO THIS.
I'M NOT LIKE OTHER PEOPLE HERE. YEAH, SURE, I'VE HEARD ALL ABOUT THE BIG BAD PUNISHER AND YOUR REP...BUT I DON'T THINK YOU'RE A "BAD GUY."
I ALSO DON'T THINK YOU WANT TO GO OUT LIKE THIS. FOOLISHLY, IN A NO-WIN SITUATION.
THAT'S WHAT THE ACTUAL BAD GUYS WANT. TO FINALLY PUT AN END TO YOU ONCE AND FOR ALL. AND IF THERE IS ONE THING I THINK I DO KNOW ABOUT YOU...
...THE PUNISHER NEVER DOES WHAT THE BAD GUYS WANT.

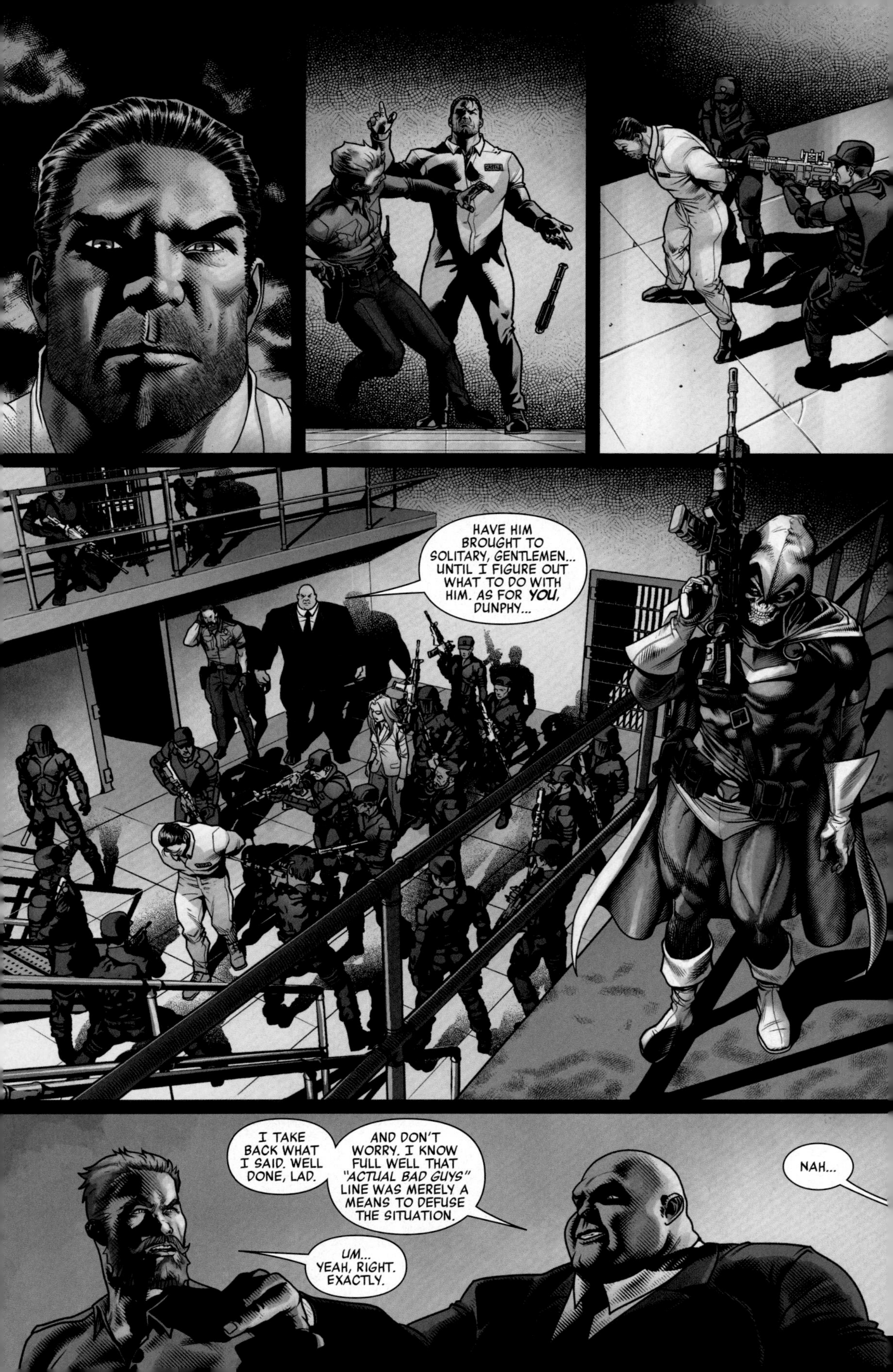
HAVE HIM BROUGHT TO SOLITARY, GENTLEMEN... UNTIL I FIGURE OUT WHAT TO DO WITH HIM. AS FOR *YOU*, DUNPHY...
I TAKE BACK WHAT I SAID. WELL DONE, LAD.
AND DON'T WORRY. I KNOW FULL WELL THAT *"ACTUAL BAD GUYS"* LINE WAS MERELY A MEANS TO DEFUSE THE SITUATION.
UM... YEAH, RIGHT. EXACTLY.
NAH...

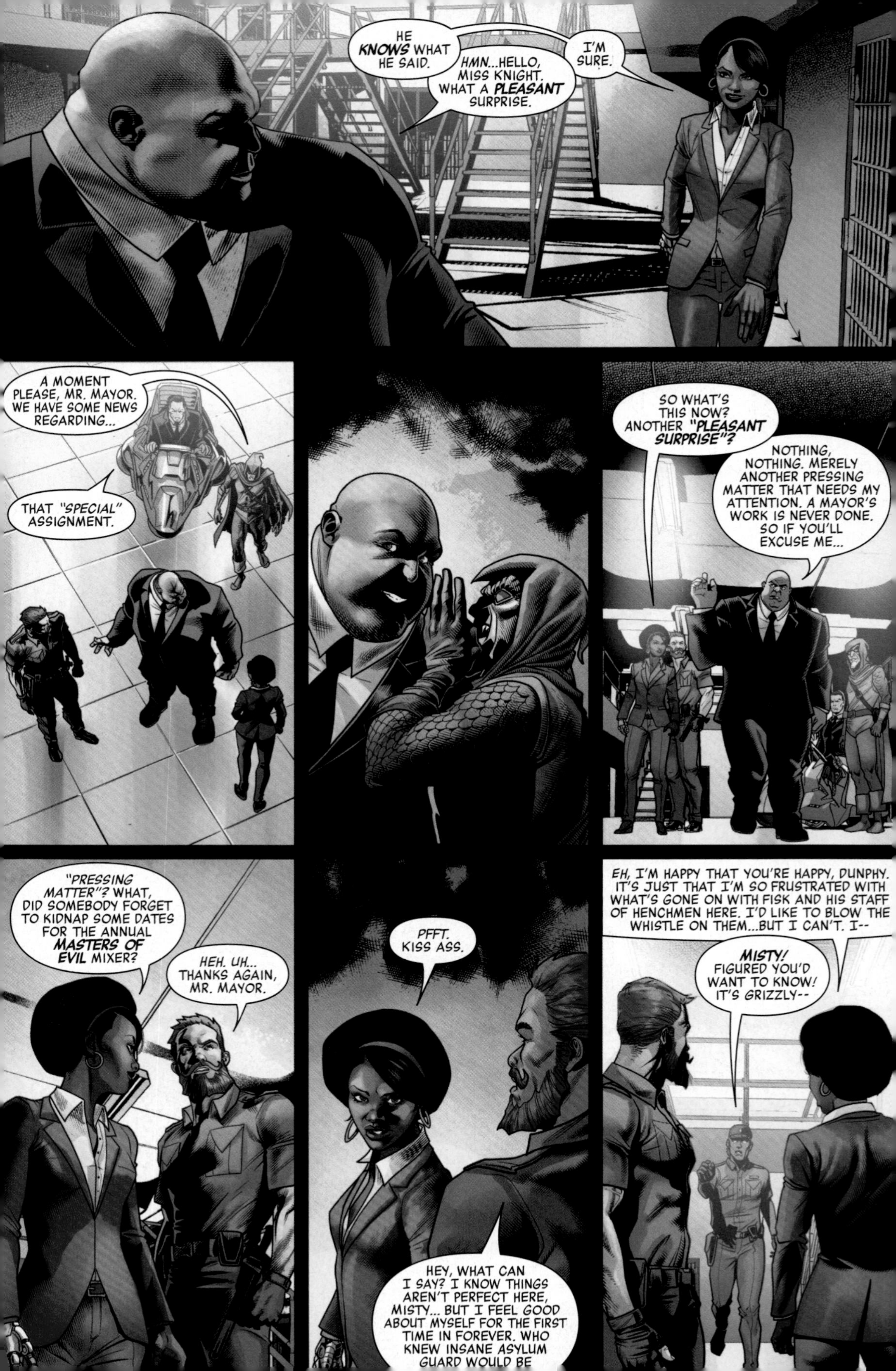
HE KNOWS WHAT HE SAID.
HMN...HELLO, MISS KNIGHT. WHAT A PLEASANT SURPRISE.
I'M SURE.
A MOMENT PLEASE, MR. MAYOR. WE HAVE SOME NEWS REGARDING...
THAT "SPECIAL" ASSIGNMENT.
SO WHAT'S THIS NOW? ANOTHER "PLEASANT SURPRISE"?
NOTHING, NOTHING. MERELY ANOTHER PRESSING MATTER THAT NEEDS MY ATTENTION. A MAYOR'S WORK IS NEVER DONE. SO IF YOU'LL EXCUSE ME...
"PRESSING MATTER"? WHAT, DID SOMEBODY FORGET TO KIDNAP SOME DATES FOR THE ANNUAL MASTERS OF EVIL MIXER?
HEH. UH... THANKS AGAIN, MR. MAYOR.
PFFT. KISS ASS.
HEY, WHAT CAN I SAY? I KNOW THINGS AREN'T PERFECT HERE, MISTY... BUT I FEEL GOOD ABOUT MYSELF FOR THE FIRST TIME IN FOREVER. WHO KNEW INSANE ASYLUM GUARD WOULD BE
EH, I'M HAPPY THAT YOU'RE HAPPY, DUNPHY. IT'S JUST THAT I'M SO FRUSTRATED WITH WHAT'S GONE ON WITH FISK AND HIS STAFF OF HENCHMEN HERE. I'D LIKE TO BLOW THE WHISTLE ON THEM...BUT I CAN'T. I--
MISTY! FIGURED YOU'D WANT TO KNOW! IT'S GRIZZLY--

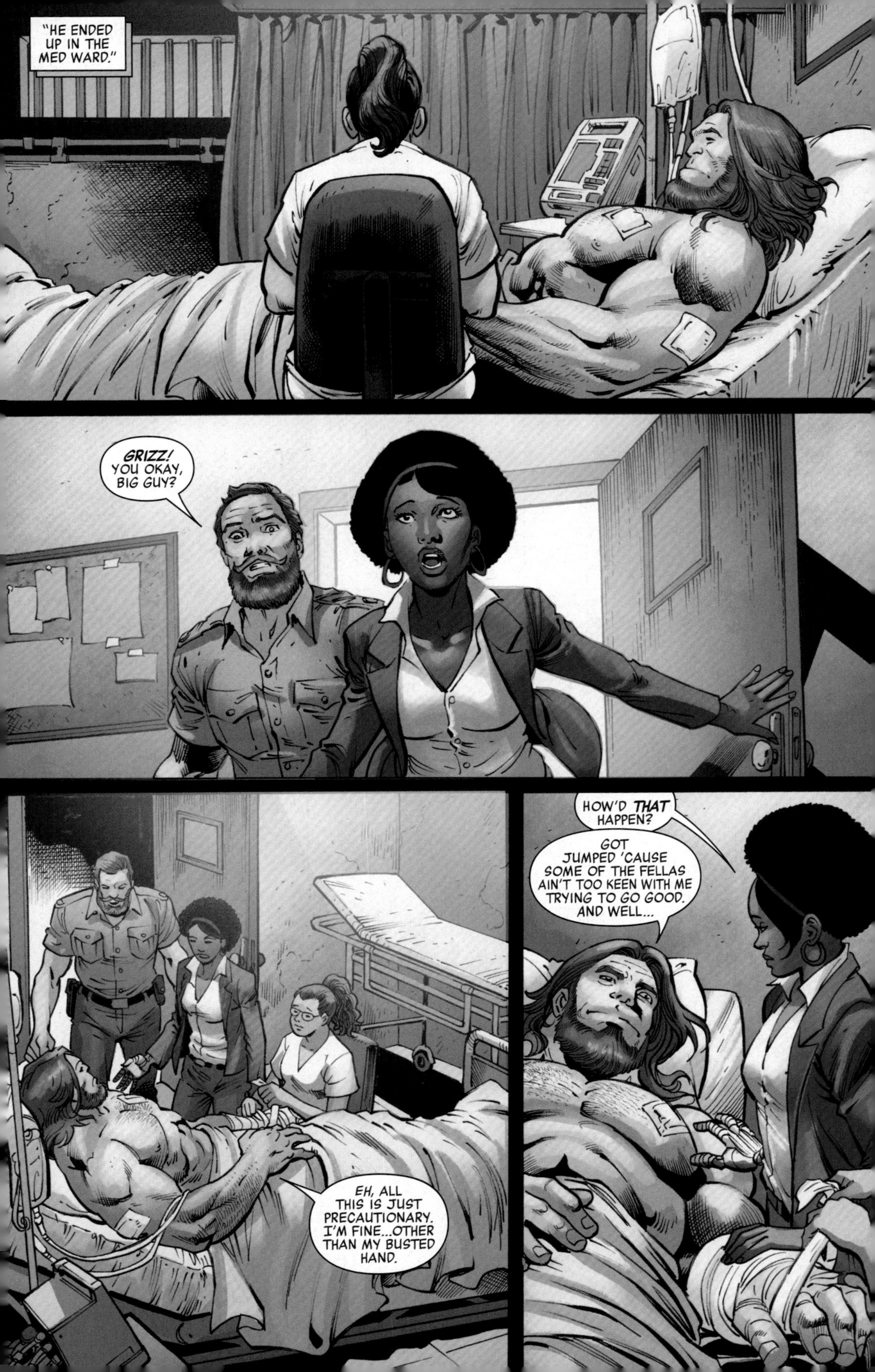
"HE ENDED UP IN THE MED WARD."
GRIZZ! YOU OKAY, BIG GUY?
EH, ALL THIS IS JUST PRECAUTIONARY. I'M FINE...OTHER THAN MY BUSTED HAND.
HOW'D THAT HAPPEN?
GOT JUMPED 'CAUSE SOME OF THE FELLAS AIN'T TOO KEEN WITH ME TRYING TO GO GOOD. AND WELL...

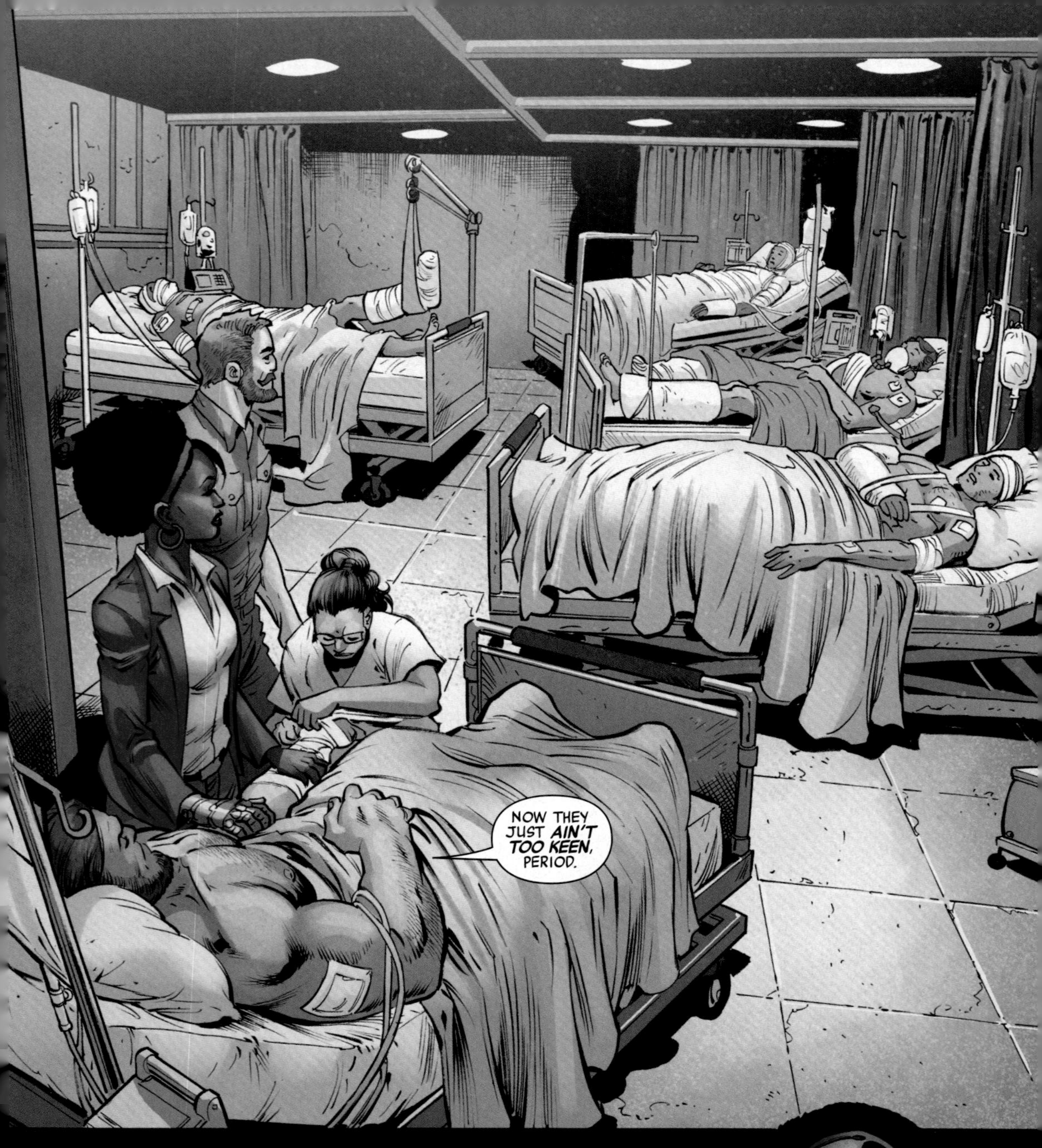
NOW THEY JUST AIN'T TOO KEEN, PERIOD.

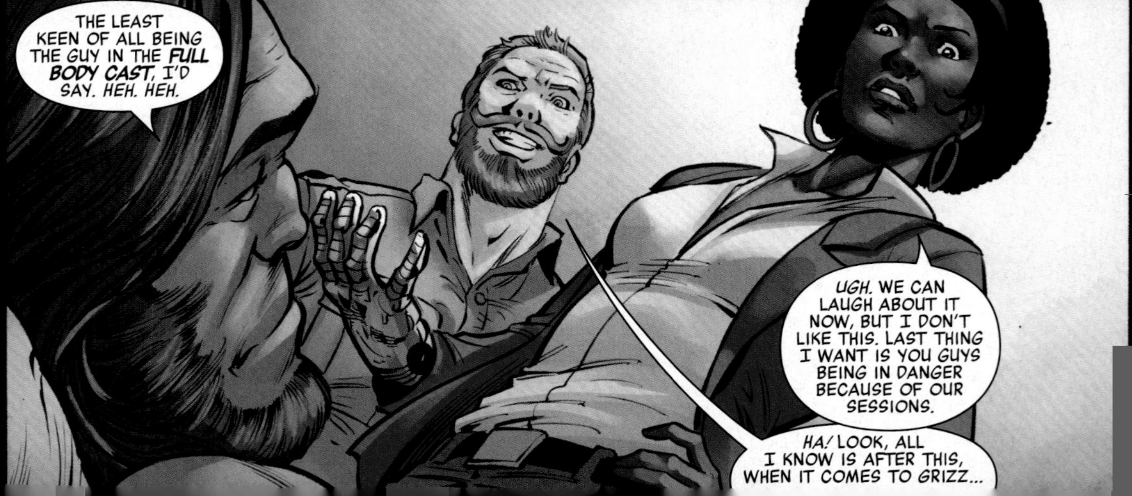
THE LEAST KEEN OF ALL BEING THE GUY IN THE FULL BODY CAST, I'D SAY. HEH. HEH.
UGH. WE CAN LAUGH ABOUT IT NOW, BUT I DON'T LIKE THIS. LAST THING I WANT IS YOU GUYS BEING IN DANGER BECAUSE OF OUR SESSIONS.
HA! LOOK, ALL I KNOW IS AFTER THIS, WHEN IT COMES TO GRIZZ...

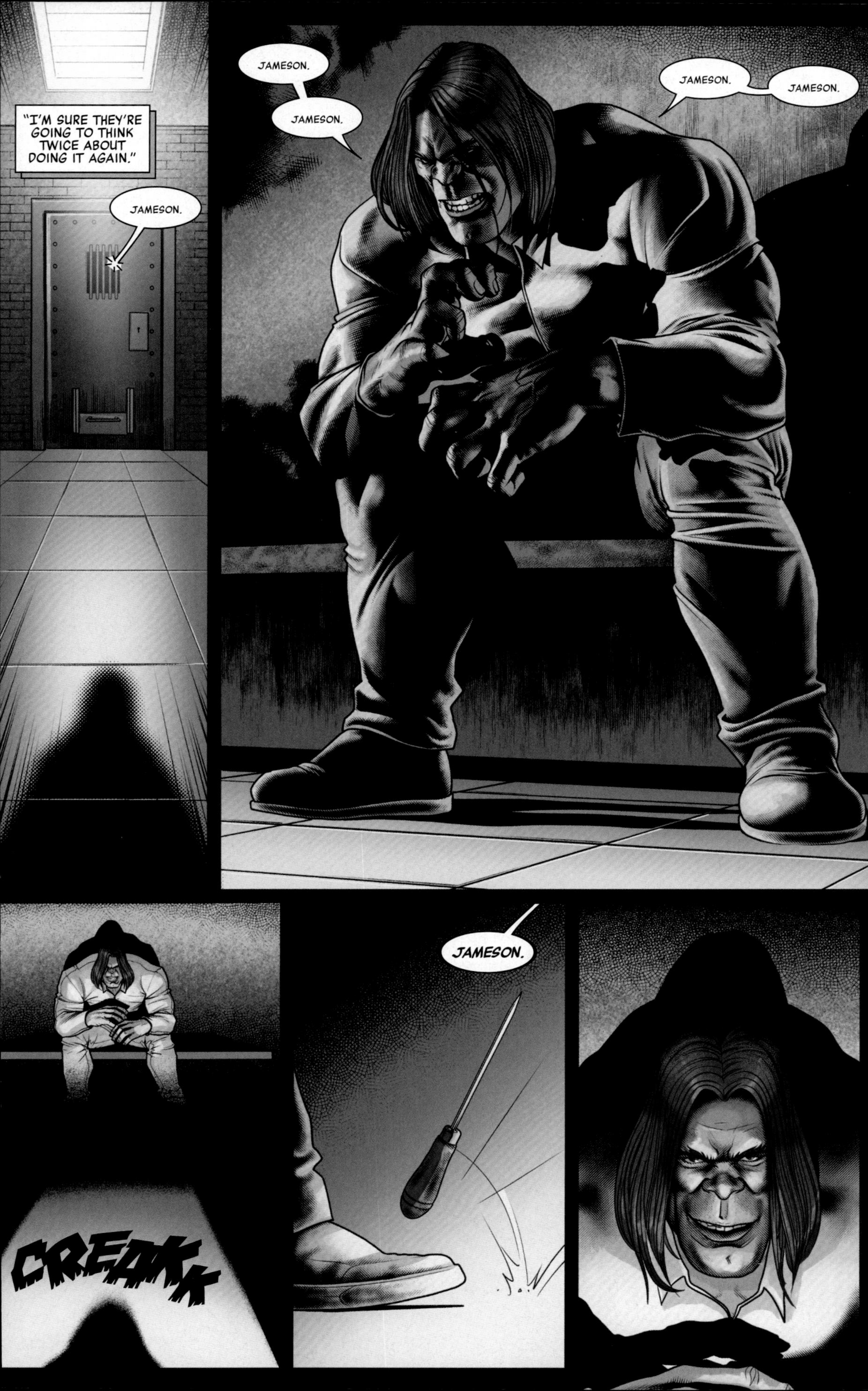
"I'M SURE THEY'RE GOING TO THINK TWICE ABOUT DOING IT AGAIN."
JAMESON.
JAMESON.
JAMESON.
JAMESON.
JAMESON.
CREAKK
JAMESON.

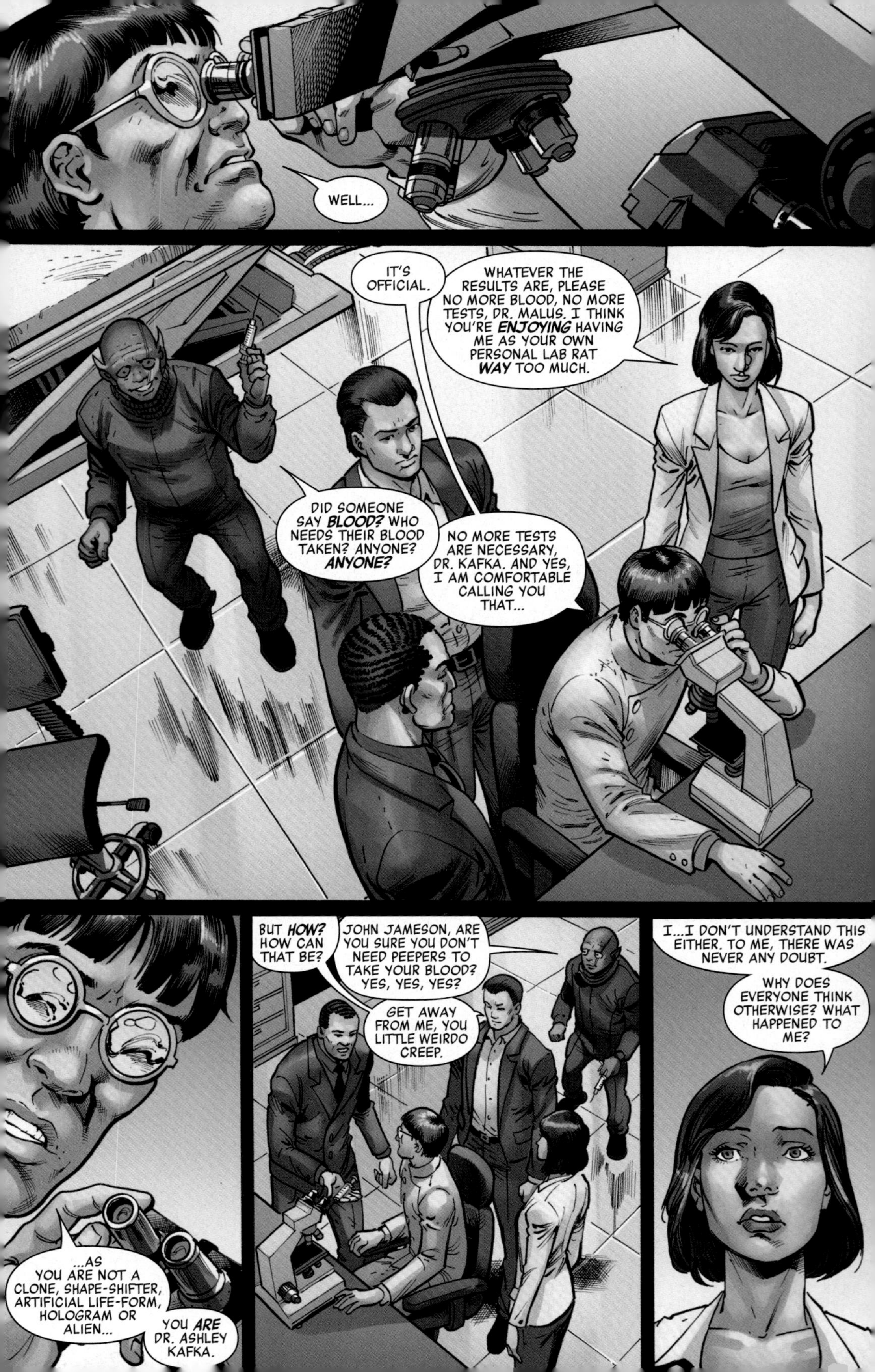
WELL...
IT'S OFFICIAL.
WHATEVER THE RESULTS ARE, PLEASE NO MORE BLOOD, NO MORE TESTS, DR. MALUS. I THINK YOU'RE ENJOYING HAVING ME AS YOUR OWN PERSONAL LAB RAT WAY TOO MUCH.
DID SOMEONE SAY BLOOD? WHO NEEDS THEIR BLOOD TAKEN? ANYONE? ANYONE?
NO MORE TESTS ARE NECESSARY, DR. KAFKA. AND YES, I AM COMFORTABLE CALLING YOU THAT...
...AS YOU ARE NOT A CLONE, SHAPE-SHIFTER, ARTIFICIAL LIFE-FORM, HOLOGRAM OR ALIEN...
YOU ARE DR. ASHLEY KAFKA.
BUT HOW? HOW CAN THAT BE?
JOHN JAMESON, ARE YOU SURE YOU DON'T NEED PEEPERS TO TAKE YOUR BLOOD? YES, YES, YES?
GET AWAY FROM ME, YOU LITTLE WEIRDO CREEP.
I...I DON'T UNDERSTAND THIS EITHER. TO ME, THERE WAS NEVER ANY DOUBT.
WHY DOES EVERYONE THINK OTHERWISE? WHAT HAPPENED TO ME?

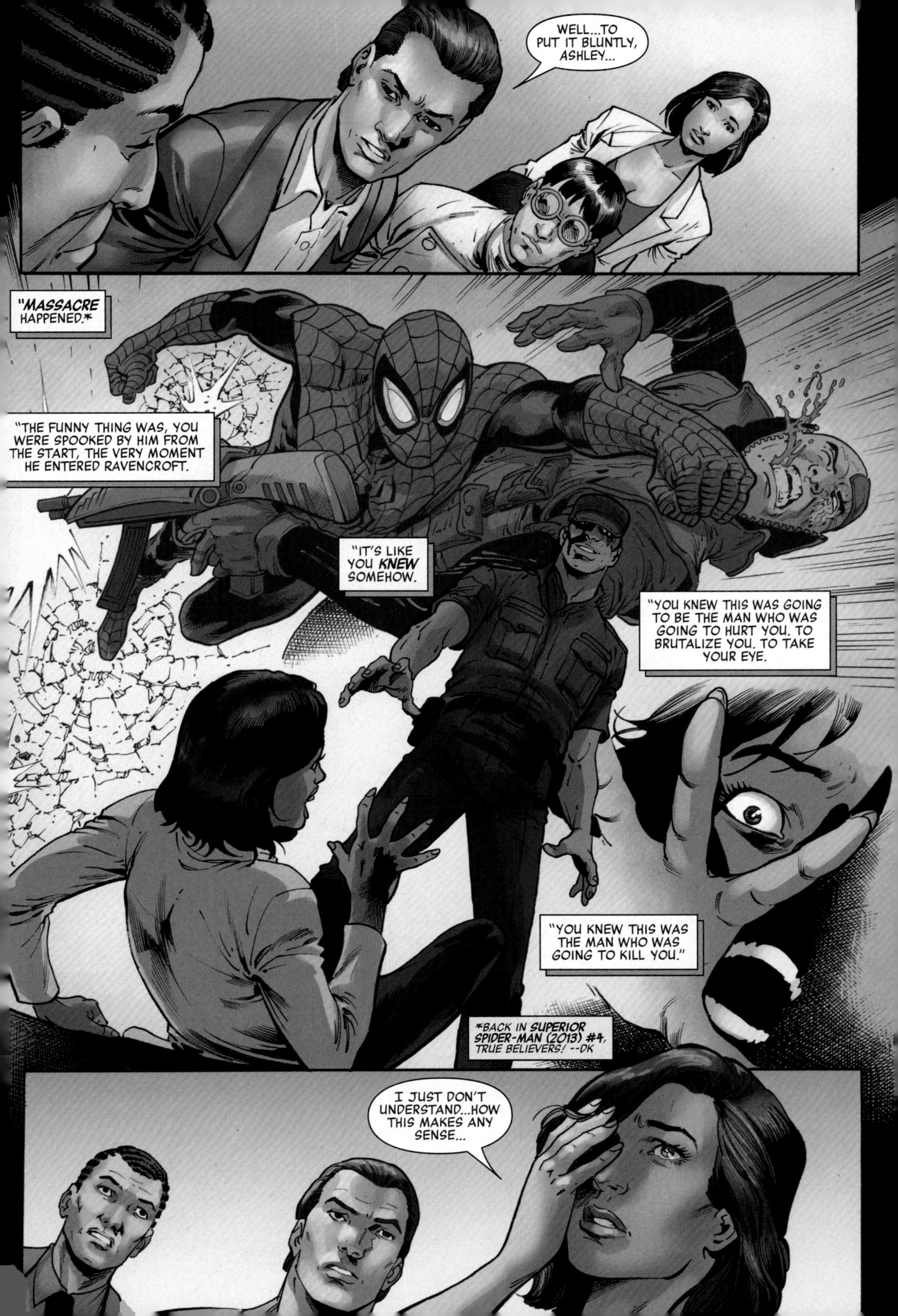
WELL...TO PUT IT BLUNTLY, ASHLEY...
"MASSACRE HAPPENED.*
"THE FUNNY THING WAS, YOU WERE SPOOKED BY HIM FROM THE START, THE VERY MOMENT HE ENTERED RAVENCROFT.
"IT'S LIKE YOU KNEW SOMEHOW.
"YOU KNEW THIS WAS GOING TO BE THE MAN WHO WAS GOING TO HURT YOU. TO BRUTALIZE YOU. TO TAKE YOUR EYE.
"YOU KNEW THIS WAS THE MAN WHO WAS GOING TO KILL YOU."
*BACK IN SUPERIOR SPIDER-MAN (2013) #4, TRUE BELIEVERS! --DK
I JUST DON'T UNDERSTAND...HOW THIS MAKES ANY SENSE...

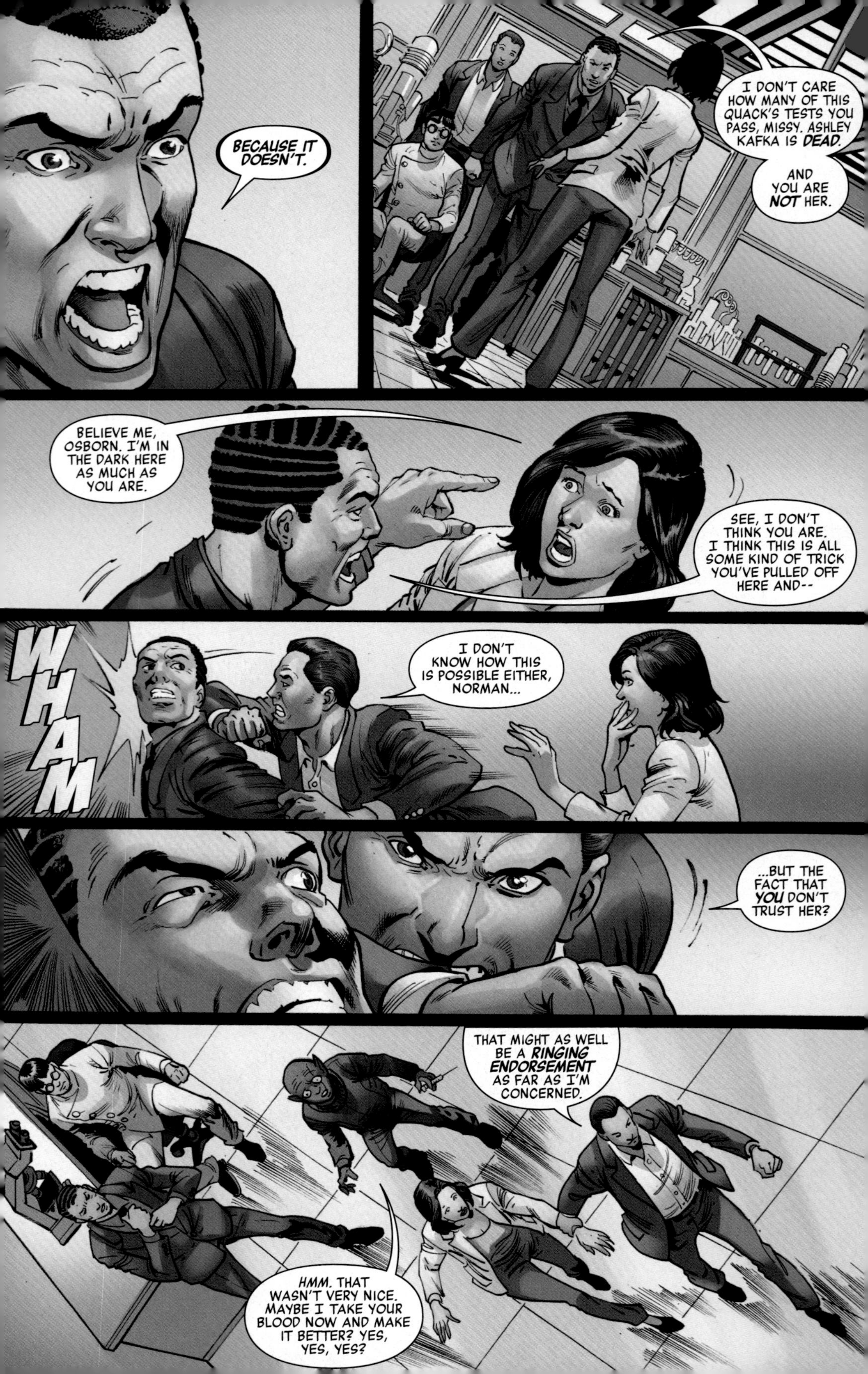

BECAUSE IT DOESN'T.
I DON'T CARE HOW MANY OF THIS QUACK'S TESTS YOU PASS, MISSY. ASHLEY KAFKA IS DEAD.
AND YOU ARE NOT HER.
BELIEVE ME, OSBORN. I'M IN THE DARK HERE AS MUCH AS YOU ARE.
SEE, I DON'T THINK YOU ARE. I THINK THIS IS ALL SOME KIND OF TRICK YOU'VE PULLED OFF HERE AND--
WHAM
I DON'T KNOW HOW THIS IS POSSIBLE EITHER, NORMAN...
...BUT THE FACT THAT YOU DON'T TRUST HER?
THAT MIGHT AS WELL BE A RINGING ENDORSEMENT AS FAR AS I'M CONCERNED.
HMM. THAT WASN'T VERY NICE. MAYBE I TAKE YOUR BLOOD NOW AND MAKE IT BETTER? YES, YES, YES?

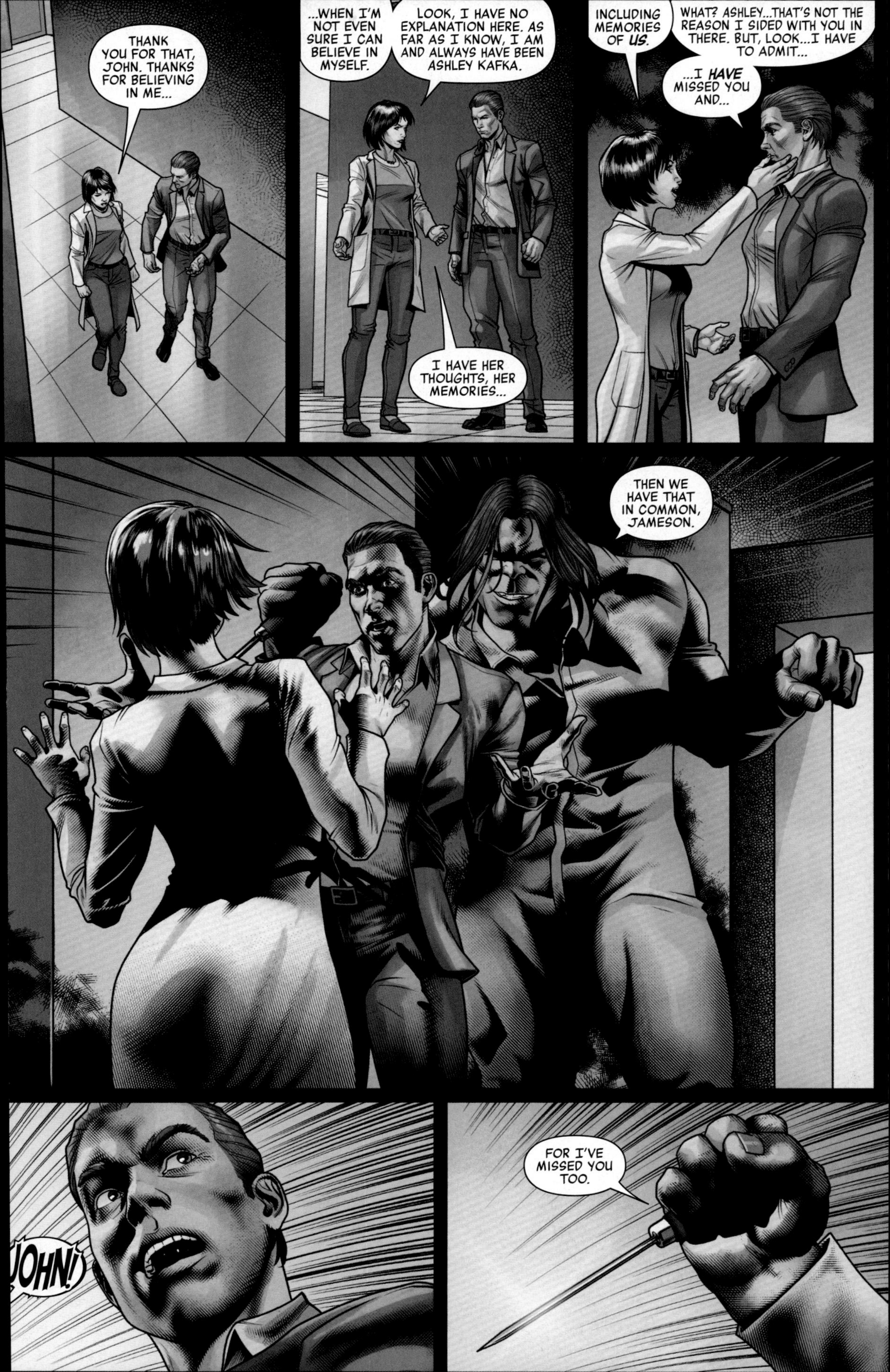
THANK YOU FOR THAT, JOHN. THANKS FOR BELIEVING IN ME...
...WHEN I'M NOT EVEN SURE I CAN BELIEVE IN MYSELF.
LOOK, I HAVE NO EXPLANATION HERE. AS FAR AS I KNOW, I AM AND ALWAYS HAVE BEEN ASHLEY KAFKA.
I HAVE HER THOUGHTS, HER MEMORIES...
INCLUDING MEMORIES OF US.
WHAT? ASHLEY...THAT'S NOT THE REASON I SIDED WITH YOU IN THERE. BUT, LOOK...I HAVE TO ADMIT...
...I HAVE MISSED YOU AND...
THEN WE HAVE THAT IN COMMON, JAMESON.
JOHN!
FOR I'VE MISSED YOU TOO.

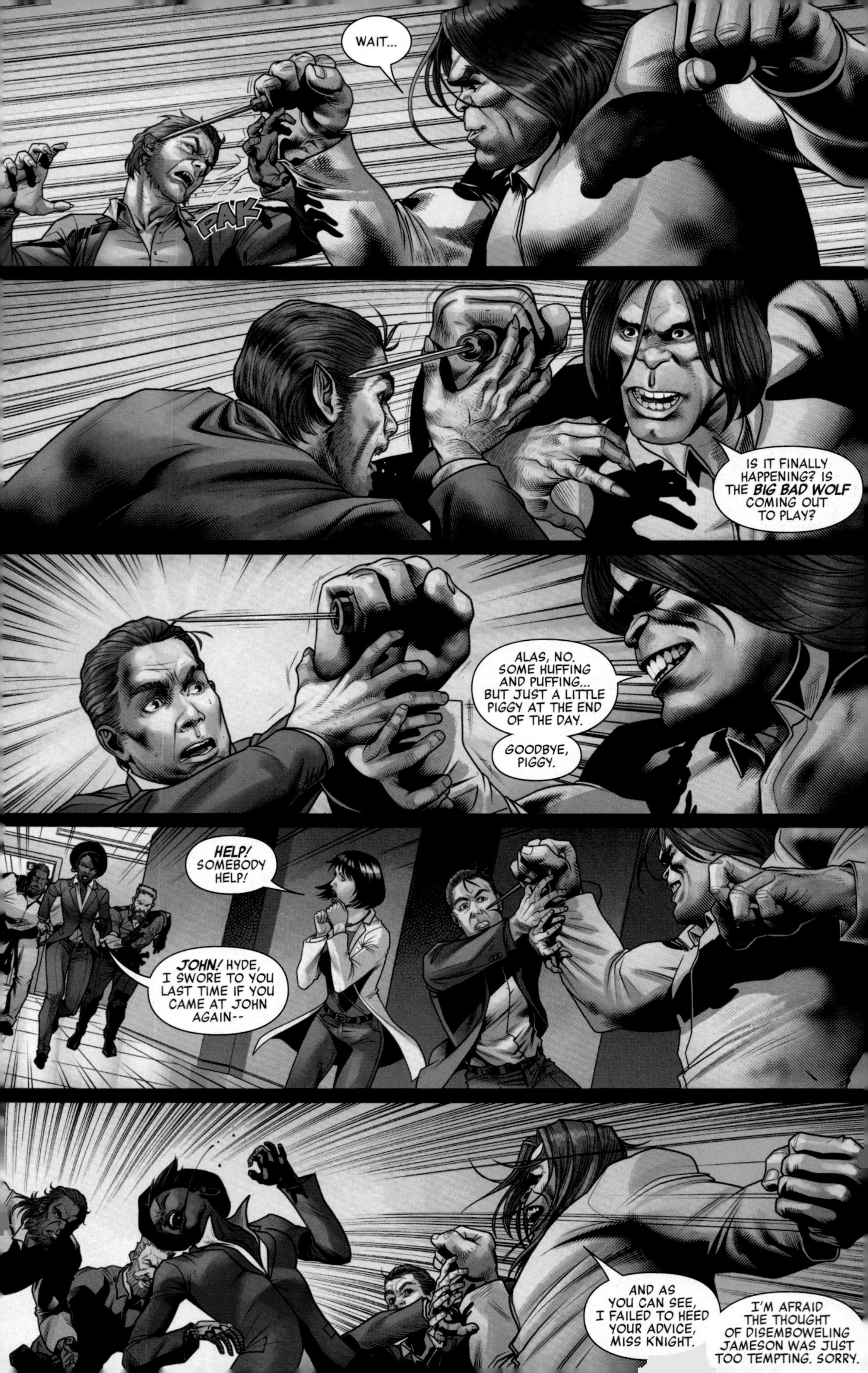

WAIT...
PAK
IS IT FINALLY HAPPENING? IS THE BIG BAD WOLF COMING OUT TO PLAY?
ALAS, NO. SOME HUFFING AND PUFFING... BUT JUST A LITTLE PIGGY AT THE END OF THE DAY.
GOODBYE, PIGGY.
HELP! SOMEBODY HELP!
JOHN! HYDE, I SWORE TO YOU LAST TIME IF YOU CAME AT JOHN AGAIN--
AND AS YOU CAN SEE, I FAILED TO HEED YOUR ADVICE, MISS KNIGHT.
I'M AFRAID THE THOUGHT OF DISEMBOWELING JAMESON WAS JUST TOO TEMPTING. SORRY.

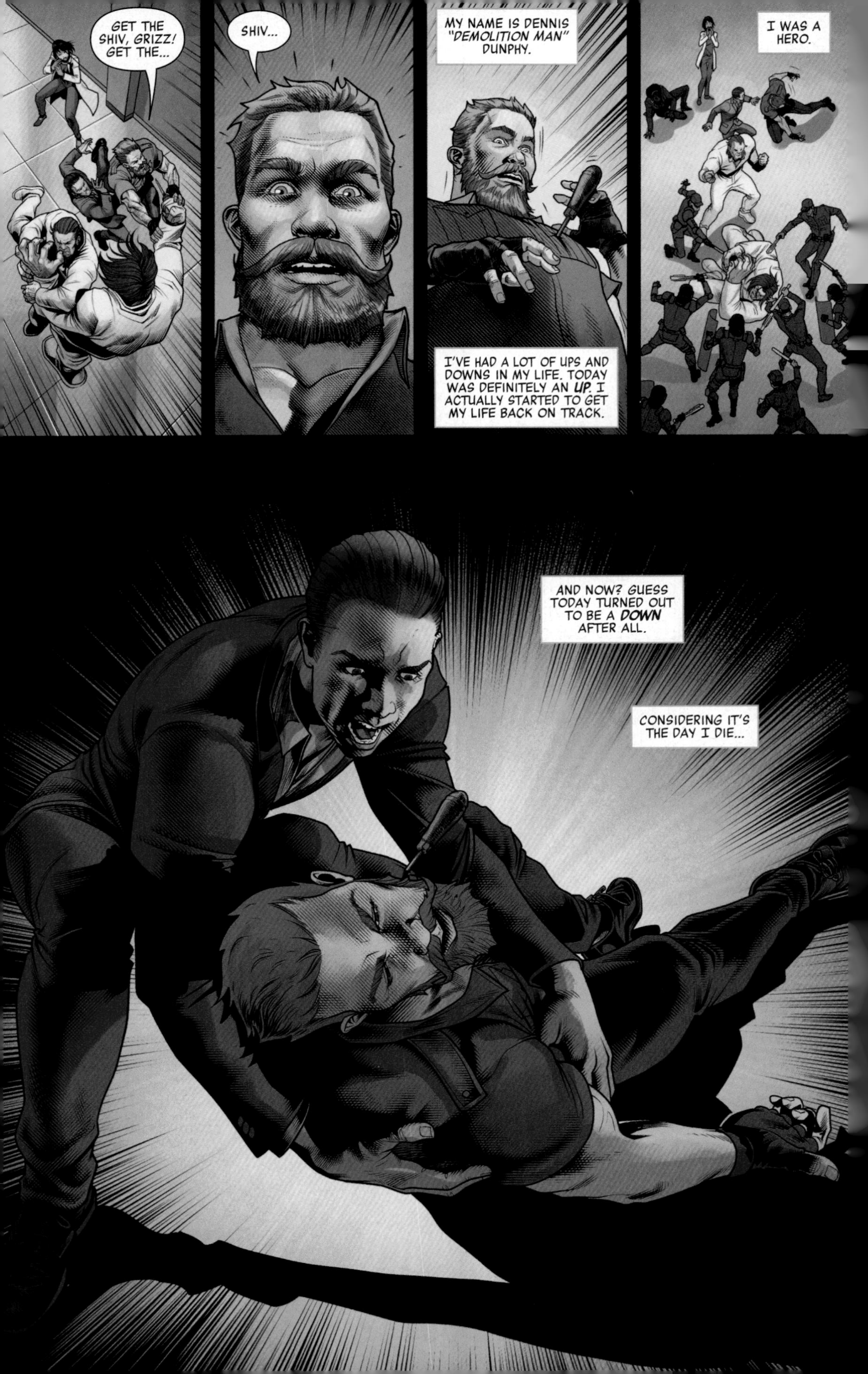
GET THE SHIV, GRIZZ! GET THE...
SHIV...
MY NAME IS DENNIS "DEMOLITION MAN" DUNPHY.
I'VE HAD A LOT OF UPS AND DOWNS IN MY LIFE. TODAY WAS DEFINITELY AN *UP*. I ACTUALLY STARTED TO GET MY LIFE BACK ON TRACK.
I WAS A HERO.
AND NOW? GUESS TODAY TURNED OUT TO BE A *DOWN* AFTER ALL.
CONSIDERING IT'S THE DAY I DIE...

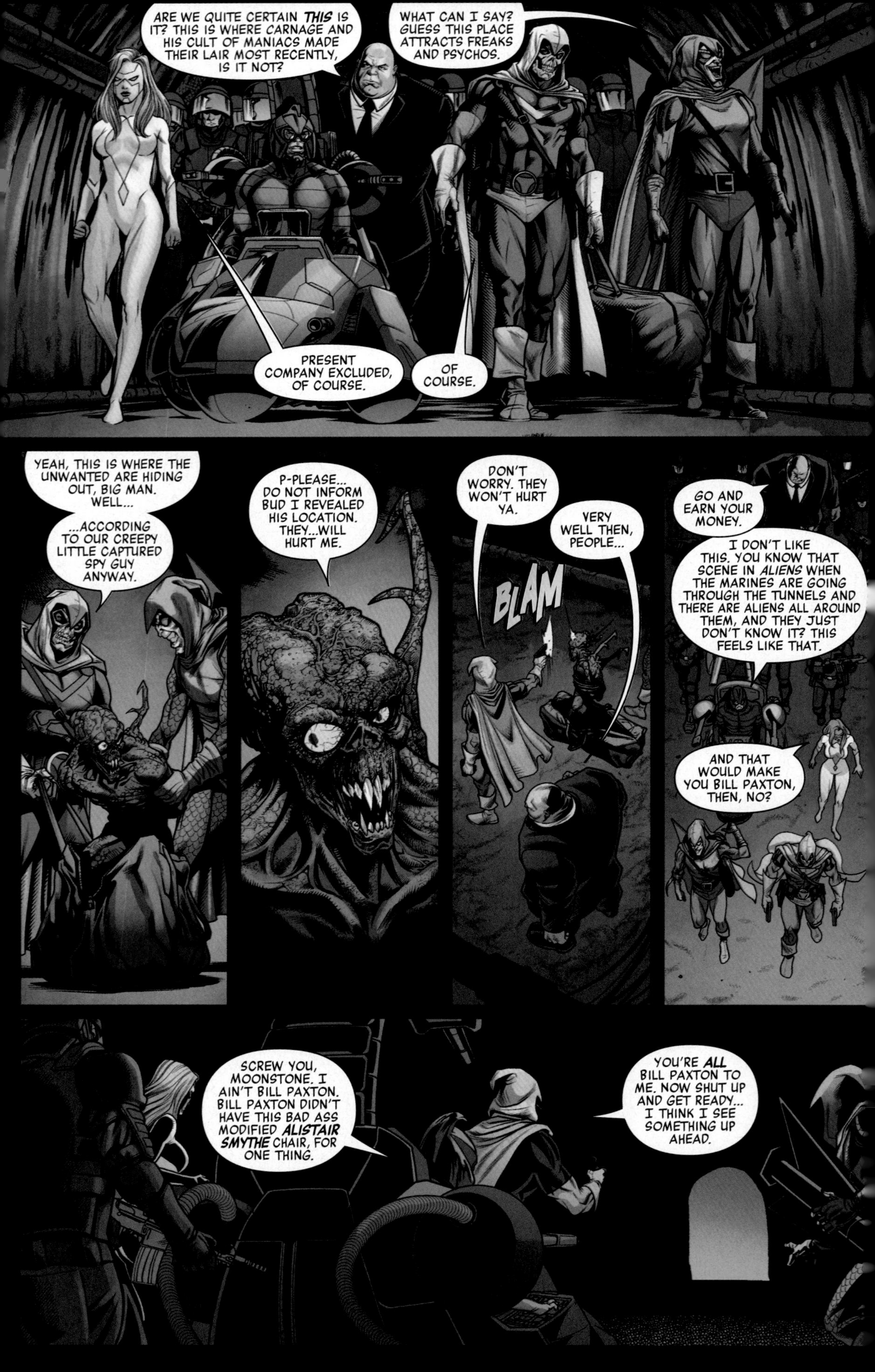
ARE WE QUITE CERTAIN THIS IS IT? THIS IS WHERE CARNAGE AND HIS CULT OF MANIACS MADE THEIR LAIR MOST RECENTLY, IS IT NOT?
WHAT CAN I SAY? GUESS THIS PLACE ATTRACTS FREAKS AND PSYCHOS.
PRESENT COMPANY EXCLUDED, OF COURSE.
OF COURSE.
YEAH, THIS IS WHERE THE UNWANTED ARE HIDING OUT, BIG MAN. WELL...
...ACCORDING TO OUR CREEPY LITTLE CAPTURED SPY GUY ANYWAY.
P-PLEASE... DO NOT INFORM BUD I REVEALED HIS LOCATION. THEY...WILL HURT ME.
DON'T WORRY. THEY WON'T HURT YA.
VERY WELL THEN, PEOPLE...
BLAM
GO AND EARN YOUR MONEY.
I DON'T LIKE THIS. YOU KNOW THAT SCENE IN ALIENS WHEN THE MARINES ARE GOING THROUGH THE TUNNELS AND THERE ARE ALIENS ALL AROUND THEM, AND THEY JUST DON'T KNOW IT? THIS FEELS LIKE THAT.
AND THAT WOULD MAKE YOU BILL PAXTON, THEN, NO?
SCREW YOU, MOONSTONE. I AIN'T BILL PAXTON. BILL PAXTON DIDN'T HAVE THIS BAD ASS MODIFIED ALISTAIR SMYTHE CHAIR, FOR ONE THING.
YOU'RE ALL BILL PAXTON TO ME. NOW SHUT UP AND GET READY... I THINK I SEE SOMETHING UP AHEAD.

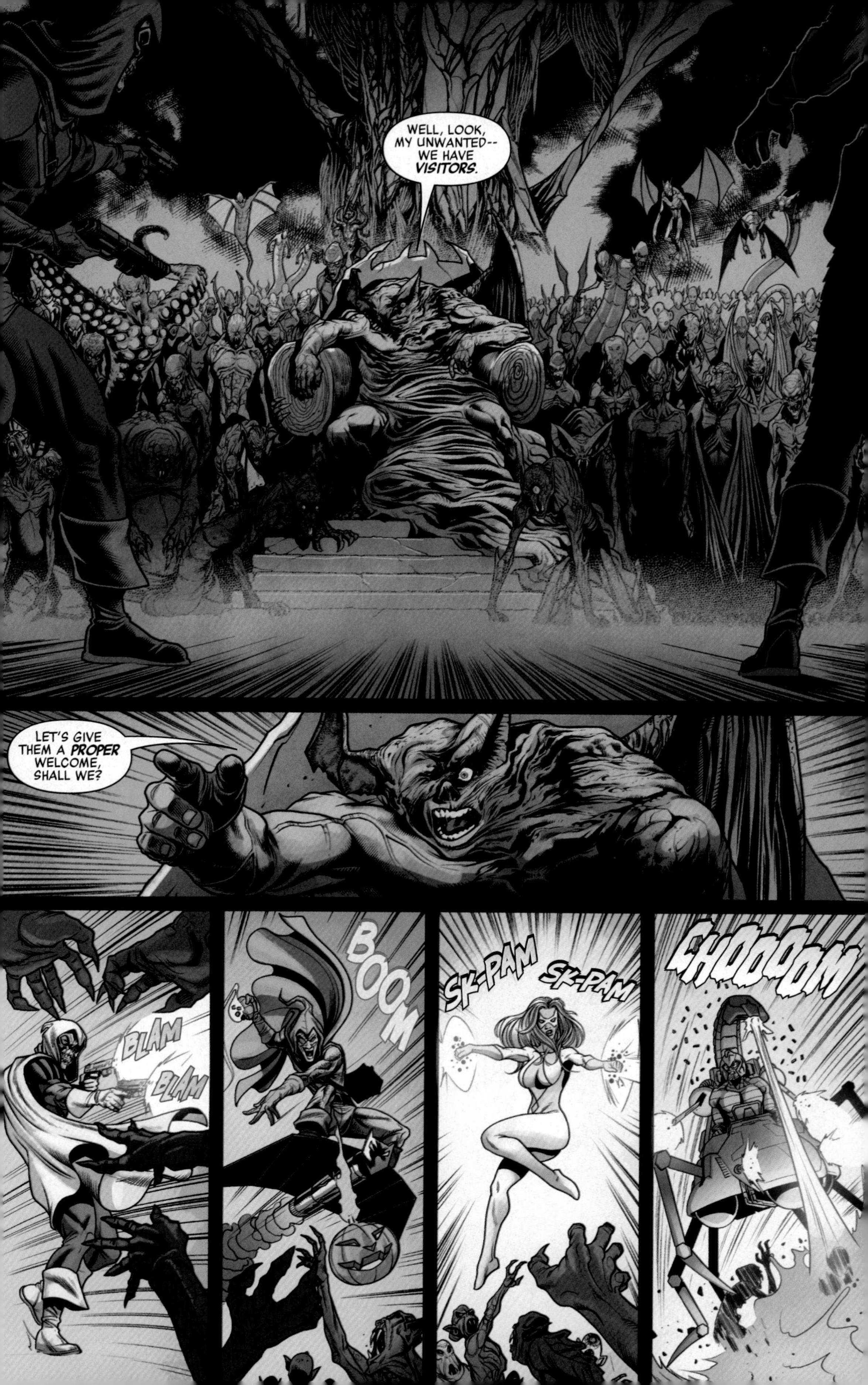
WELL, LOOK, MY UNWANTED-- WE HAVE VISITORS.
LET'S GIVE THEM A PROPER WELCOME, SHALL WE?
BLAM
BLAM
BOOM
SK-PAM
SK-PAM
CHOOOOM

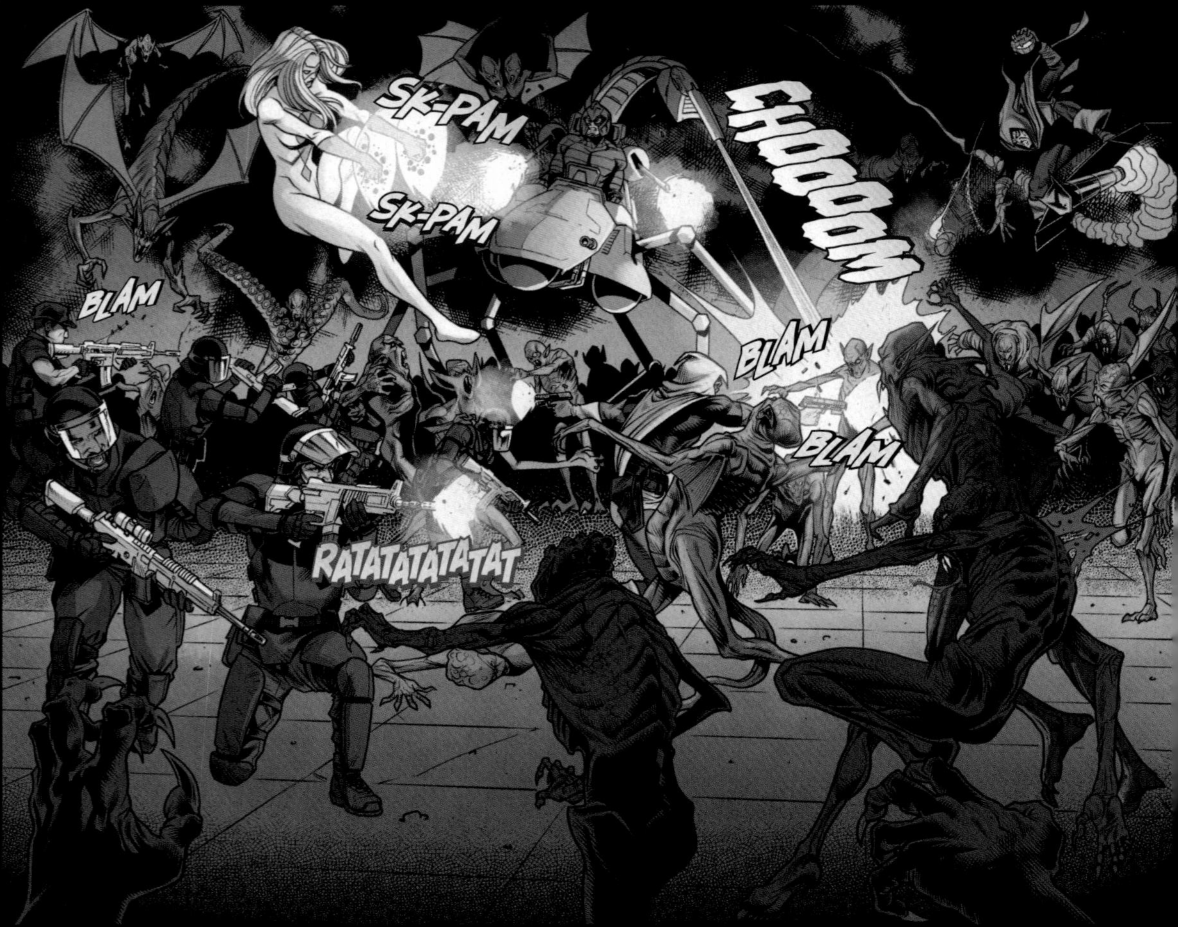
SK-PAM
SK-PAM
CHOOOOM
BLAM
BLAM
BLAM
RATATATATATAT

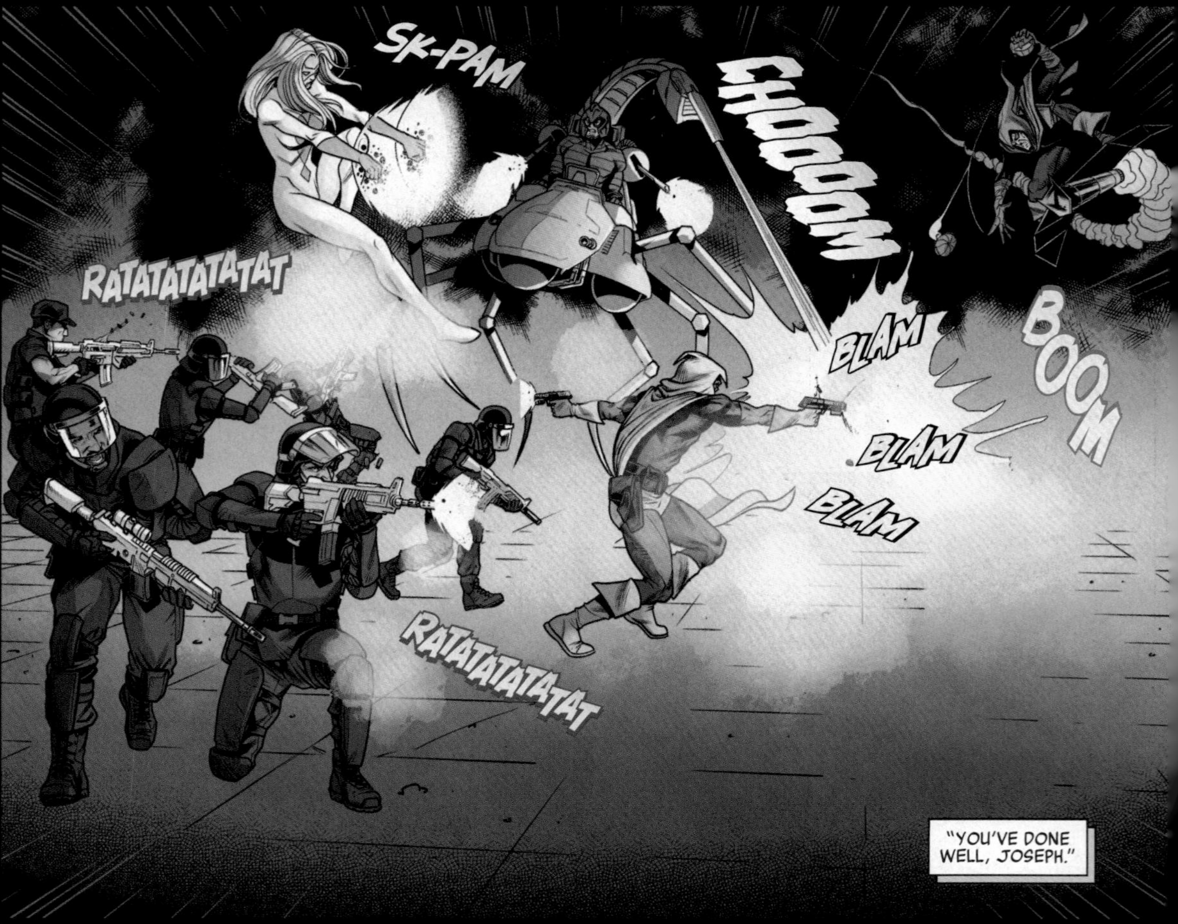
SK-PAM
CHOOOOM
RATATATATATAT
BLAM
BOOM
BLAM
BLAM
RATATATATATAT
"YOU'VE DONE WELL, JOSEPH."

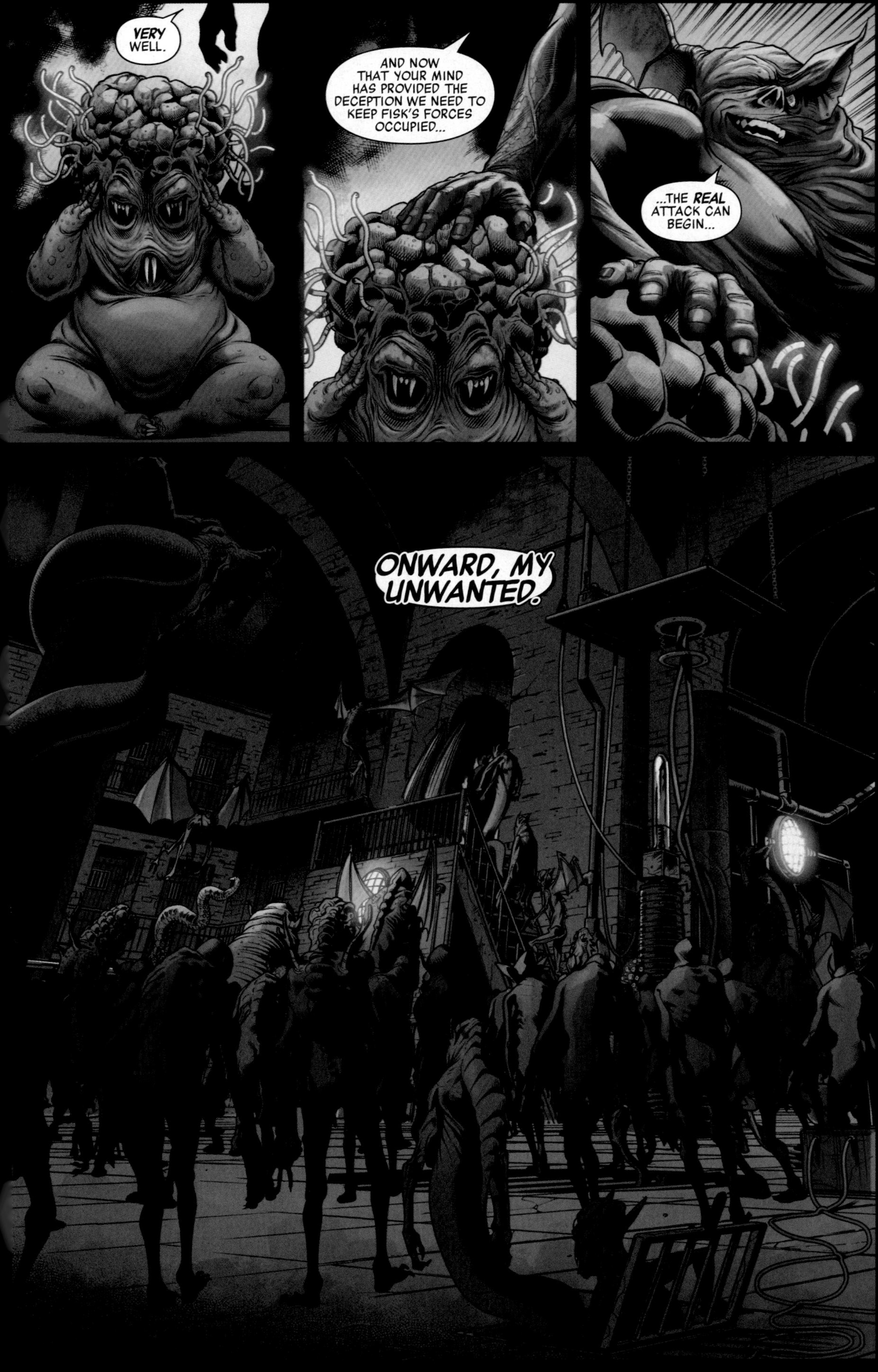
VERY WELL.
AND NOW THAT YOUR MIND HAS PROVIDED THE DECEPTION WE NEED TO KEEP FISK'S FORCES OCCUPIED...
...THE REAL ATTACK CAN BEGIN...
ONWARD, MY UNWANTED.

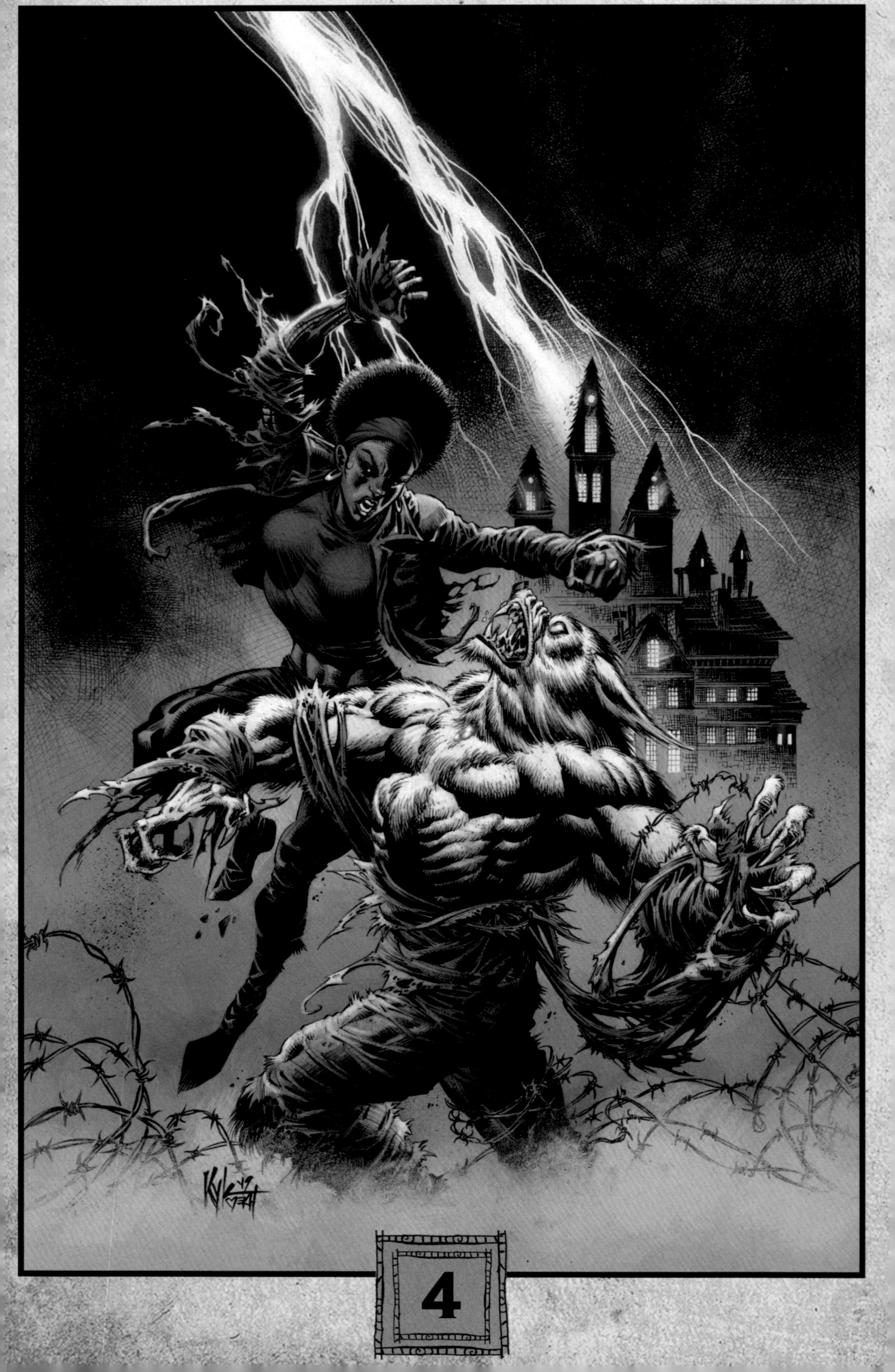

4

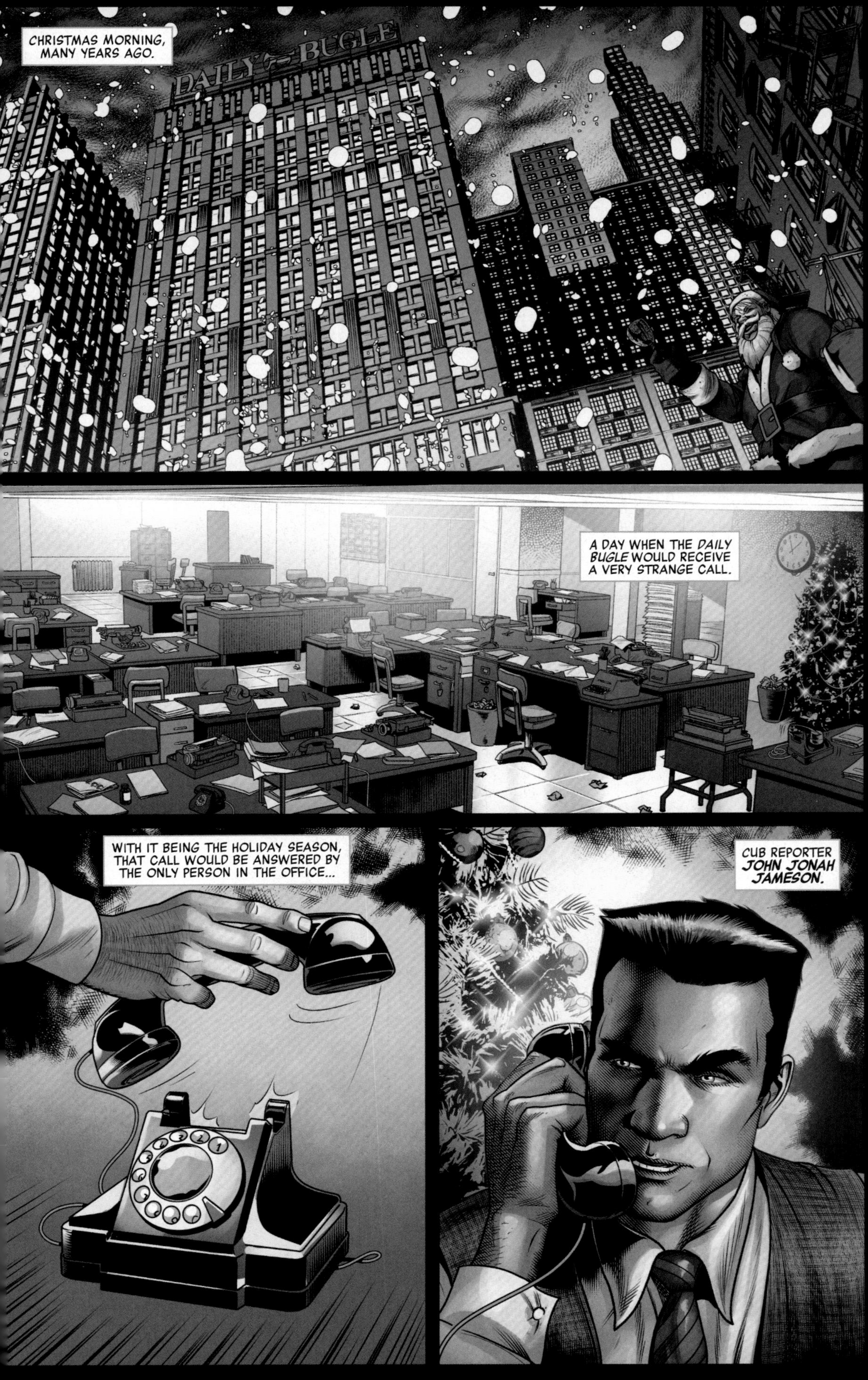
CHRISTMAS MORNING, MANY YEARS AGO.
DAILY BUGLE
A DAY WHEN THE *DAILY BUGLE* WOULD RECEIVE A VERY STRANGE CALL.
WITH IT BEING THE HOLIDAY SEASON, THAT CALL WOULD BE ANSWERED BY THE ONLY PERSON IN THE OFFICE...
CUB REPORTER ***JOHN JONAH JAMESON.***

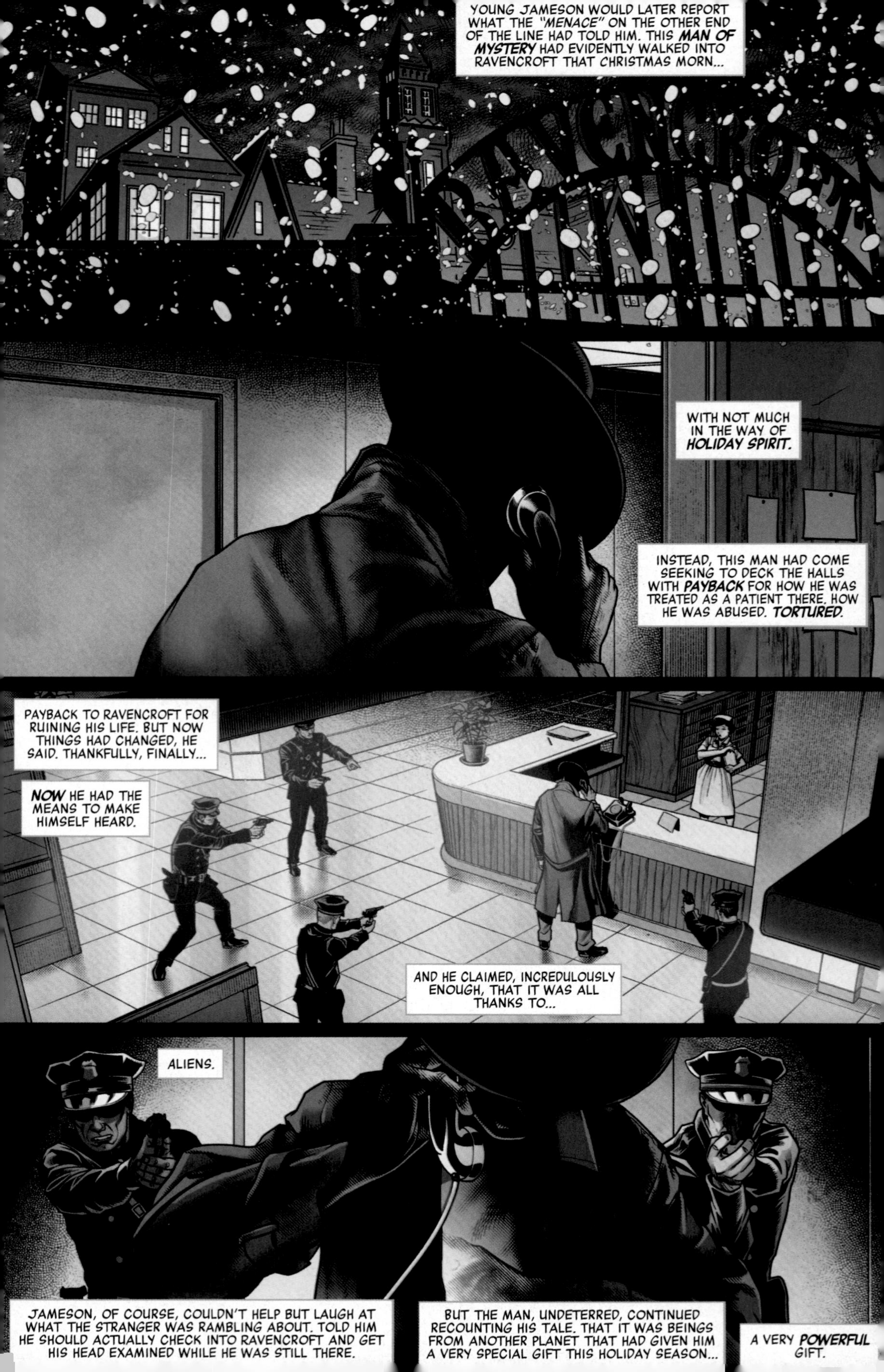
YOUNG JAMESON WOULD LATER REPORT WHAT THE "MENACE" ON THE OTHER END OF THE LINE HAD TOLD HIM. THIS MAN OF MYSTERY HAD EVIDENTLY WALKED INTO RAVENCROFT THAT CHRISTMAS MORN...
WITH NOT MUCH IN THE WAY OF HOLIDAY SPIRIT.
INSTEAD, THIS MAN HAD COME SEEKING TO DECK THE HALLS WITH PAYBACK FOR HOW HE WAS TREATED AS A PATIENT THERE. HOW HE WAS ABUSED. TORTURED.
PAYBACK TO RAVENCROFT FOR RUINING HIS LIFE. BUT NOW THINGS HAD CHANGED, HE SAID. THANKFULLY, FINALLY...
NOW HE HAD THE MEANS TO MAKE HIMSELF HEARD.
AND HE CLAIMED, INCREDULOUSLY ENOUGH, THAT IT WAS ALL THANKS TO...
ALIENS.
JAMESON, OF COURSE, COULDN'T HELP BUT LAUGH AT WHAT THE STRANGER WAS RAMBLING ABOUT. TOLD HIM HE SHOULD ACTUALLY CHECK INTO RAVENCROFT AND GET HIS HEAD EXAMINED WHILE HE WAS STILL THERE.
BUT THE MAN, UNDETERRED, CONTINUED RECOUNTING HIS TALE. THAT IT WAS BEINGS FROM ANOTHER PLANET THAT HAD GIVEN HIM A VERY SPECIAL GIFT THIS HOLIDAY SEASON...
A VERY POWERFUL GIFT.

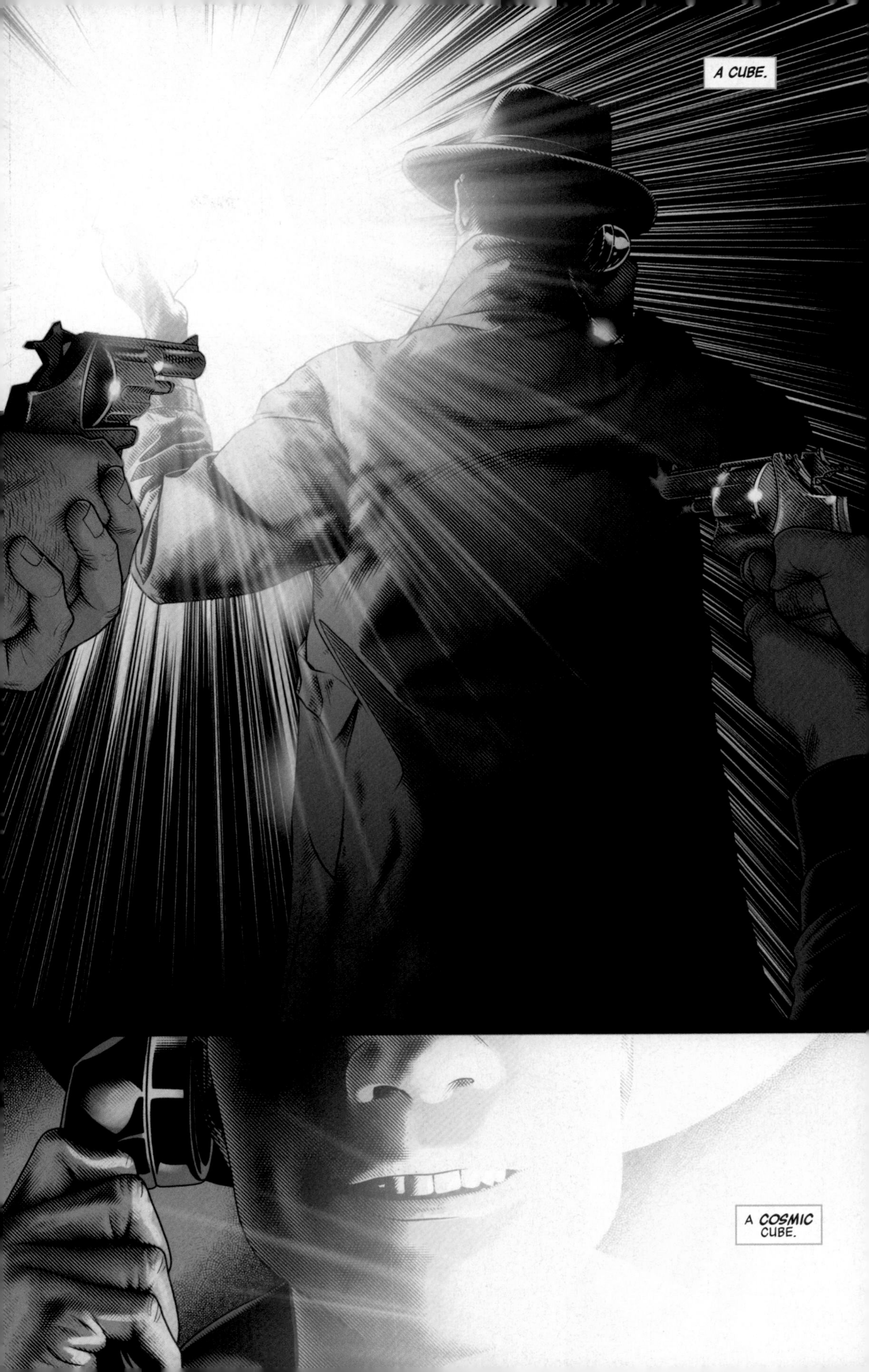
A CUBE.
A COSMIC CUBE.

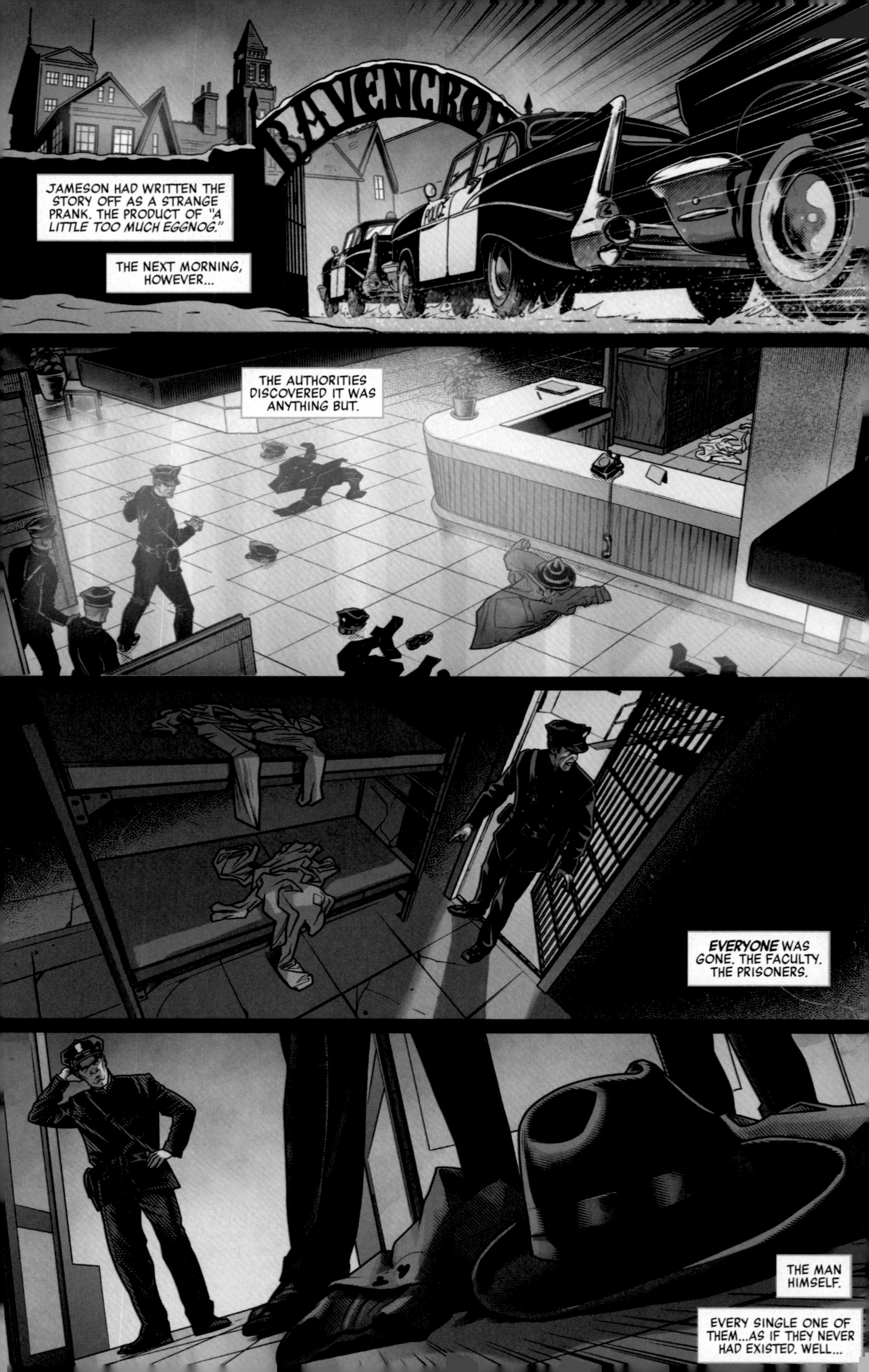
RAVENCROFT
JAMESON HAD WRITTEN THE STORY OFF AS A STRANGE PRANK. THE PRODUCT OF "A LITTLE TOO MUCH EGGNOG."
THE NEXT MORNING, HOWEVER...
POLICE
THE AUTHORITIES DISCOVERED IT WAS ANYTHING BUT.
EVERYONE WAS GONE. THE FACULTY. THE PRISONERS.
THE MAN HIMSELF.
EVERY SINGLE ONE OF THEM...AS IF THEY NEVER HAD EXISTED. WELL...

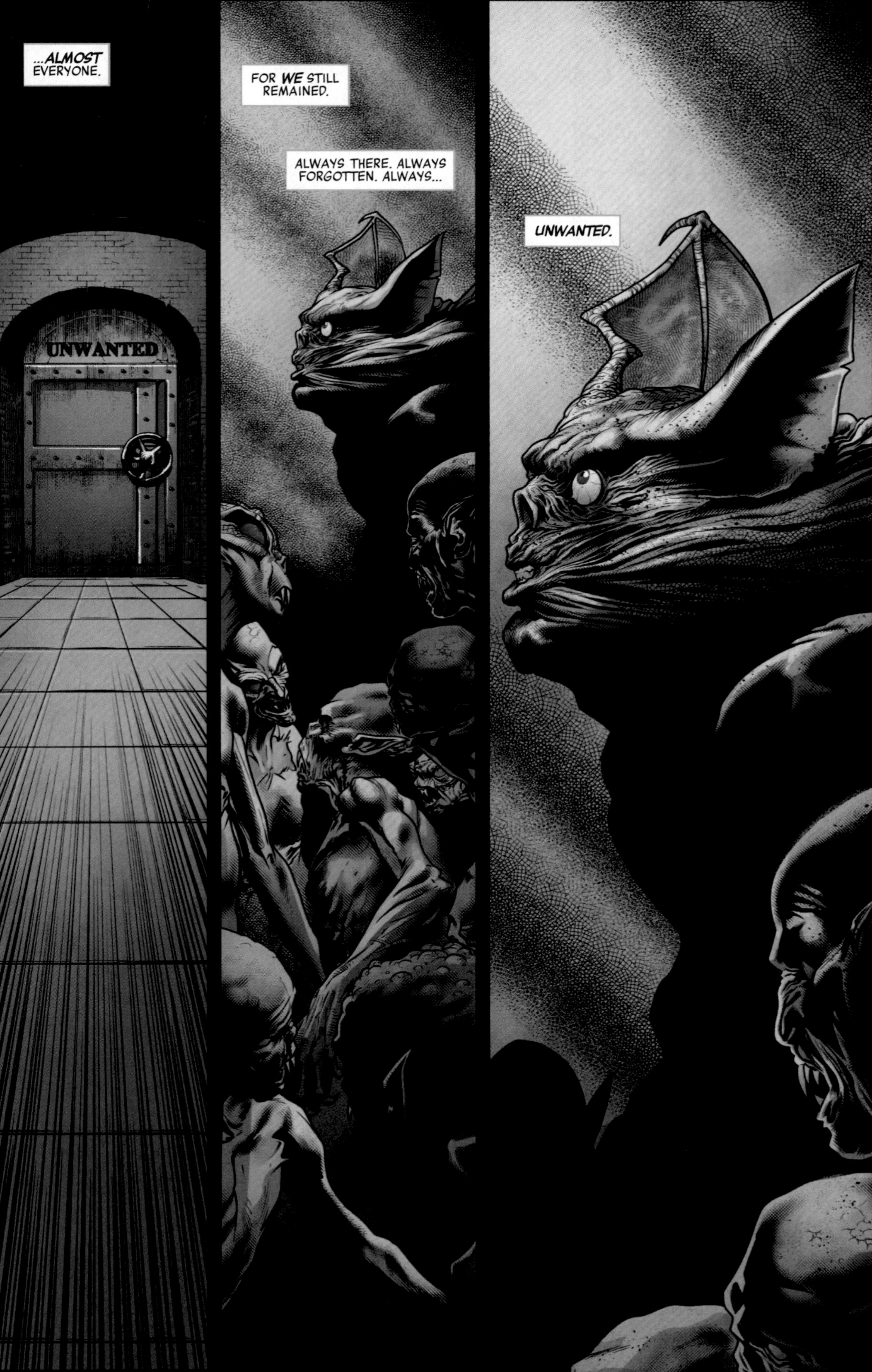
...ALMOST EVERYONE.
UNWANTED
FOR WE STILL REMAINED.
ALWAYS THERE. ALWAYS FORGOTTEN. ALWAYS...
UNWANTED.

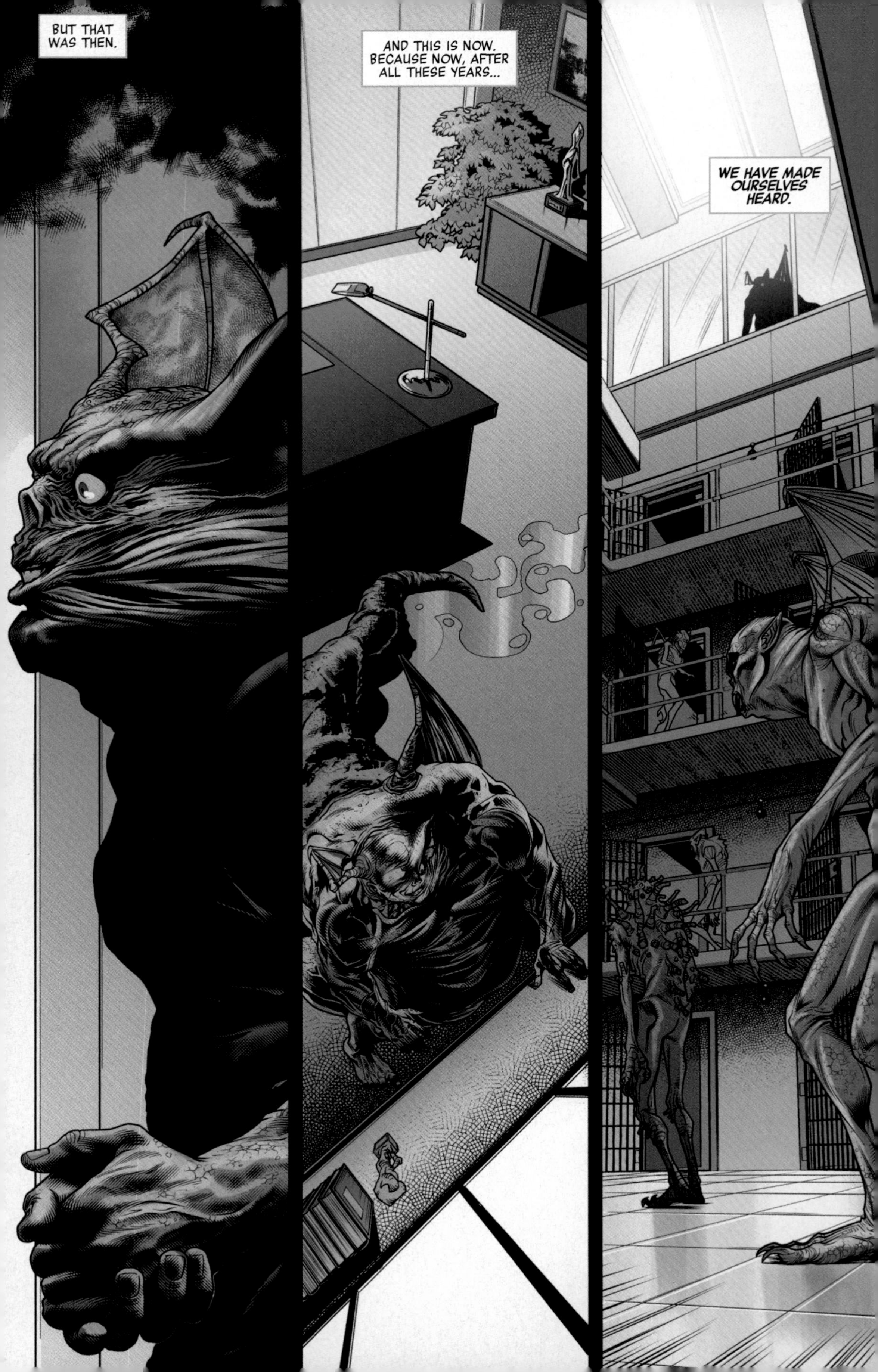
BUT THAT WAS THEN.
AND THIS IS NOW. BECAUSE NOW, AFTER ALL THESE YEARS...
WE HAVE MADE OURSELVES HEARD.

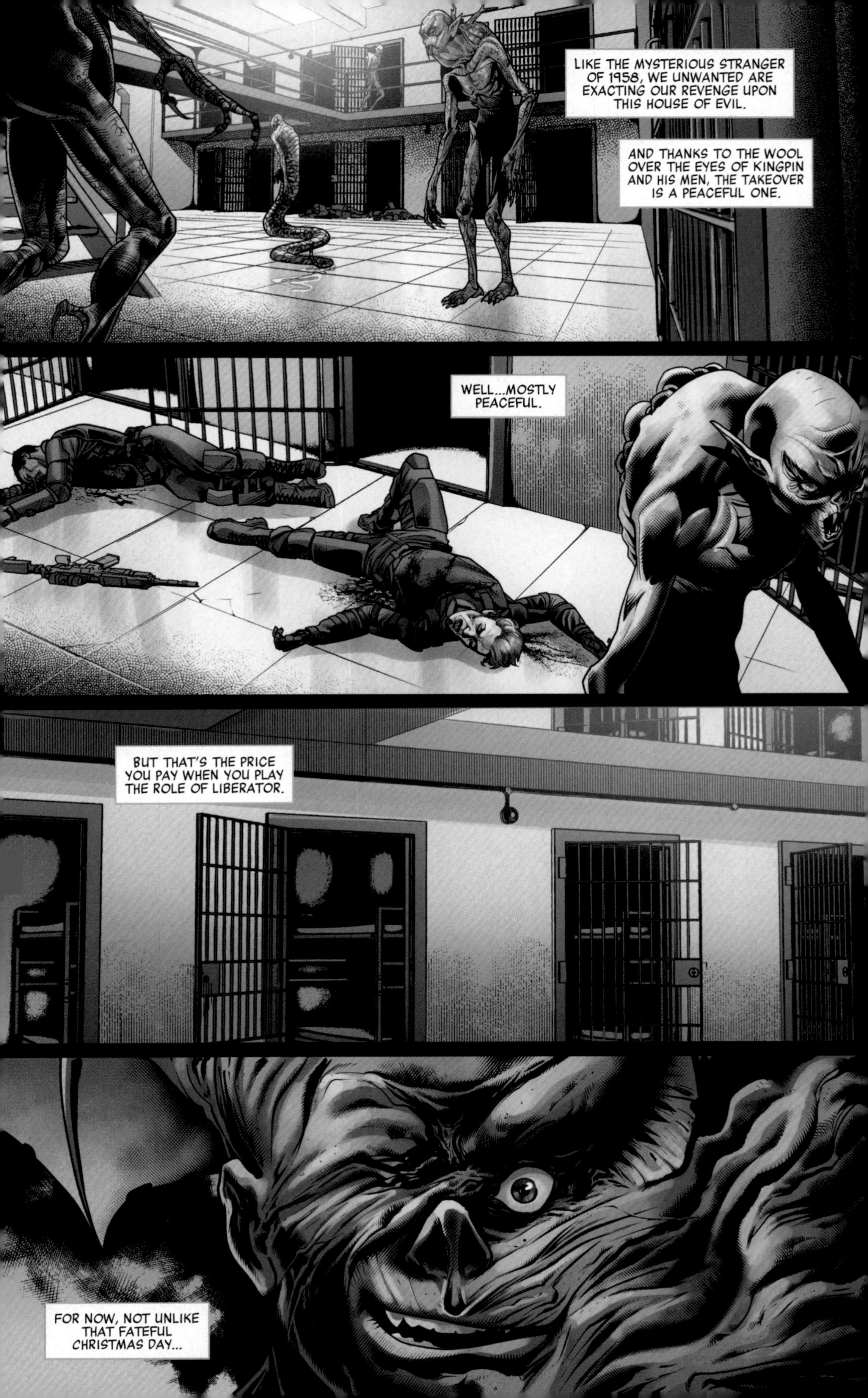
LIKE THE MYSTERIOUS STRANGER OF 1958, WE UNWANTED ARE EXACTING OUR REVENGE UPON THIS HOUSE OF EVIL.
AND THANKS TO THE WOOL OVER THE EYES OF KINGPIN AND HIS MEN, THE TAKEOVER IS A PEACEFUL ONE.
WELL...MOSTLY PEACEFUL.
BUT THAT'S THE PRICE YOU PAY WHEN YOU PLAY THE ROLE OF LIBERATOR.
FOR NOW, NOT UNLIKE THAT FATEFUL CHRISTMAS DAY...

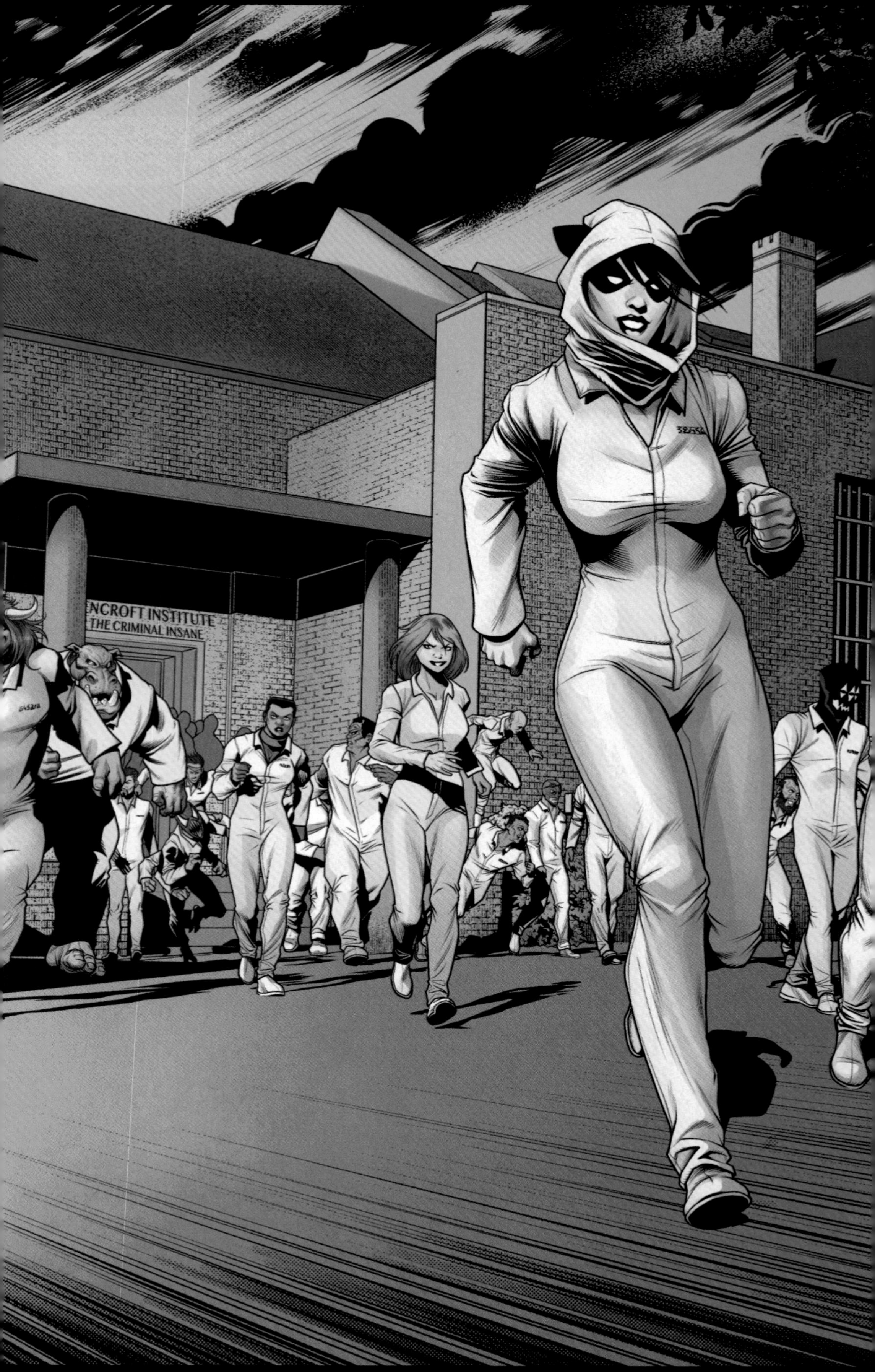
NCROFT INSTITUTE
THE CRIMINAL INSANE

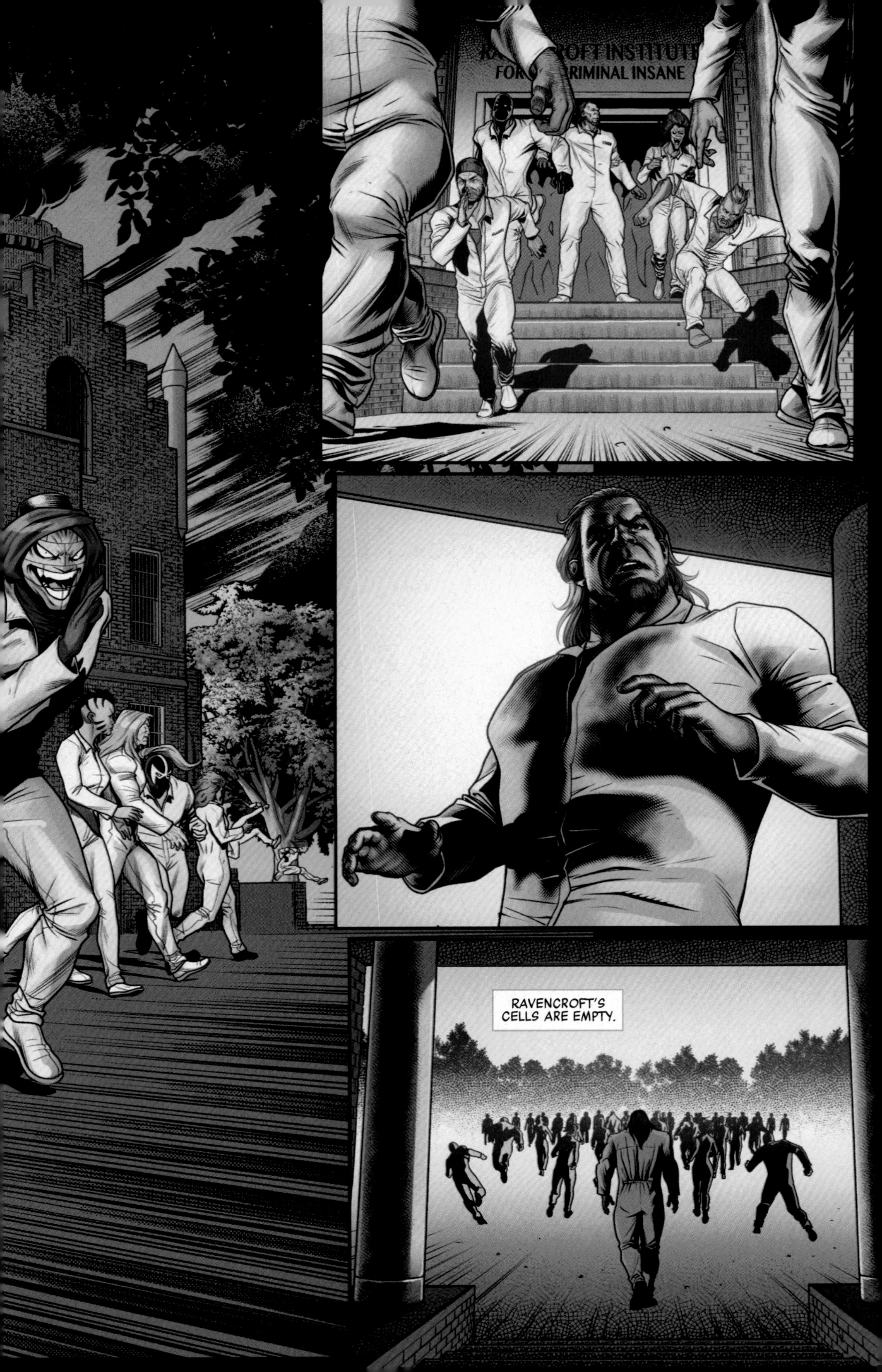
INSANE
RAVENCROFT'S CELLS ARE EMPTY.

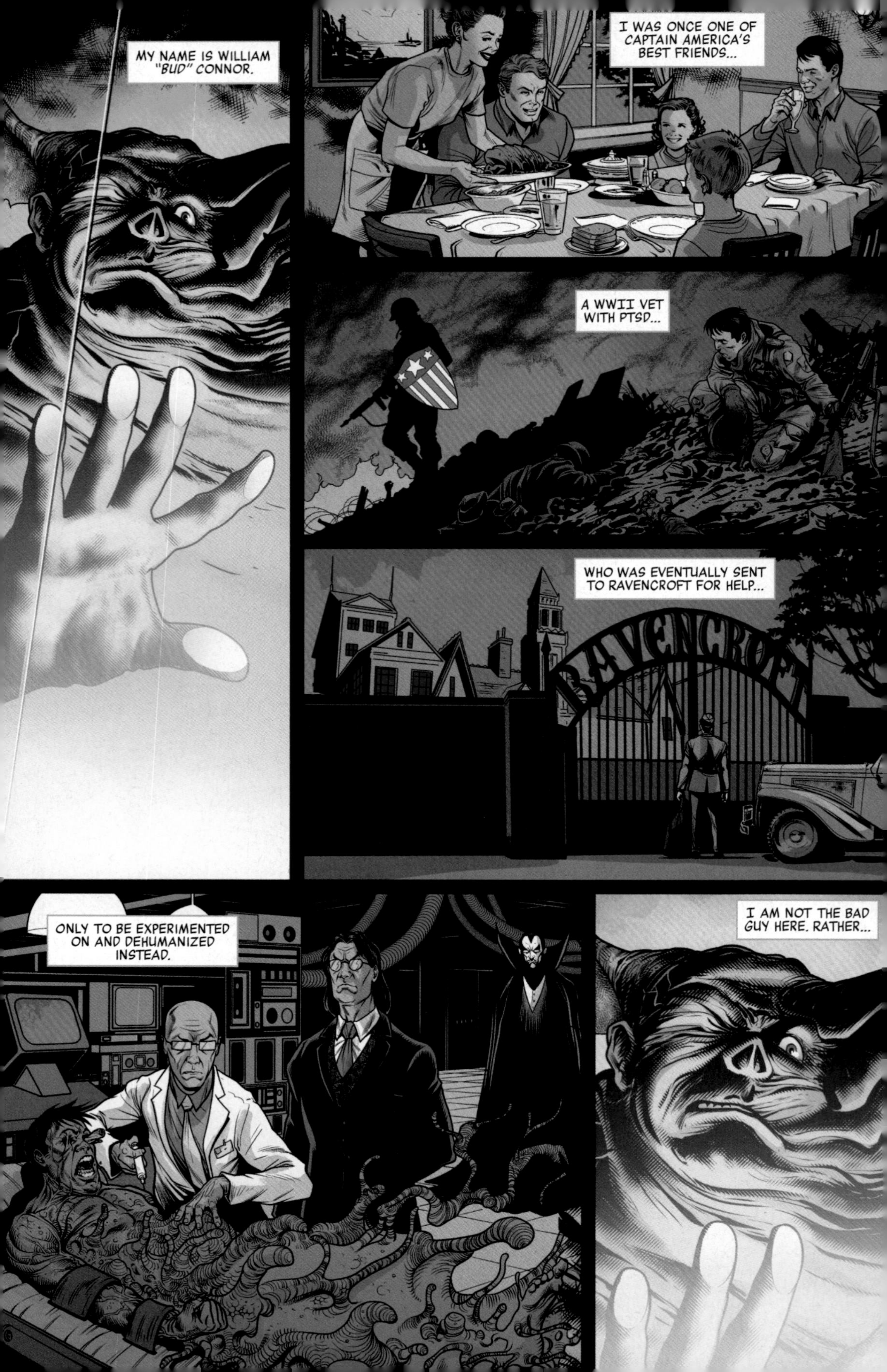
MY NAME IS WILLIAM "BUD" CONNOR.
I WAS ONCE ONE OF CAPTAIN AMERICA'S BEST FRIENDS...
A WWII VET WITH PTSD...
WHO WAS EVENTUALLY SENT TO RAVENCROFT FOR HELP...
RAVENCROFT
ONLY TO BE EXPERIMENTED ON AND DEHUMANIZED INSTEAD.
I AM NOT THE BAD GUY HERE. RATHER...

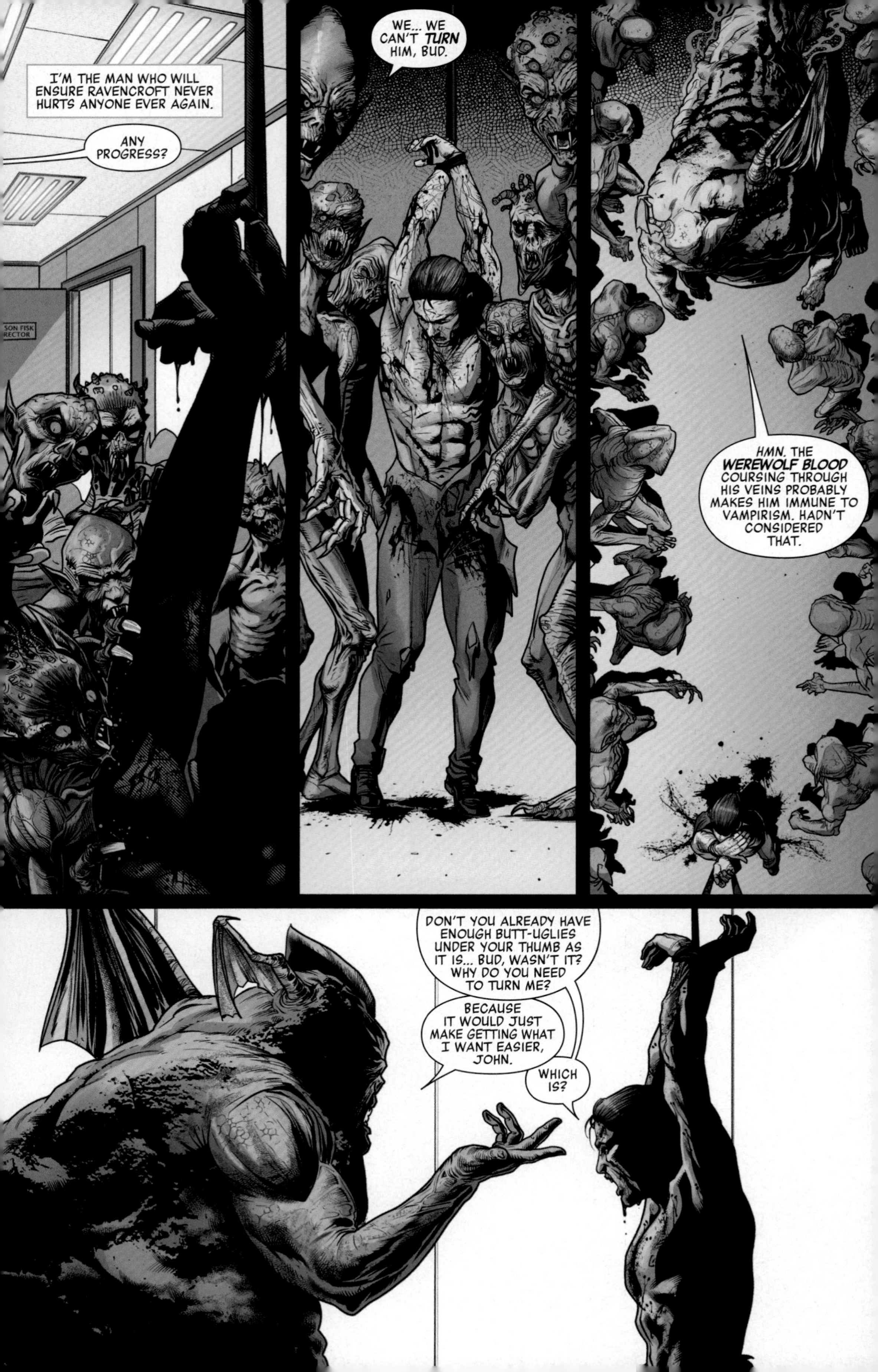
I'M THE MAN WHO WILL ENSURE RAVENCROFT NEVER HURTS ANYONE EVER AGAIN.
ANY PROGRESS?
WE... WE CAN'T TURN HIM, BUD.
HMN. THE WEREWOLF BLOOD COURSING THROUGH HIS VEINS PROBABLY MAKES HIM IMMUNE TO VAMPIRISM. HADN'T CONSIDERED THAT.
DON'T YOU ALREADY HAVE ENOUGH BUTT-UGLIES UNDER YOUR THUMB AS IT IS... BUD, WASN'T IT? WHY DO YOU NEED TO TURN ME?
BECAUSE IT WOULD JUST MAKE GETTING WHAT I WANT EASIER, JOHN.
WHICH IS?

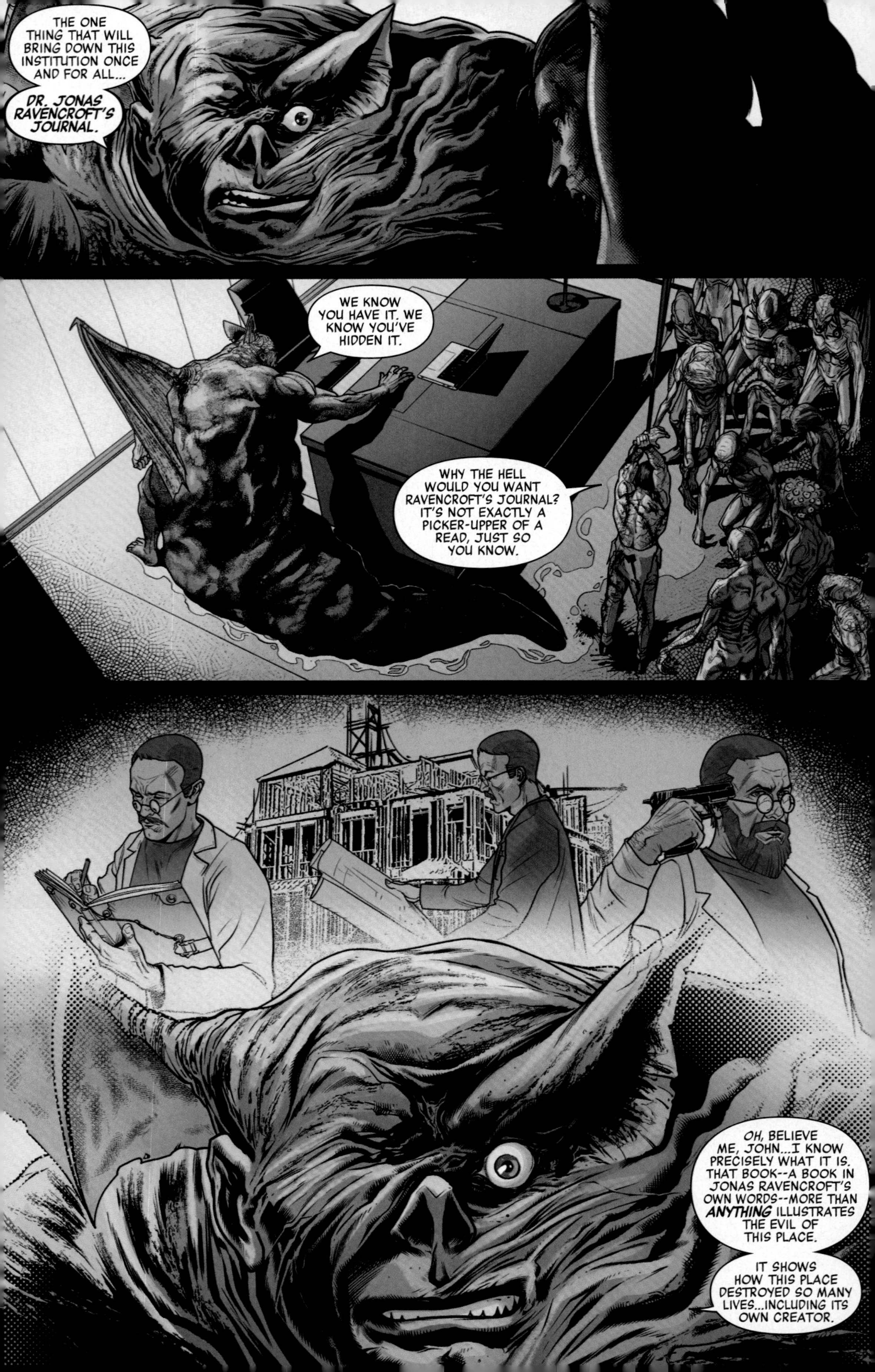
THE ONE THING THAT WILL BRING DOWN THIS INSTITUTION ONCE AND FOR ALL...
DR. JONAS RAVENCROFT'S JOURNAL.
WE KNOW YOU HAVE IT. WE KNOW YOU'VE HIDDEN IT.
WHY THE HELL WOULD YOU WANT RAVENCROFT'S JOURNAL? IT'S NOT EXACTLY A PICKER-UPPER OF A READ, JUST SO YOU KNOW.
OH, BELIEVE ME, JOHN...I KNOW PRECISELY WHAT IT IS. THAT BOOK--A BOOK IN JONAS RAVENCROFT'S OWN WORDS--MORE THAN ANYTHING ILLUSTRATES THE EVIL OF THIS PLACE.
IT SHOWS HOW THIS PLACE DESTROYED SO MANY LIVES...INCLUDING ITS OWN CREATOR.

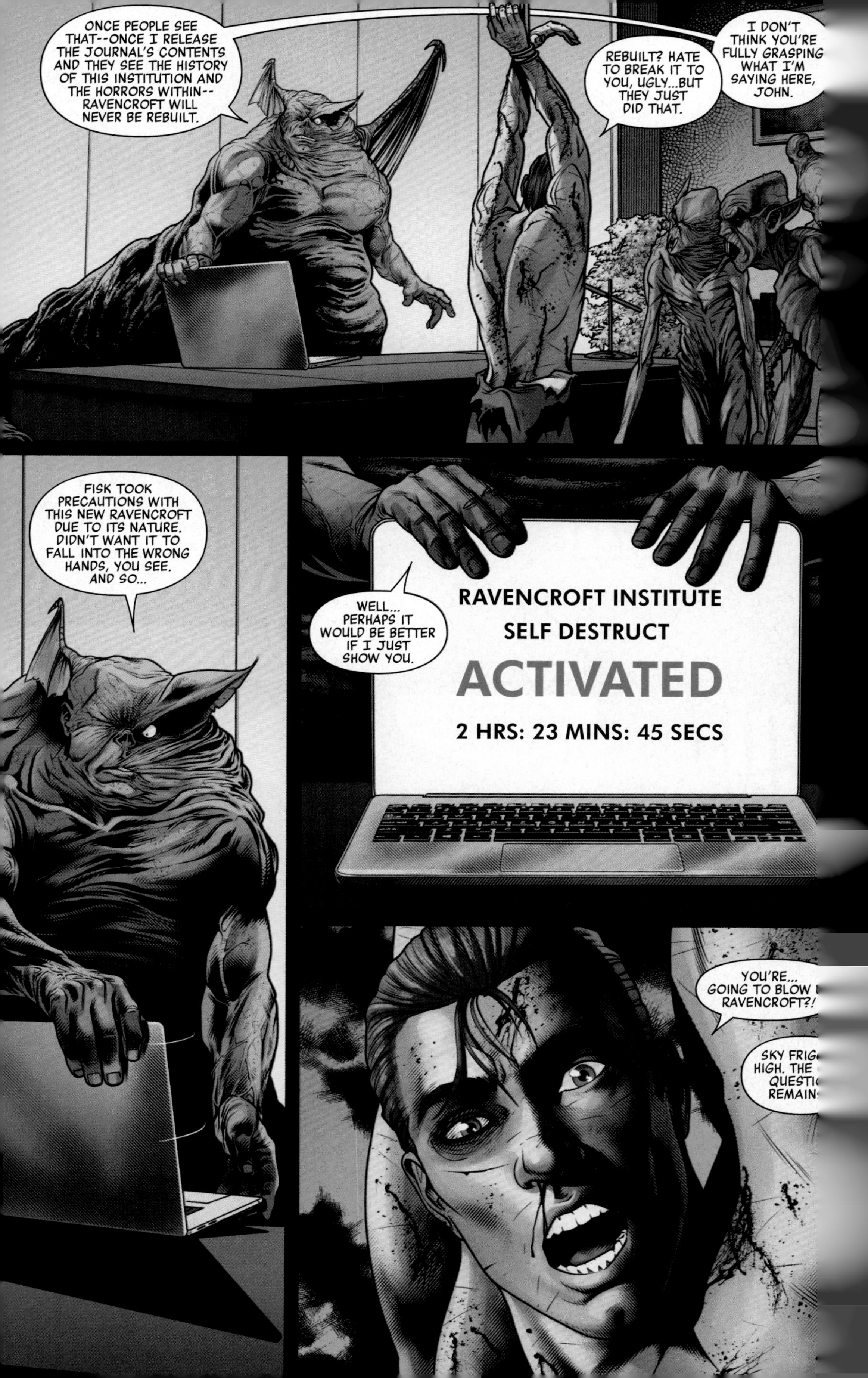
ONCE PEOPLE SEE THAT--ONCE I RELEASE THE JOURNAL'S CONTENTS AND THEY SEE THE HISTORY OF THIS INSTITUTION AND THE HORRORS WITHIN--RAVENCROFT WILL NEVER BE REBUILT.
REBUILT? HATE TO BREAK IT TO YOU, UGLY...BUT THEY JUST DID THAT.
I DON'T THINK YOU'RE FULLY GRASPING WHAT I'M SAYING HERE, JOHN.
FISK TOOK PRECAUTIONS WITH THIS NEW RAVENCROFT DUE TO ITS NATURE. DIDN'T WANT IT TO FALL INTO THE WRONG HANDS, YOU SEE. AND SO...
WELL... PERHAPS IT WOULD BE BETTER IF I JUST SHOW YOU.
RAVENCROFT INSTITUTE
SELF DESTRUCT
ACTIVATED
2 HRS: 23 MINS: 45 SECS
YOU'RE... GOING TO BLOW
RAVENCROFT?!
SKY FRIG
HIGH. THE
QUESTI
REMAIN

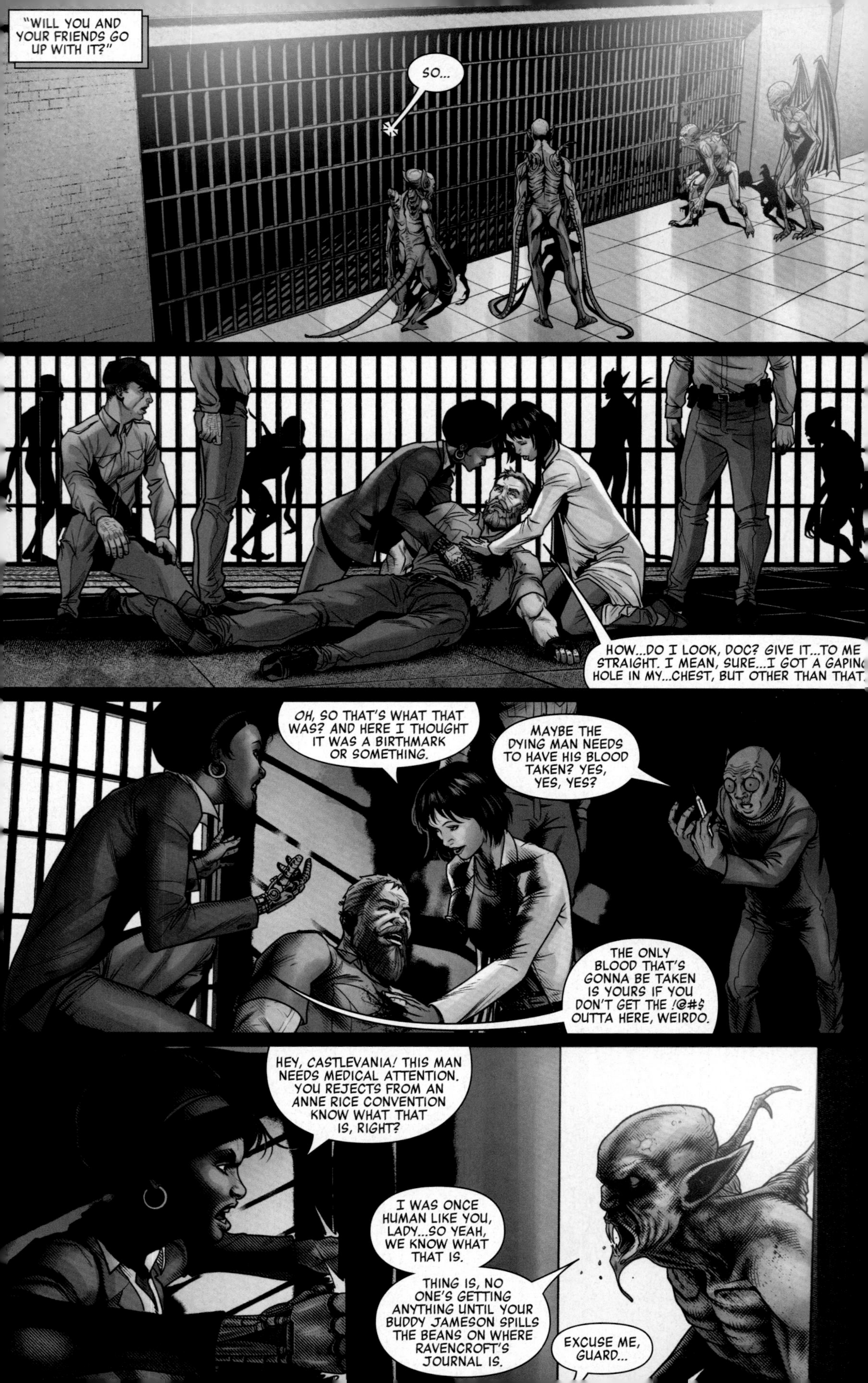
"WILL YOU AND YOUR FRIENDS GO UP WITH IT?"
SO...
HOW...DO I LOOK, DOC? GIVE IT...TO ME STRAIGHT. I MEAN, SURE...I GOT A GAPING HOLE IN MY...CHEST, BUT OTHER THAN THAT.
OH, SO THAT'S WHAT THAT WAS? AND HERE I THOUGHT IT WAS A BIRTHMARK OR SOMETHING.
MAYBE THE DYING MAN NEEDS TO HAVE HIS BLOOD TAKEN? YES, YES, YES?
THE ONLY BLOOD THAT'S GONNA BE TAKEN IS YOURS IF YOU DON'T GET THE !@#$ OUTTA HERE, WEIRDO.
HEY, CASTLEVANIA! THIS MAN NEEDS MEDICAL ATTENTION. YOU REJECTS FROM AN ANNE RICE CONVENTION KNOW WHAT THAT IS, RIGHT?
I WAS ONCE HUMAN LIKE YOU, LADY...SO YEAH, WE KNOW WHAT THAT IS.
THING IS, NO ONE'S GETTING ANYTHING UNTIL YOUR BUDDY JAMESON SPILLS THE BEANS ON WHERE RAVENCROFT'S JOURNAL IS.
EXCUSE ME, GUARD...

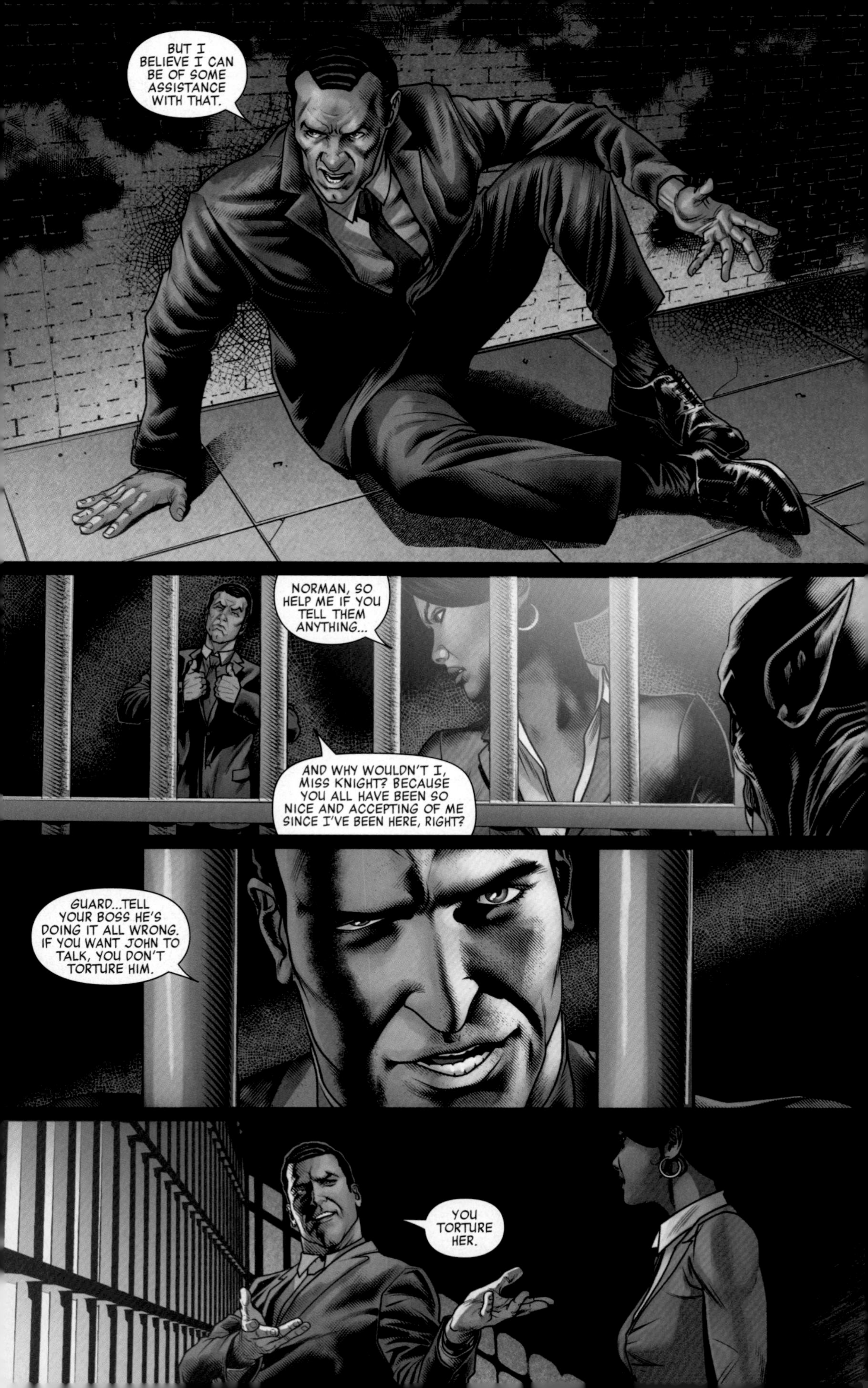
BUT I BELIEVE I CAN BE OF SOME ASSISTANCE WITH THAT.
NORMAN, SO HELP ME IF YOU TELL THEM ANYTHING...
AND WHY WOULDN'T I, MISS KNIGHT? BECAUSE YOU ALL HAVE BEEN SO NICE AND ACCEPTING OF ME SINCE I'VE BEEN HERE, RIGHT?
GUARD...TELL YOUR BOSS HE'S DOING IT ALL WRONG. IF YOU WANT JOHN TO TALK, YOU DON'T TORTURE HIM.
YOU TORTURE HER.

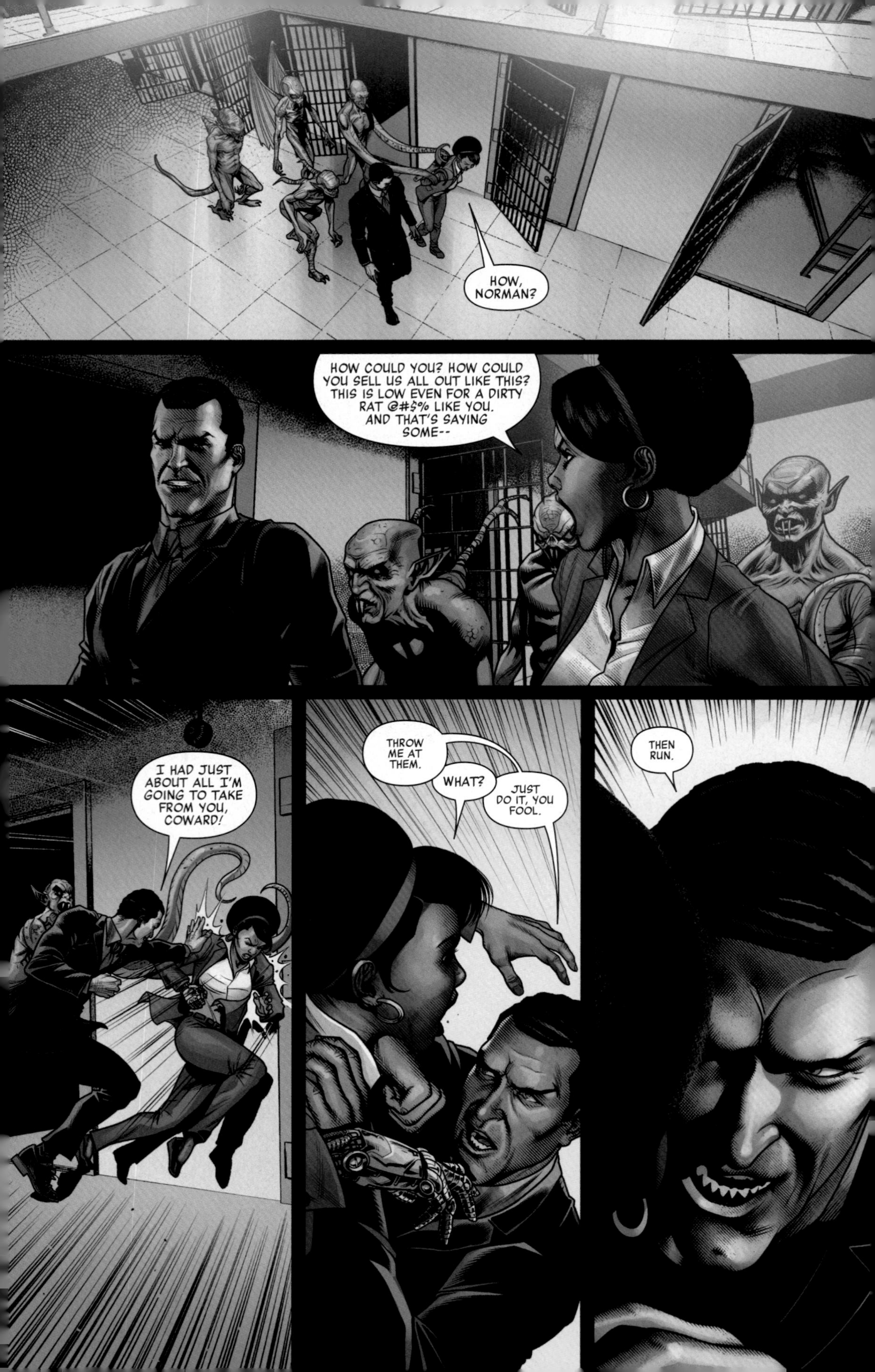
HOW, NORMAN?
HOW COULD YOU? HOW COULD YOU SELL US ALL OUT LIKE THIS? THIS IS LOW EVEN FOR A DIRTY RAT @#$% LIKE YOU. AND THAT'S SAYING SOME--
I HAD JUST ABOUT ALL I'M GOING TO TAKE FROM YOU, COWARD!
THROW ME AT THEM.
WHAT?
JUST DO IT, YOU FOOL.
THEN RUN.

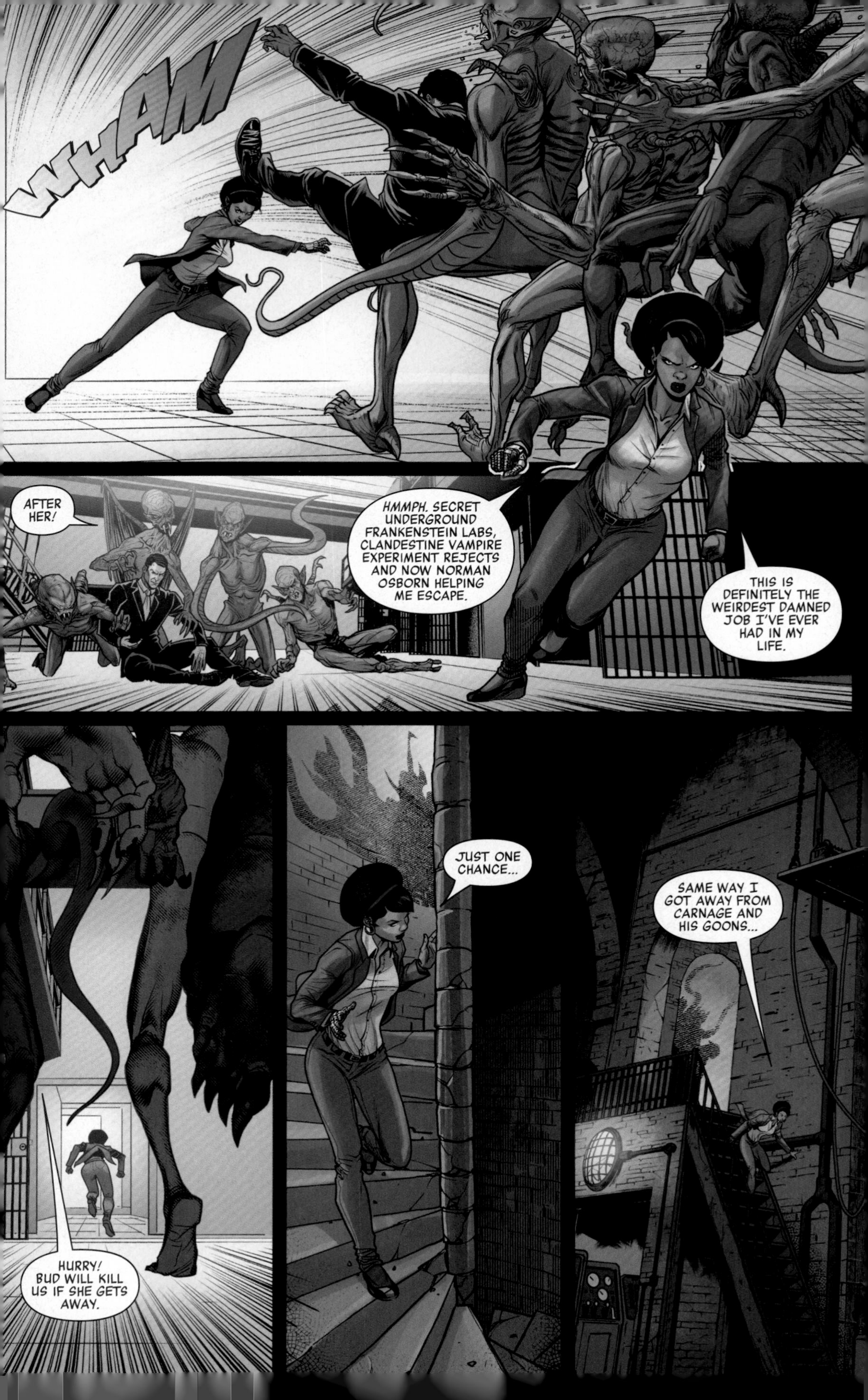
WHAM
AFTER HER!
HMMPH. SECRET UNDERGROUND FRANKENSTEIN LABS, CLANDESTINE VAMPIRE EXPERIMENT REJECTS AND NOW NORMAN OSBORN HELPING ME ESCAPE.
THIS IS DEFINITELY THE WEIRDEST DAMNED JOB I'VE EVER HAD IN MY LIFE.
HURRY! BUD WILL KILL US IF SHE GETS AWAY.
JUST ONE CHANCE...
SAME WAY I GOT AWAY FROM CARNAGE AND HIS GOONS...

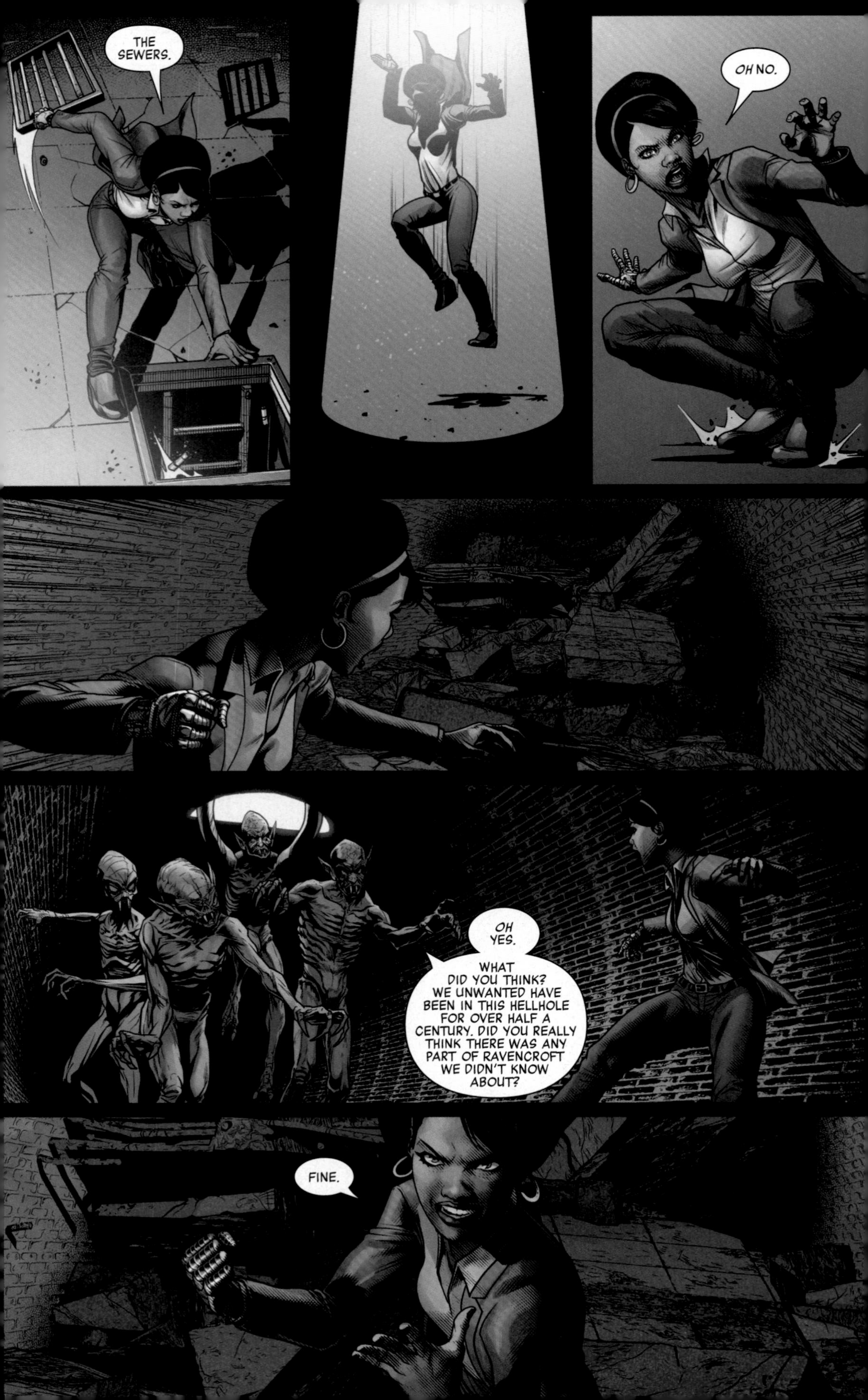
THE SEWERS.
OH NO.
OH YES.
WHAT DID YOU THINK? WE UNWANTED HAVE BEEN IN THIS HELLHOLE FOR OVER HALF A CENTURY. DID YOU REALLY THINK THERE WAS ANY PART OF RAVENCROFT WE DIDN'T KNOW ABOUT?
FINE.

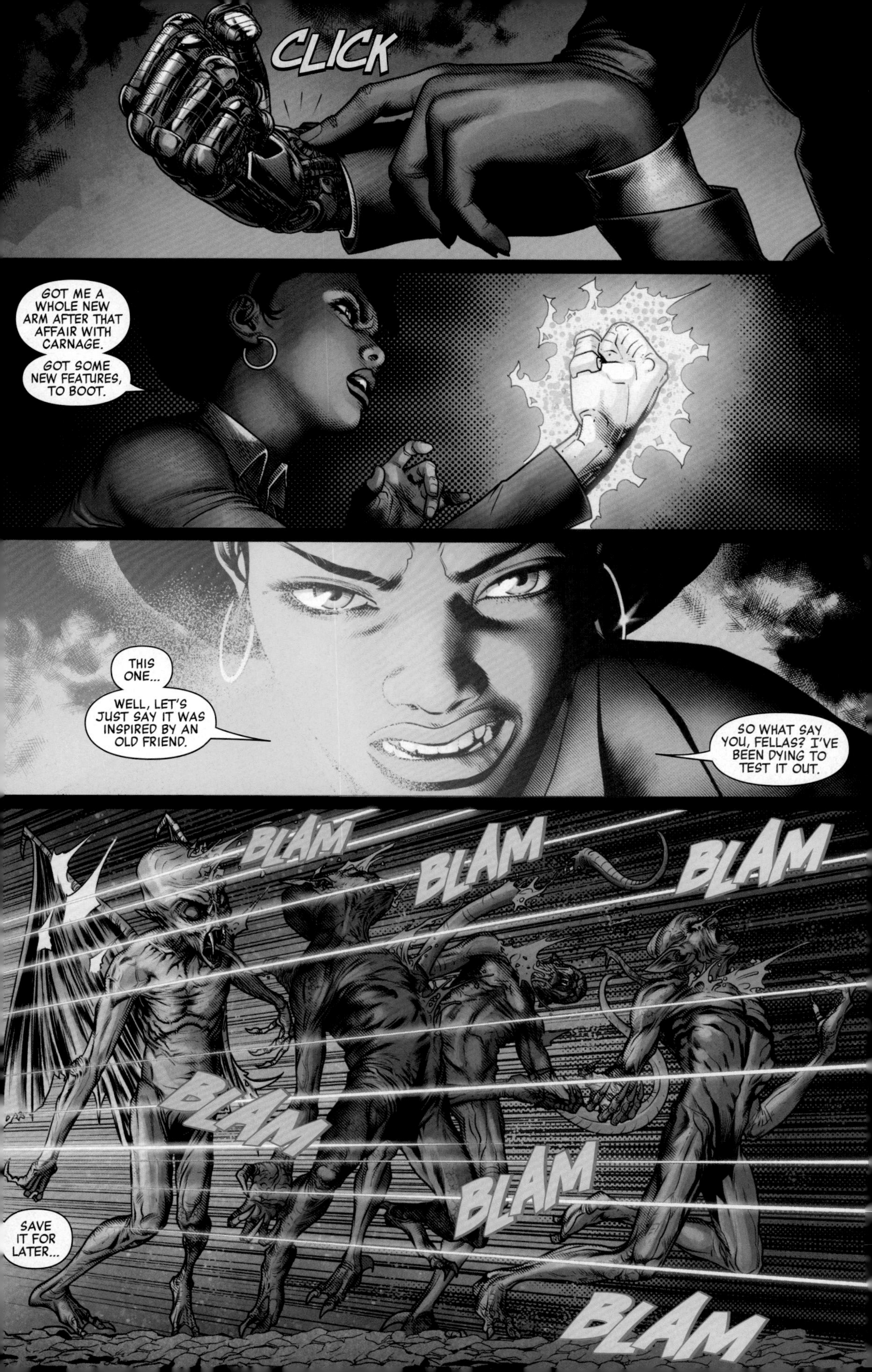
CLICK
GOT ME A WHOLE NEW ARM AFTER THAT AFFAIR WITH CARNAGE.
GOT SOME NEW FEATURES, TO BOOT.
THIS ONE...
WELL, LET'S JUST SAY IT WAS INSPIRED BY AN OLD FRIEND.
SO WHAT SAY YOU, FELLAS? I'VE BEEN DYING TO TEST IT OUT.
BLAM
BLAM
BLAM
BLAM
BLAM
SAVE IT FOR LATER...
BLAM

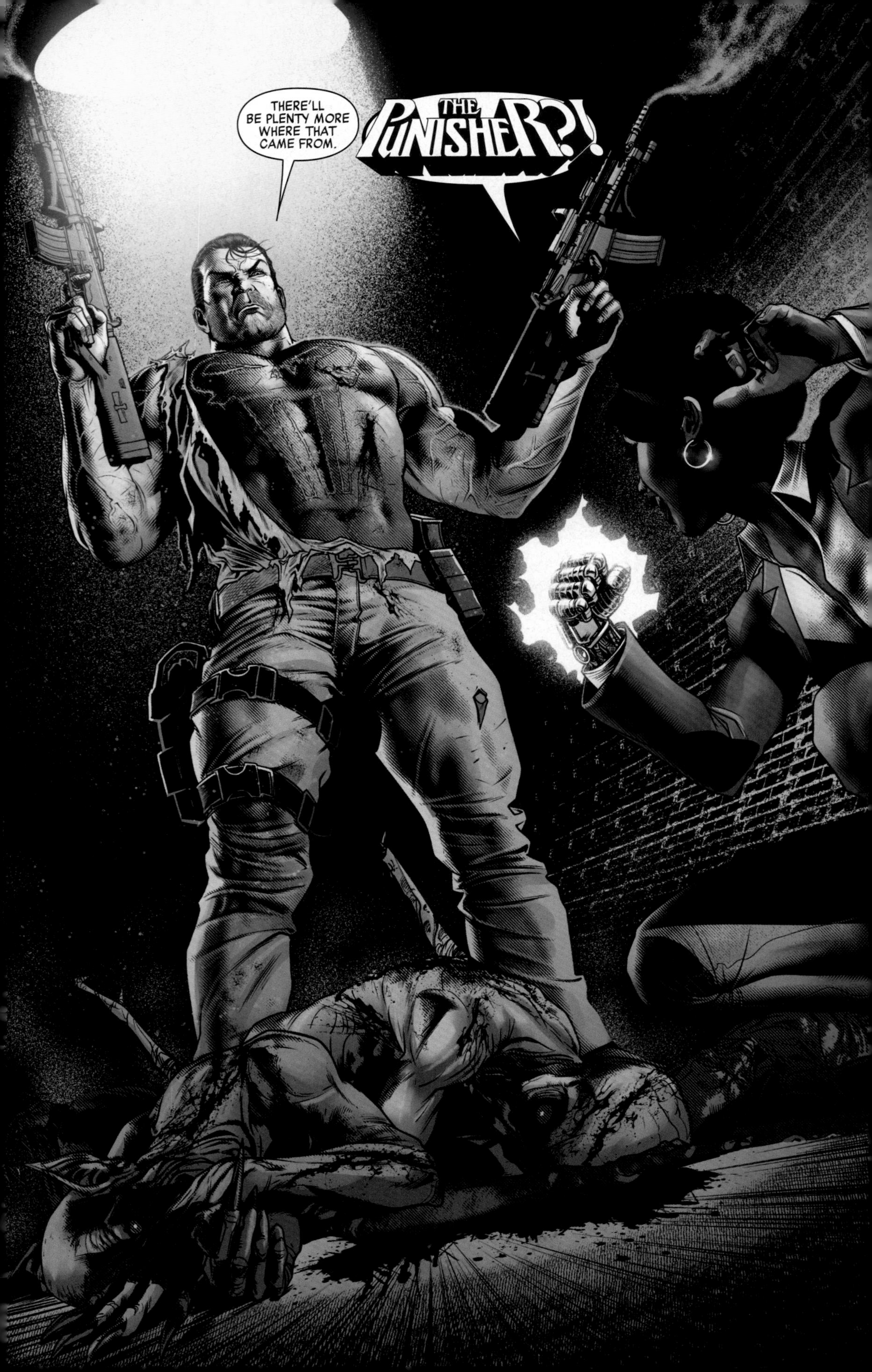
THERE'LL BE PLENTY MORE WHERE THAT CAME FROM.
THE PUNISHER?!

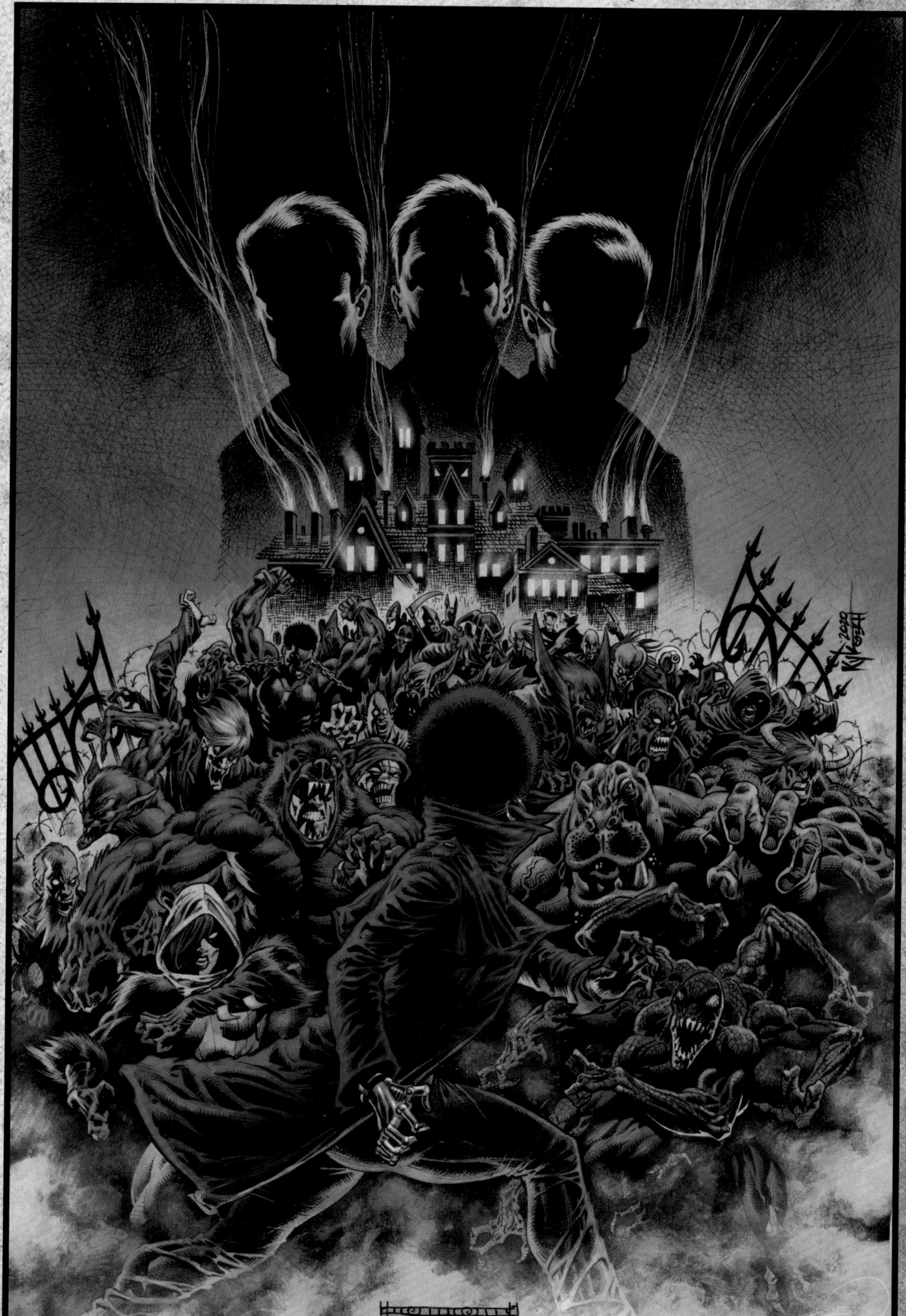

5

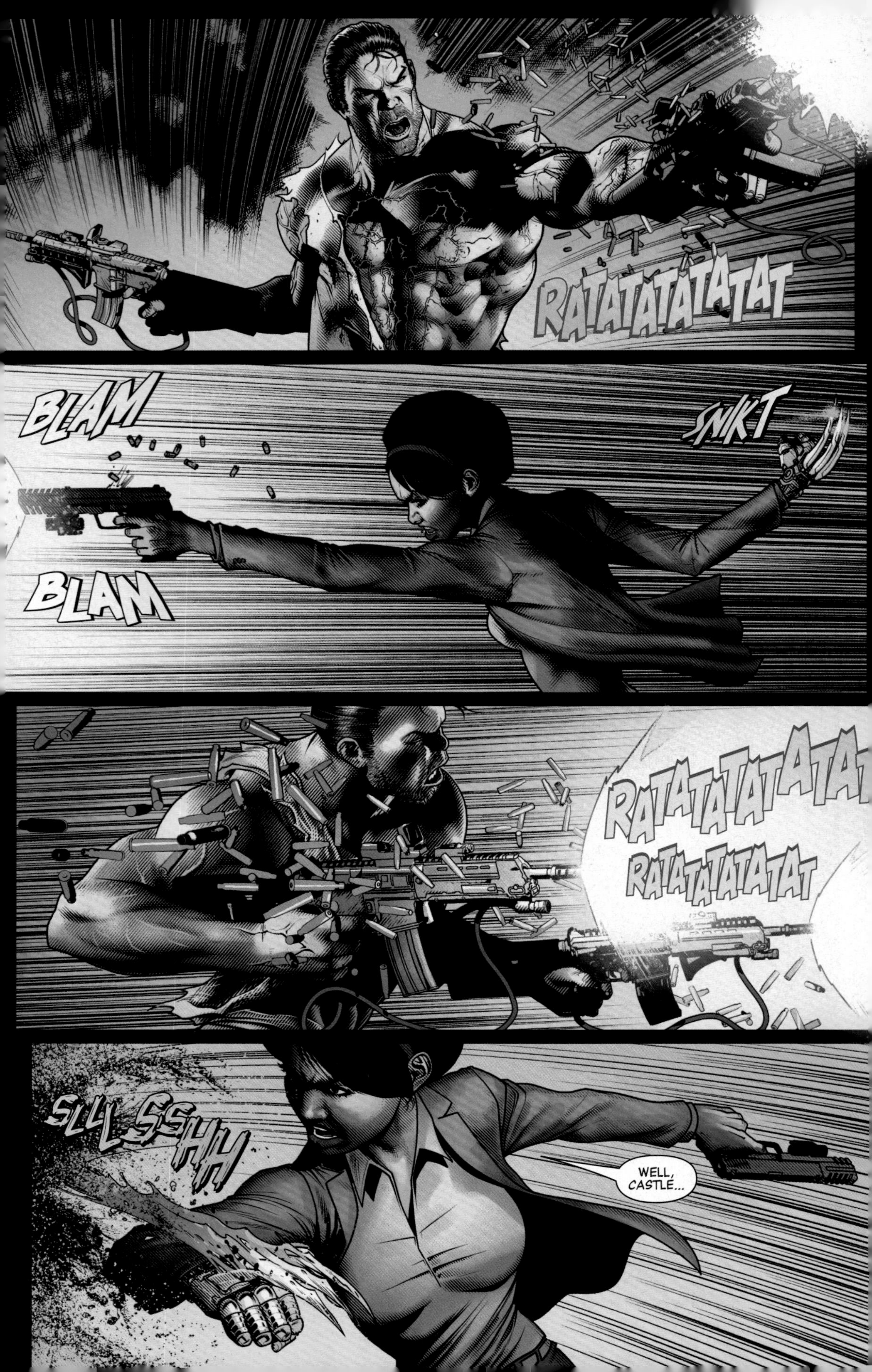
RATATATATATAT
BLAM
SNIKT
BLAM
RATATATATATAT
RATATATATATAT
SLLLSSHH
WELL, CASTLE...

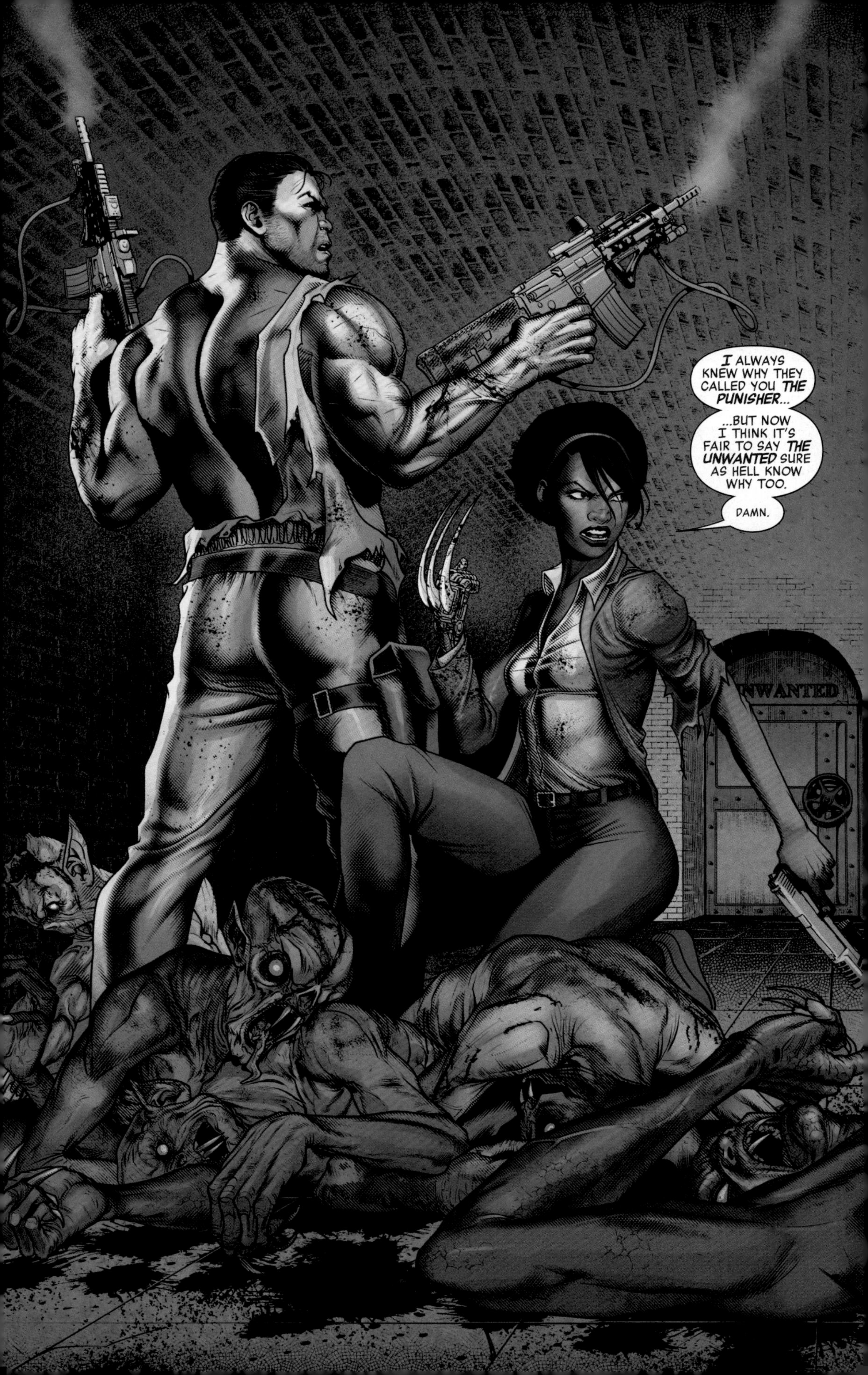
I ALWAYS KNEW WHY THEY CALLED YOU THE PUNISHER...
...BUT NOW I THINK IT'S FAIR TO SAY THE UNWANTED SURE AS HELL KNOW WHY TOO.
DAMN.
UNWANTED

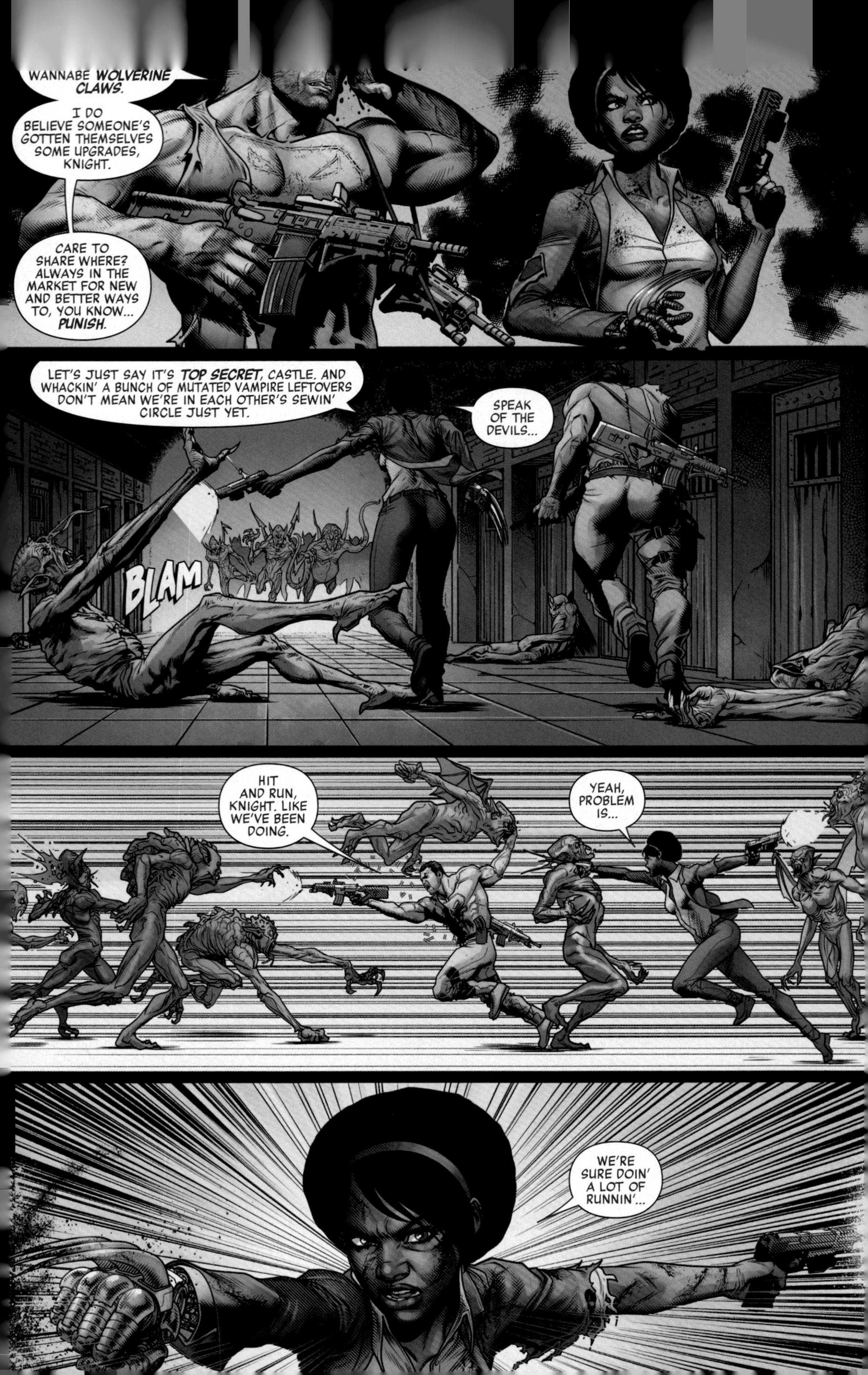
WANNABE WOLVERINE CLAWS.
I DO BELIEVE SOMEONE'S GOTTEN THEMSELVES SOME UPGRADES, KNIGHT.
CARE TO SHARE WHERE? ALWAYS IN THE MARKET FOR NEW AND BETTER WAYS TO, YOU KNOW... PUNISH.
LET'S JUST SAY IT'S TOP SECRET, CASTLE. AND WHACKIN' A BUNCH OF MUTATED VAMPIRE LEFTOVERS DON'T MEAN WE'RE IN EACH OTHER'S SEWIN' CIRCLE JUST YET.
SPEAK OF THE DEVILS...
BLAM
HIT AND RUN, KNIGHT. LIKE WE'VE BEEN DOING.
YEAH, PROBLEM IS...
WE'RE SURE DOIN' A LOT OF RUNNIN'...

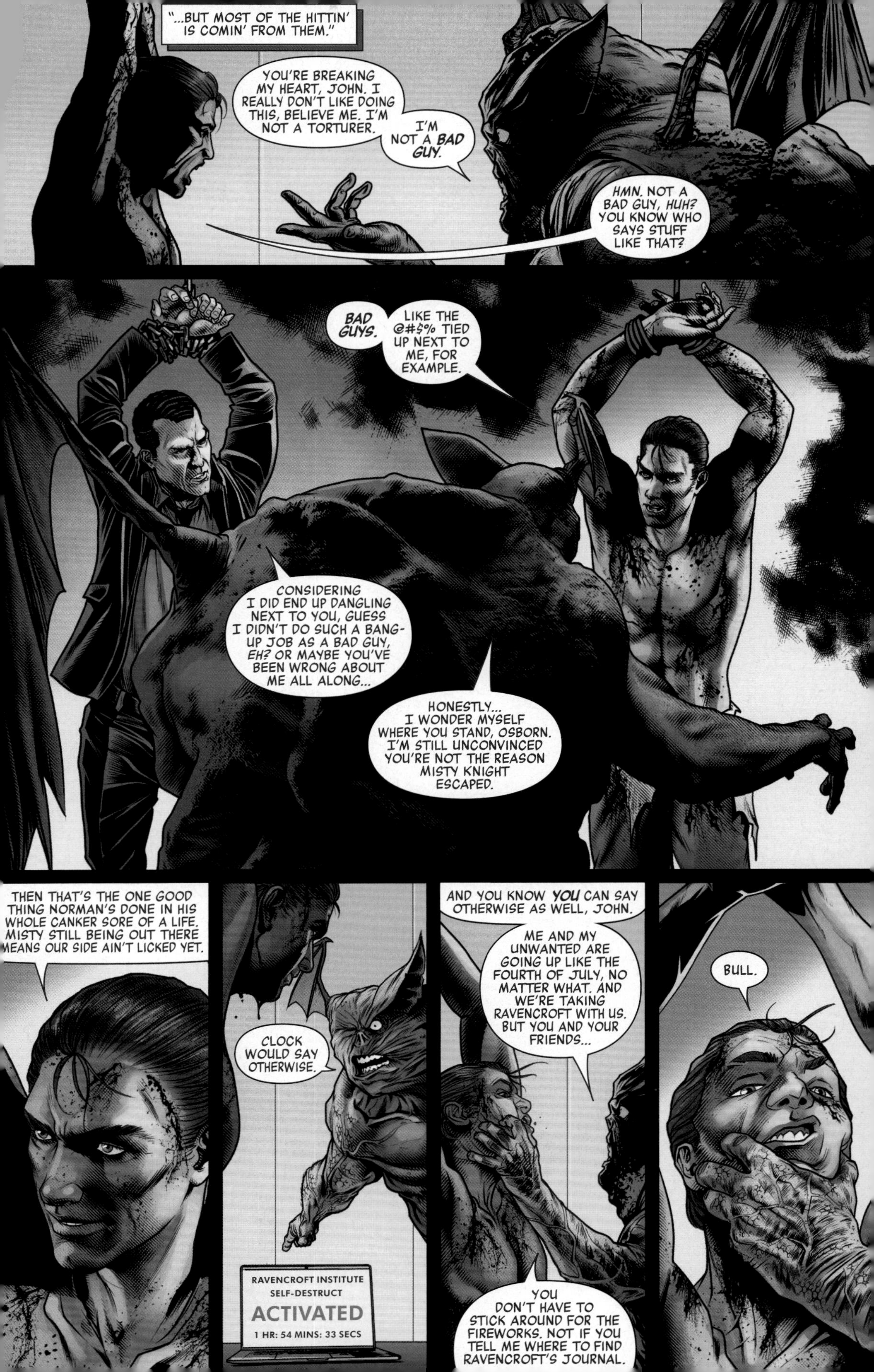
"...BUT MOST OF THE HITTIN' IS COMIN' FROM THEM."
YOU'RE BREAKING MY HEART, JOHN. I REALLY DON'T LIKE DOING THIS, BELIEVE ME. I'M NOT A TORTURER.
I'M NOT A BAD GUY.
HMN. NOT A BAD GUY, HUH? YOU KNOW WHO SAYS STUFF LIKE THAT?
BAD GUYS.
LIKE THE @#$% TIED UP NEXT TO ME, FOR EXAMPLE.
CONSIDERING I DID END UP DANGLING NEXT TO YOU, GUESS I DIDN'T DO SUCH A BANG-UP JOB AS A BAD GUY, EH? OR MAYBE YOU'VE BEEN WRONG ABOUT ME ALL ALONG...
HONESTLY... I WONDER MYSELF WHERE YOU STAND, OSBORN. I'M STILL UNCONVINCED YOU'RE NOT THE REASON MISTY KNIGHT ESCAPED.
THEN THAT'S THE ONE GOOD THING NORMAN'S DONE IN HIS WHOLE CANKER SORE OF A LIFE. MISTY STILL BEING OUT THERE MEANS OUR SIDE AIN'T LICKED YET.
CLOCK WOULD SAY OTHERWISE.
RAVENCROFT INSTITUTE
SELF-DESTRUCT
ACTIVATED
1 HR: 54 MINS: 33 SECS
AND YOU KNOW YOU CAN SAY OTHERWISE AS WELL, JOHN.
ME AND MY UNWANTED ARE GOING UP LIKE THE FOURTH OF JULY, NO MATTER WHAT. AND WE'RE TAKING RAVENCROFT WITH US. BUT YOU AND YOUR FRIENDS...
YOU DON'T HAVE TO STICK AROUND FOR THE FIREWORKS. NOT IF YOU TELL ME WHERE TO FIND RAVENCROFT'S JOURNAL.
BULL.

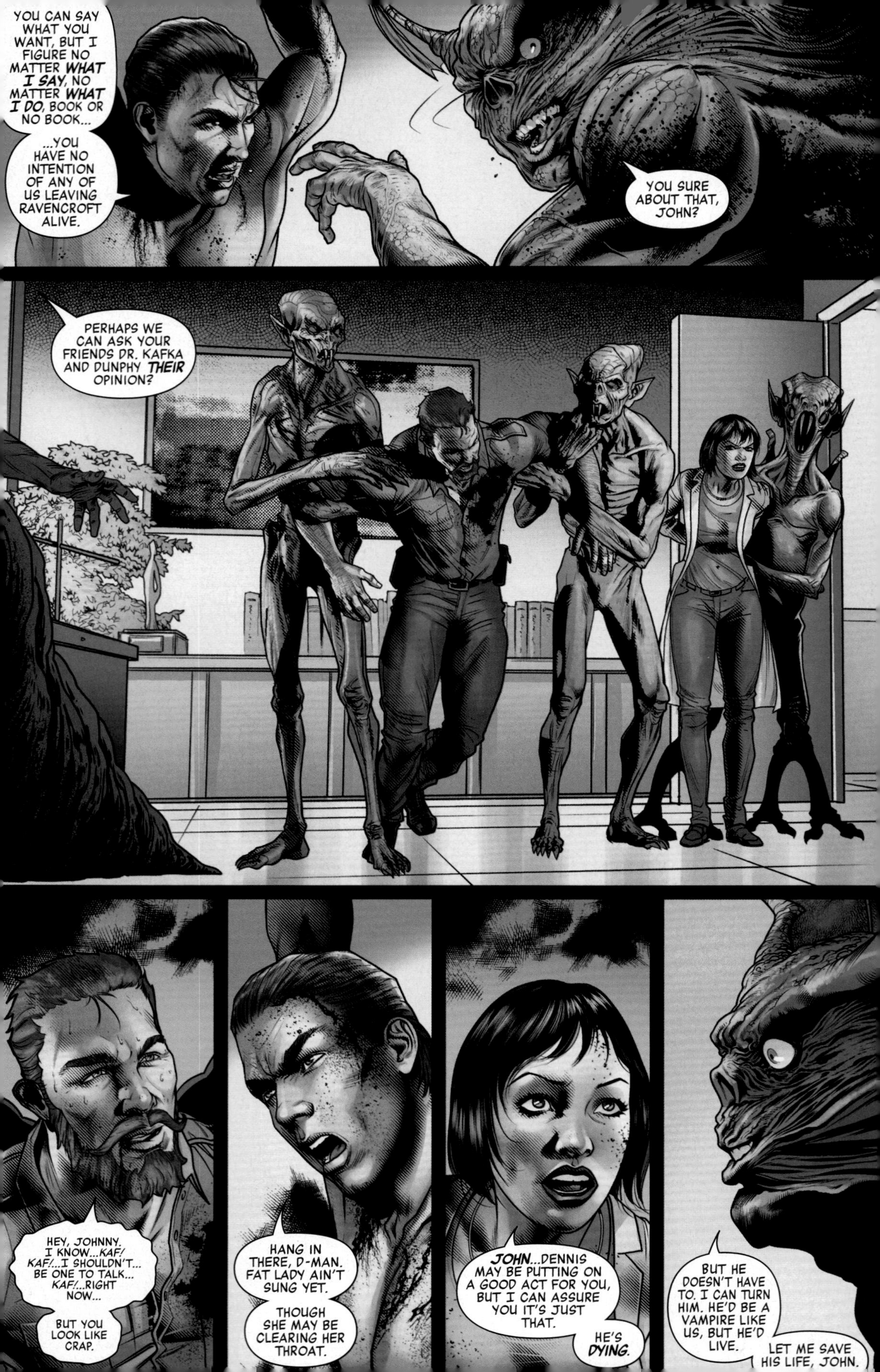

YOU CAN SAY WHAT YOU WANT, BUT I FIGURE NO MATTER WHAT I SAY, NO MATTER WHAT I DO, BOOK OR NO BOOK...
...YOU HAVE NO INTENTION OF ANY OF US LEAVING RAVENCROFT ALIVE.
YOU SURE ABOUT THAT, JOHN?
PERHAPS WE CAN ASK YOUR FRIENDS DR. KAFKA AND DUNPHY THEIR OPINION?
HEY, JOHNNY. I KNOW...KAF! KAF!...I SHOULDN'T... BE ONE TO TALK... KAF!...RIGHT NOW...
BUT YOU LOOK LIKE CRAP.
HANG IN THERE, D-MAN. FAT LADY AIN'T SUNG YET.
THOUGH SHE MAY BE CLEARING HER THROAT.
JOHN...DENNIS MAY BE PUTTING ON A GOOD ACT FOR YOU, BUT I CAN ASSURE YOU IT'S JUST THAT.
HE'S DYING.
BUT HE DOESN'T HAVE TO. I CAN TURN HIM. HE'D BE A VAMPIRE LIKE US, BUT HE'D LIVE.
LET ME SAVE HIS LIFE, JOHN.

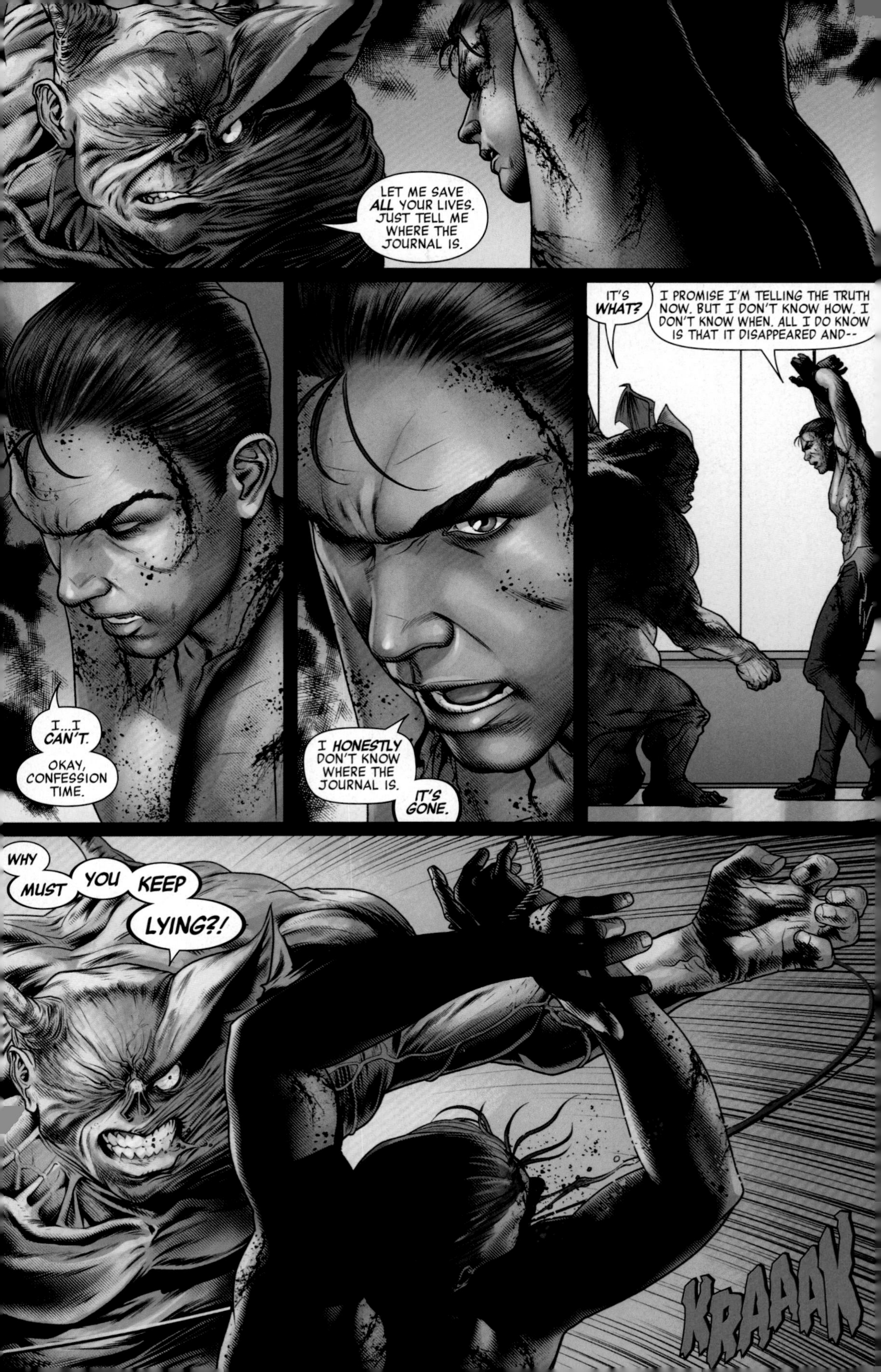
LET ME SAVE ALL YOUR LIVES. JUST TELL ME WHERE THE JOURNAL IS.
I...I CAN'T.
OKAY, CONFESSION TIME.
I HONESTLY DON'T KNOW WHERE THE JOURNAL IS.
IT'S GONE.
IT'S WHAT?
I PROMISE I'M TELLING THE TRUTH NOW. BUT I DON'T KNOW HOW. I DON'T KNOW WHEN. ALL I DO KNOW IS THAT IT DISAPPEARED AND--
WHY MUST YOU KEEP LYING?!
KRAAAK

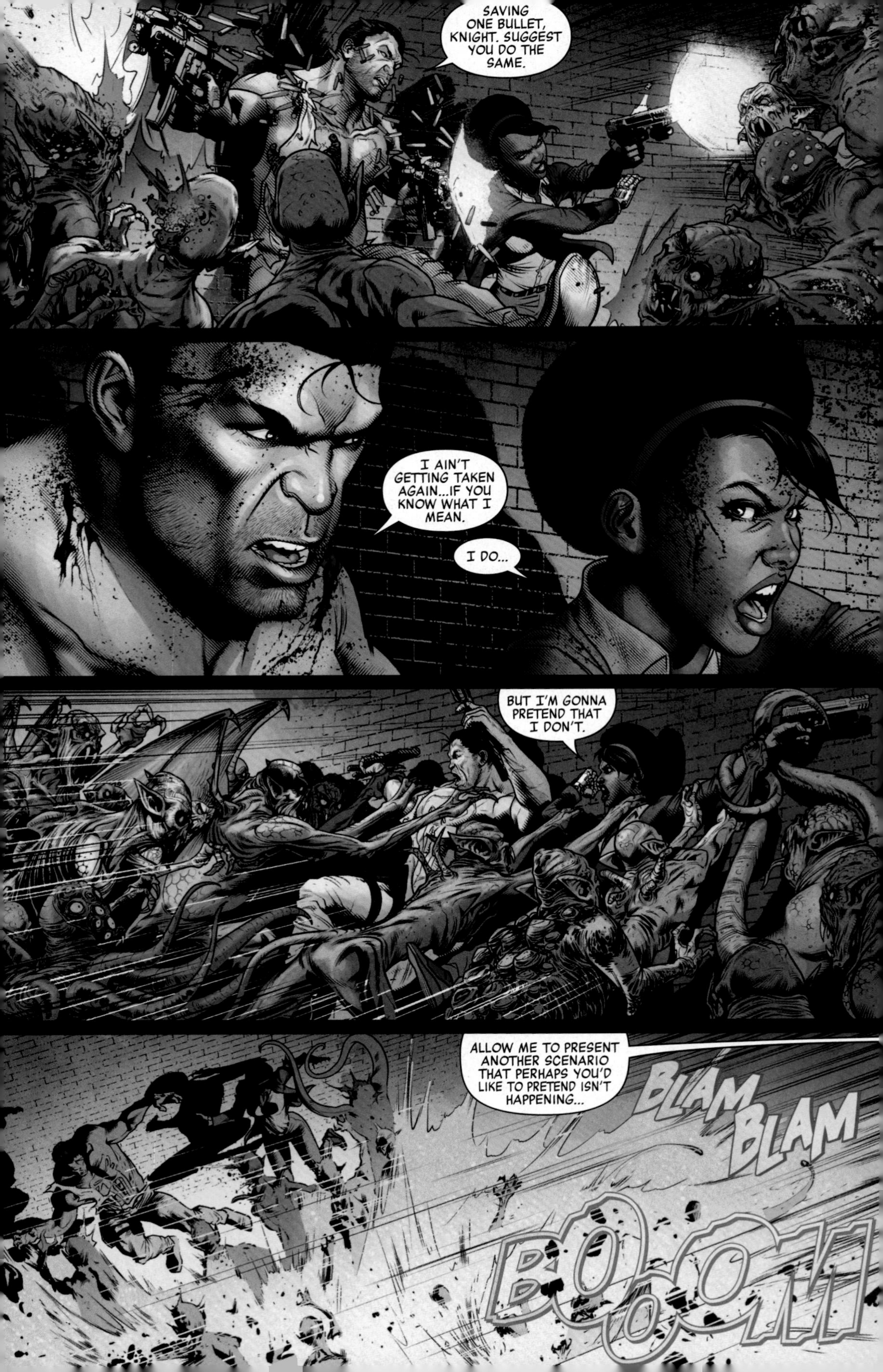
SAVING ONE BULLET, KNIGHT. SUGGEST YOU DO THE SAME.
I AIN'T GETTING TAKEN AGAIN...IF YOU KNOW WHAT I MEAN.
I DO...
BUT I'M GONNA PRETEND THAT I DON'T.
ALLOW ME TO PRESENT ANOTHER SCENARIO THAT PERHAPS YOU'D LIKE TO PRETEND ISN'T HAPPENING...
BLAM
BLAM
BOOOOM

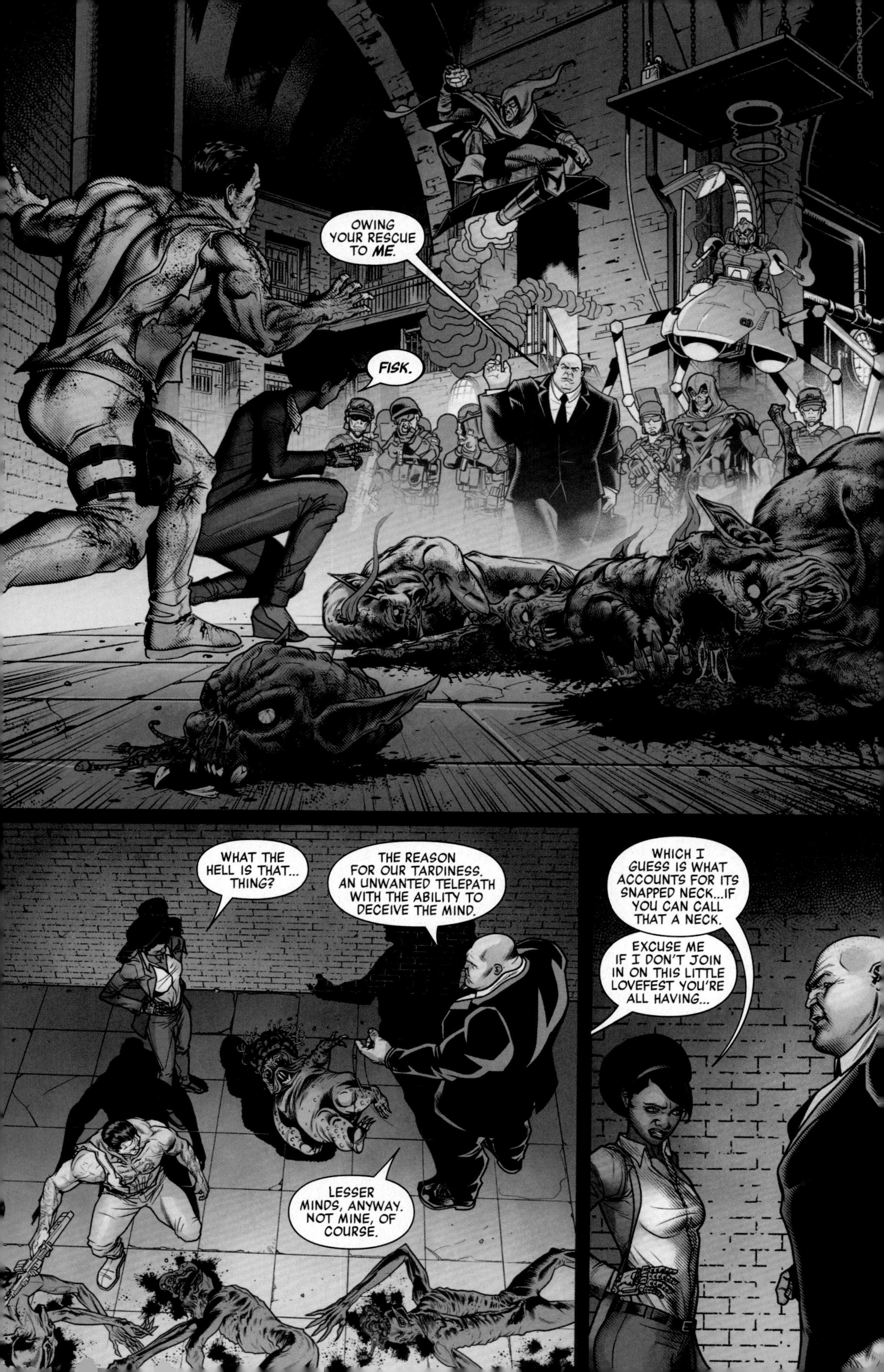
OWING YOUR RESCUE TO ME.
FISK.
WHAT THE HELL IS THAT... THING?
THE REASON FOR OUR TARDINESS. AN UNWANTED TELEPATH WITH THE ABILITY TO DECEIVE THE MIND.
LESSER MINDS, ANYWAY. NOT MINE, OF COURSE.
WHICH I GUESS IS WHAT ACCOUNTS FOR ITS SNAPPED NECK...IF YOU CAN CALL THAT A NECK.
EXCUSE ME IF I DON'T JOIN IN ON THIS LITTLE LOVEFEST YOU'RE ALL HAVING...

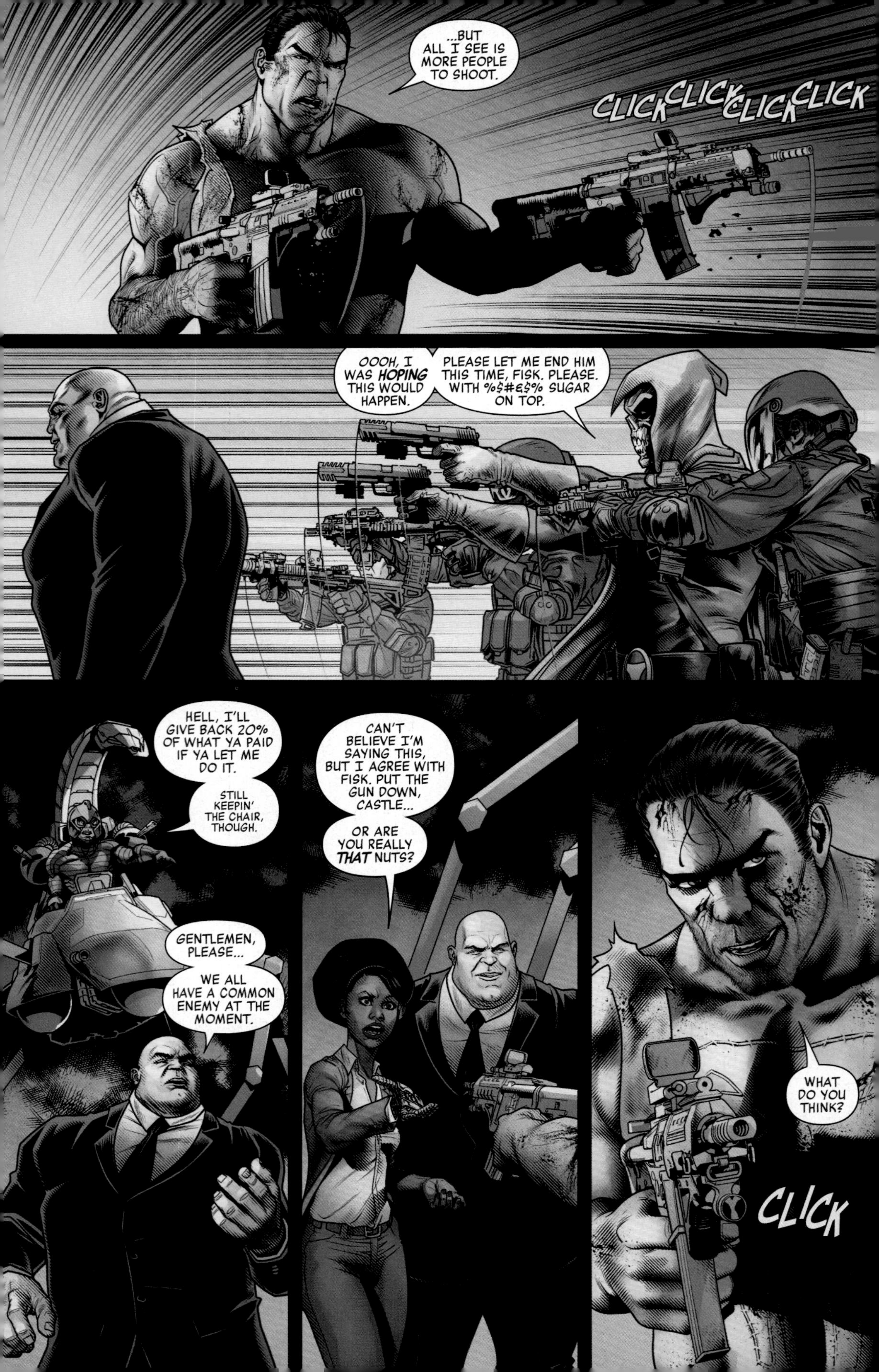
...BUT ALL I SEE IS MORE PEOPLE TO SHOOT.
CLICKCLICKCLICKCLICK
OOOH, I WAS HOPING THIS WOULD HAPPEN.
PLEASE LET ME END HIM THIS TIME, FISK. PLEASE. WITH %$#&$% SUGAR ON TOP.
HELL, I'LL GIVE BACK 20% OF WHAT YA PAID IF YA LET ME DO IT.
STILL KEEPIN' THE CHAIR, THOUGH.
GENTLEMEN, PLEASE...
WE ALL HAVE A COMMON ENEMY AT THE MOMENT.
CAN'T BELIEVE I'M SAYING THIS, BUT I AGREE WITH FISK. PUT THE GUN DOWN, CASTLE...
OR ARE YOU REALLY THAT NUTS?
WHAT DO YOU THINK?
CLICK

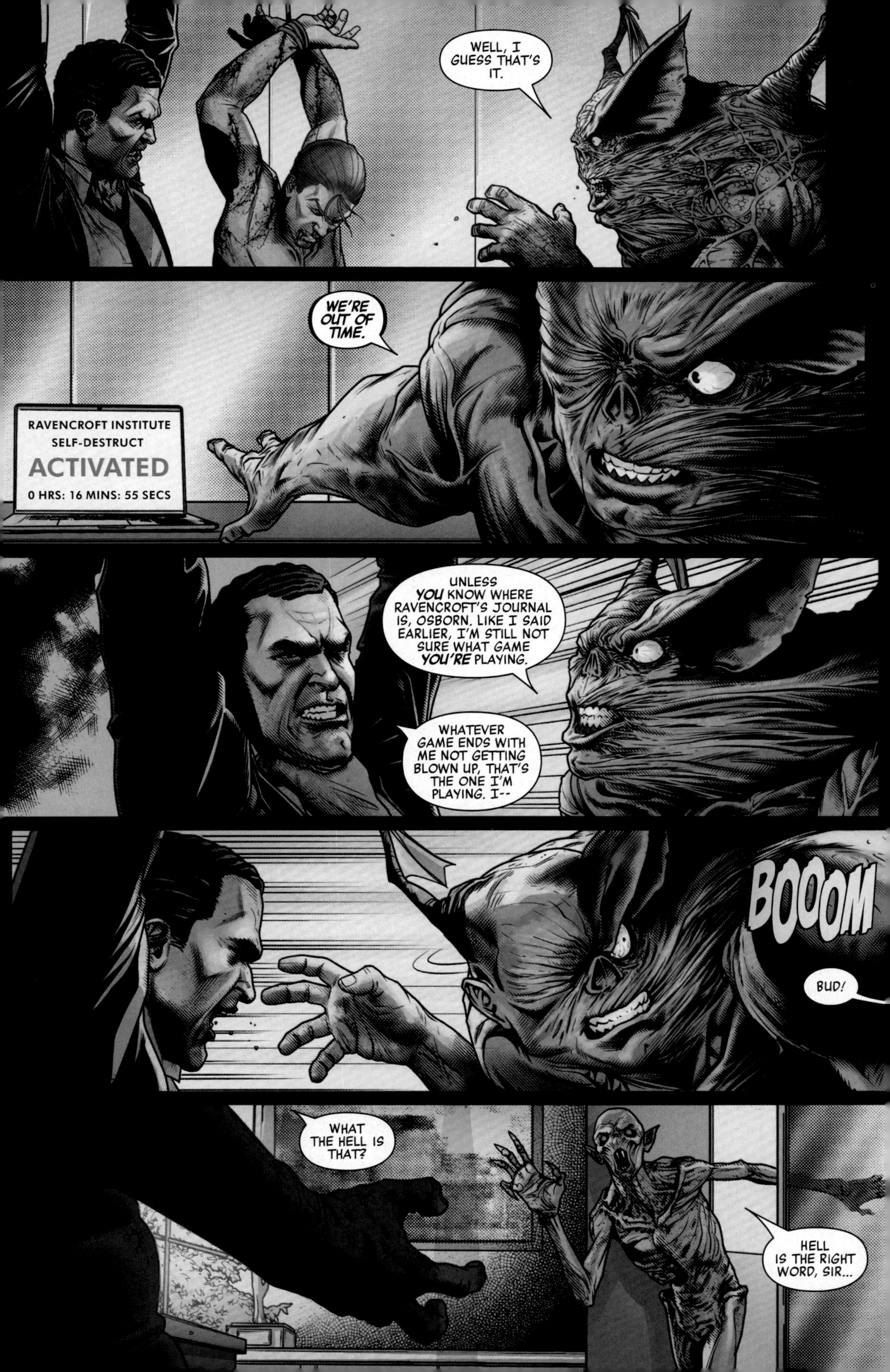
WELL, I GUESS THAT'S IT.
WE'RE OUT OF TIME.
RAVENCROFT INSTITUTE
SELF-DESTRUCT
ACTIVATED
0 HRS: 16 MINS: 55 SECS
UNLESS YOU KNOW WHERE RAVENCROFT'S JOURNAL IS, OSBORN. LIKE I SAID EARLIER, I'M STILL NOT SURE WHAT GAME YOU'RE PLAYING.
WHATEVER GAME ENDS WITH ME NOT GETTING BLOWN UP, THAT'S THE ONE I'M PLAYING. I--
BOOOM
BUD!
WHAT THE HELL IS THAT?
HELL IS THE RIGHT WORD, SIR...

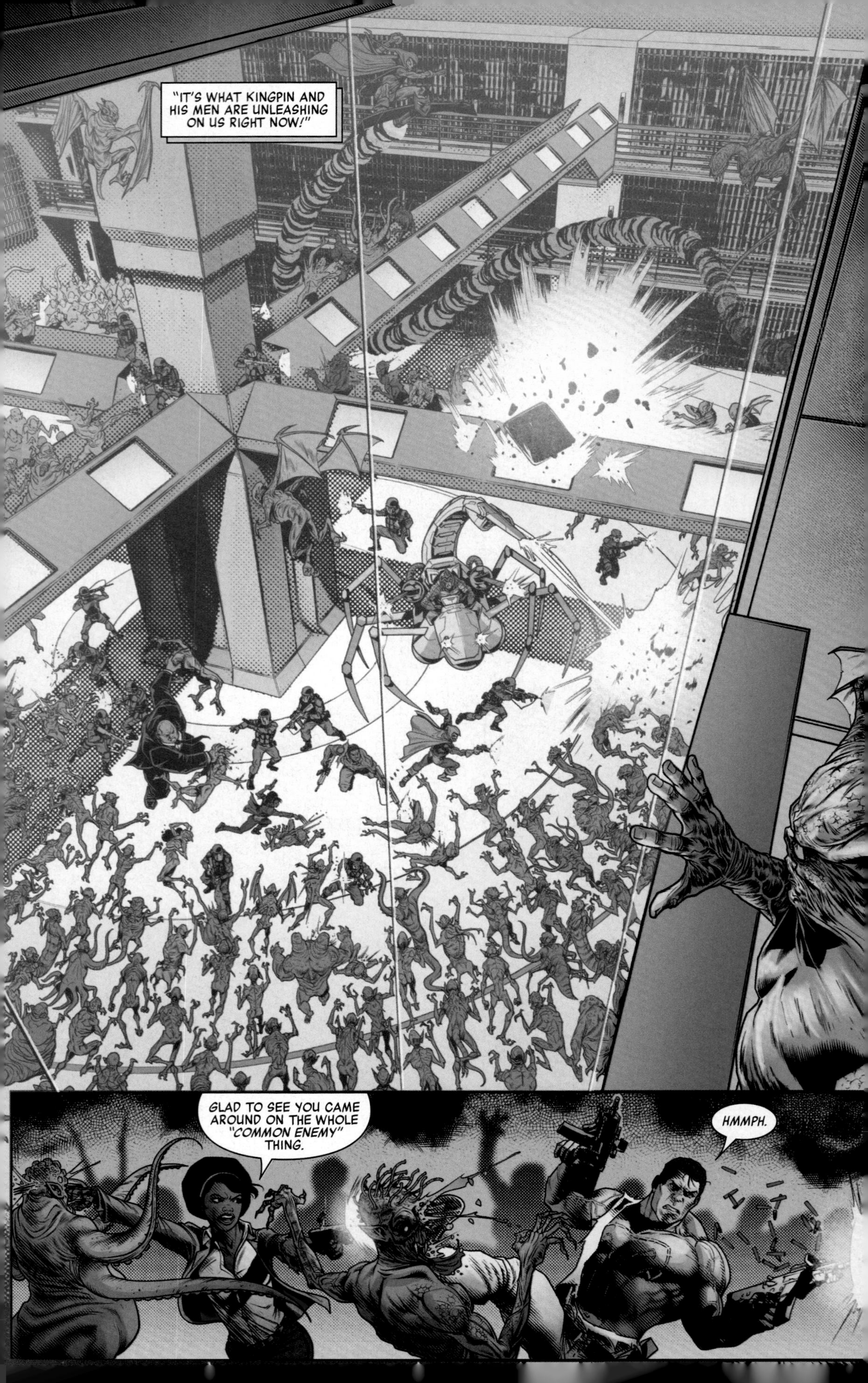
"IT'S WHAT KINGPIN AND HIS MEN ARE UNLEASHING ON US RIGHT NOW!"
GLAD TO SEE YOU CAME AROUND ON THE WHOLE "COMMON ENEMY" THING.
HMMPH.

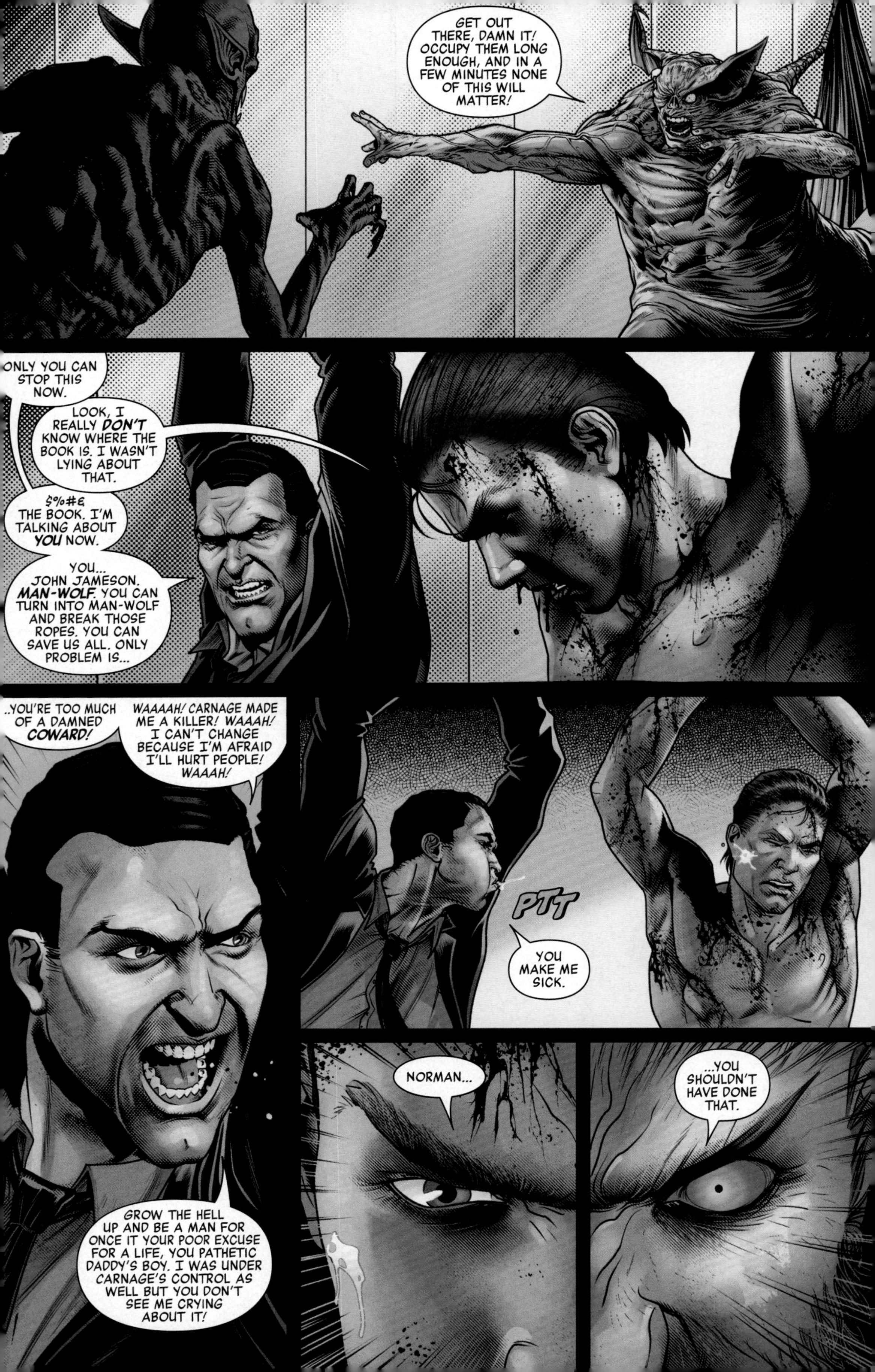
GET OUT THERE, DAMN IT! OCCUPY THEM LONG ENOUGH, AND IN A FEW MINUTES NONE OF THIS WILL MATTER!
ONLY YOU CAN STOP THIS NOW.
LOOK, I REALLY DON'T KNOW WHERE THE BOOK IS. I WASN'T LYING ABOUT THAT.
$%#& THE BOOK. I'M TALKING ABOUT YOU NOW.
YOU... JOHN JAMESON. MAN-WOLF. YOU CAN TURN INTO MAN-WOLF AND BREAK THOSE ROPES. YOU CAN SAVE US ALL. ONLY PROBLEM IS...
..YOU'RE TOO MUCH OF A DAMNED COWARD!
WAAAAH! CARNAGE MADE ME A KILLER! WAAAH! I CAN'T CHANGE BECAUSE I'M AFRAID I'LL HURT PEOPLE! WAAAH!
GROW THE HELL UP AND BE A MAN FOR ONCE IT YOUR POOR EXCUSE FOR A LIFE, YOU PATHETIC DADDY'S BOY. I WAS UNDER CARNAGE'S CONTROL AS WELL BUT YOU DON'T SEE ME CRYING ABOUT IT!
PTT
YOU MAKE ME SICK.
NORMAN...
...YOU SHOULDN'T HAVE DONE THAT.

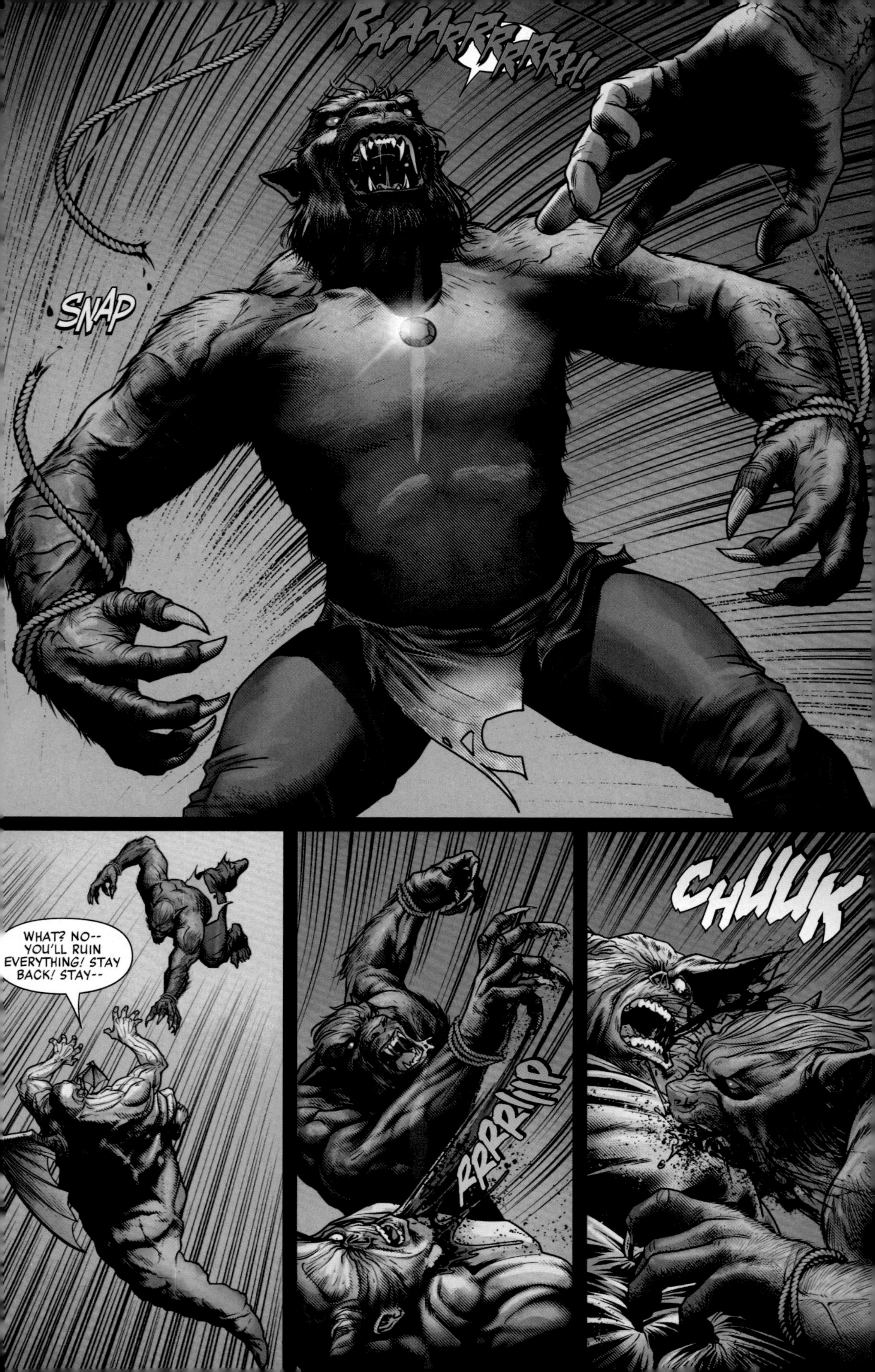
RAAARRRRRRH!!
SNAP
WHAT? NO-- YOU'LL RUIN EVERYTHING! STAY BACK! STAY--
RRRRIIIP
CHUUK

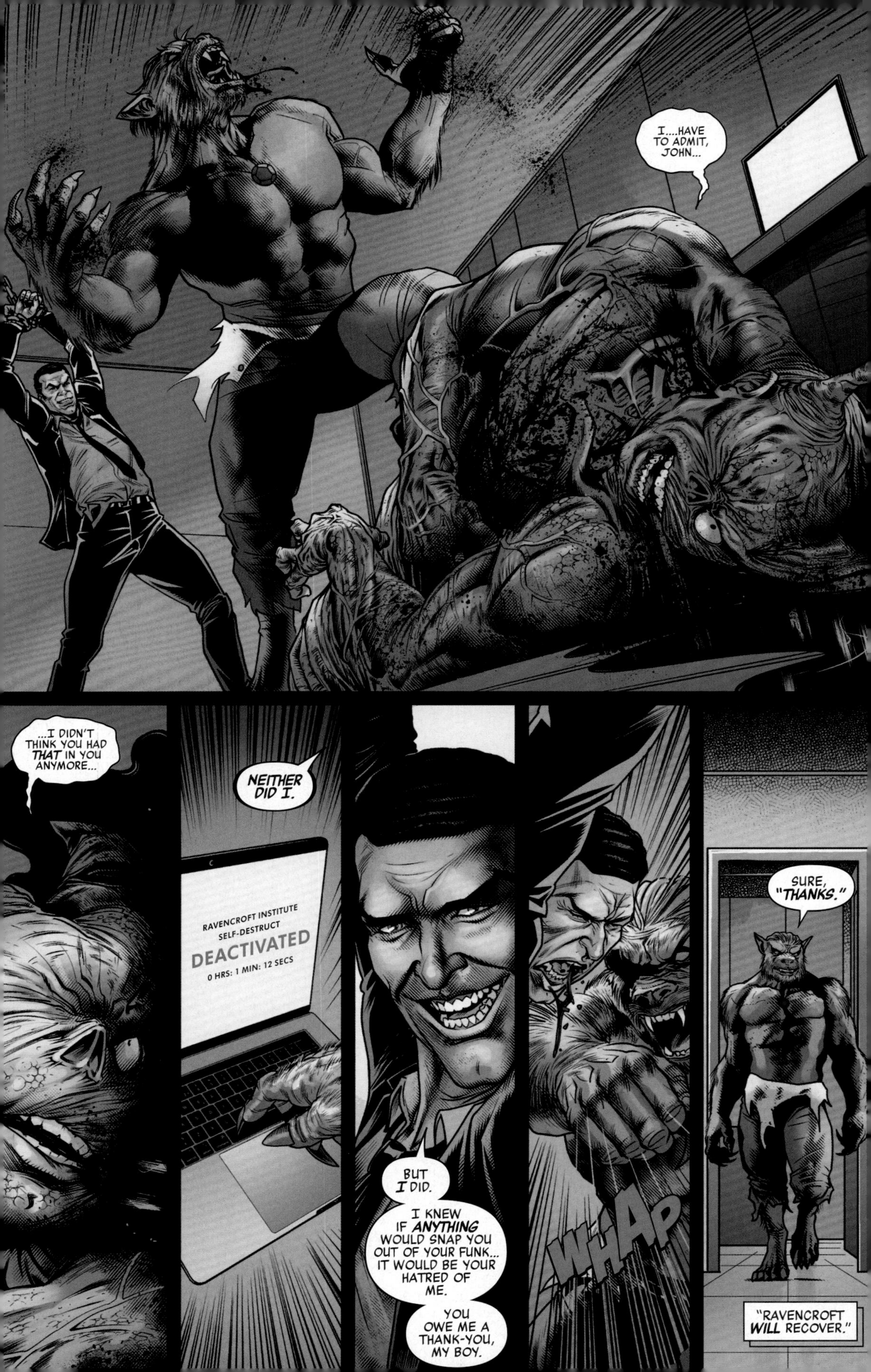
I....HAVE TO ADMIT, JOHN...
...I DIDN'T THINK YOU HAD THAT IN YOU ANYMORE...
NEITHER DID I.
RAVENCROFT INSTITUTE
SELF-DESTRUCT
DEACTIVATED
0 HRS: 1 MIN: 12 SECS
BUT I DID.
I KNEW IF ANYTHING WOULD SNAP YOU OUT OF YOUR FUNK... IT WOULD BE YOUR HATRED OF ME.
YOU OWE ME A THANK-YOU, MY BOY.
WHAP
SURE, "THANKS."
"RAVENCROFT WILL RECOVER."

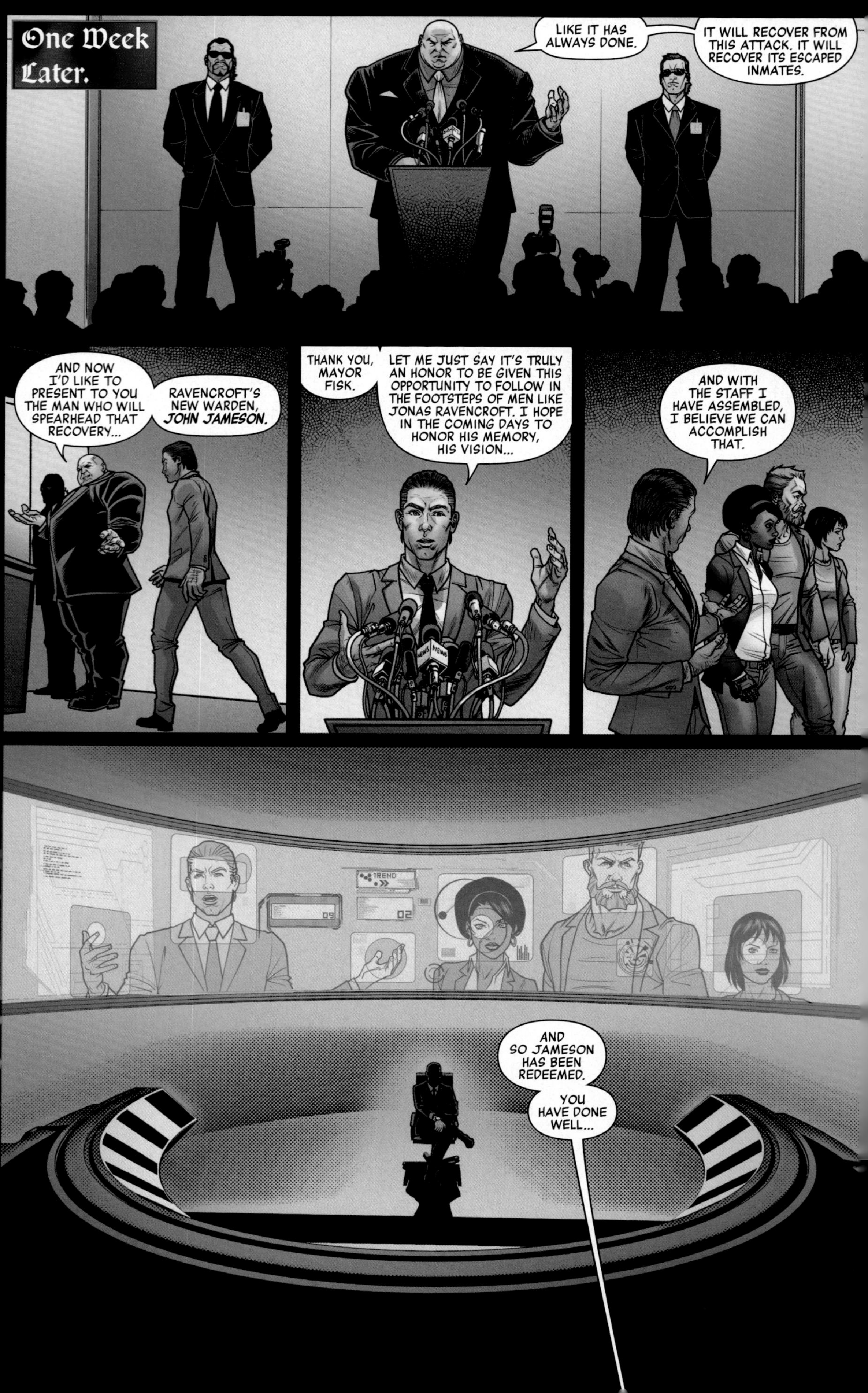
One Week Later.
LIKE IT HAS ALWAYS DONE.
IT WILL RECOVER FROM THIS ATTACK. IT WILL RECOVER ITS ESCAPED INMATES.
AND NOW I'D LIKE TO PRESENT TO YOU THE MAN WHO WILL SPEARHEAD THAT RECOVERY...
RAVENCROFT'S NEW WARDEN, JOHN JAMESON.
THANK YOU, MAYOR FISK.
LET ME JUST SAY IT'S TRULY AN HONOR TO BE GIVEN THIS OPPORTUNITY TO FOLLOW IN THE FOOTSTEPS OF MEN LIKE JONAS RAVENCROFT. I HOPE IN THE COMING DAYS TO HONOR HIS MEMORY, HIS VISION...
NEWS
AND WITH THE STAFF I HAVE ASSEMBLED, I BELIEVE WE CAN ACCOMPLISH THAT.
TREND
09
02
AND SO JAMESON HAS BEEN REDEEMED.
YOU HAVE DONE WELL...

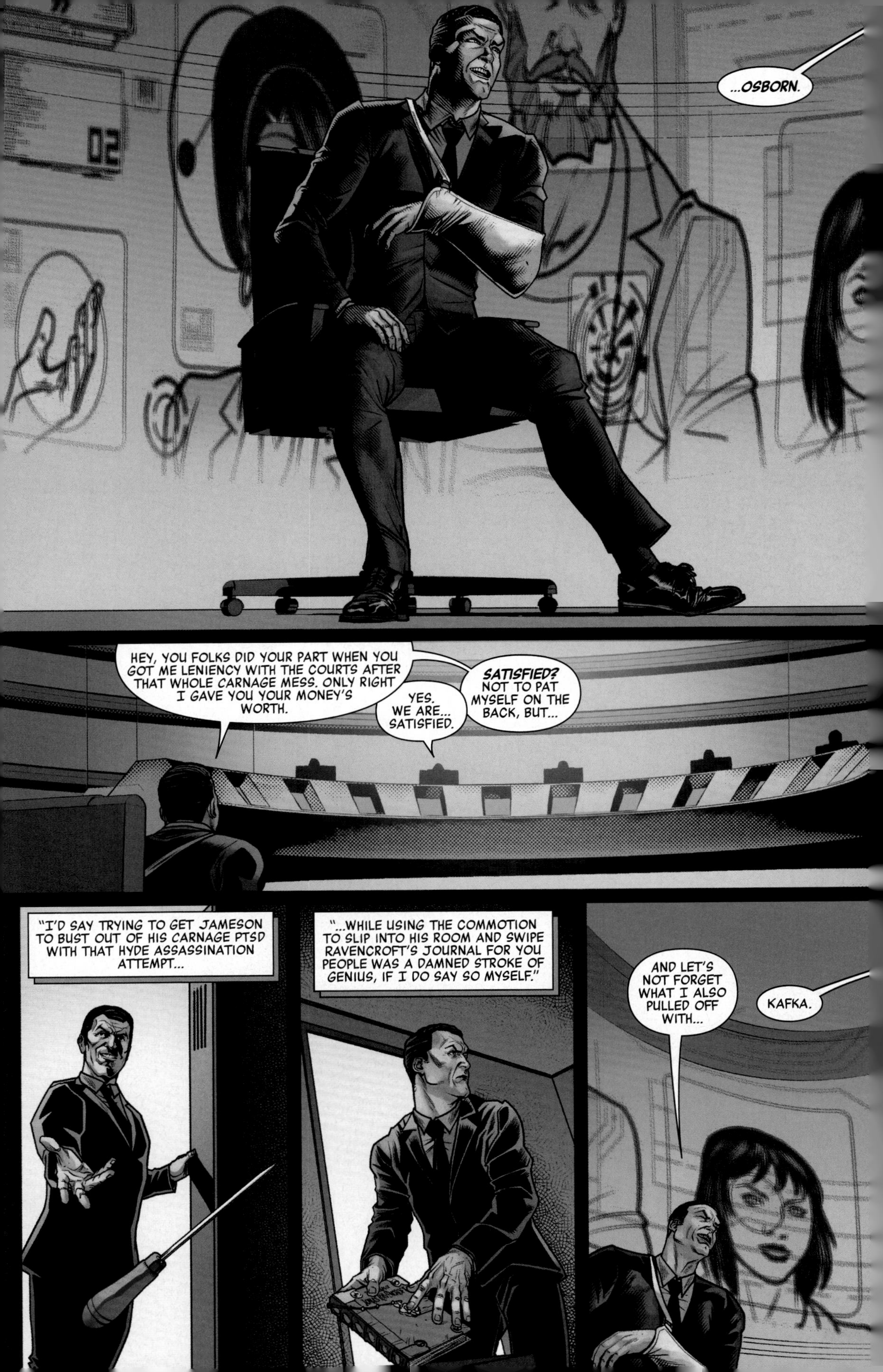
...OSBORN.
HEY, YOU FOLKS DID YOUR PART WHEN YOU GOT ME LENIENCY WITH THE COURTS AFTER THAT WHOLE CARNAGE MESS. ONLY RIGHT I GAVE YOU YOUR MONEY'S WORTH.
SATISFIED? NOT TO PAT MYSELF ON THE BACK, BUT...
YES. WE ARE... SATISFIED.
"I'D SAY TRYING TO GET JAMESON TO BUST OUT OF HIS CARNAGE PTSD WITH THAT HYDE ASSASSINATION ATTEMPT...
"...WHILE USING THE COMMOTION TO SLIP INTO HIS ROOM AND SWIPE RAVENCROFT'S JOURNAL FOR YOU PEOPLE WAS A DAMNED STROKE OF GENIUS, IF I DO SAY SO MYSELF."
AND LET'S NOT FORGET WHAT I ALSO PULLED OFF WITH...
KAFKA.

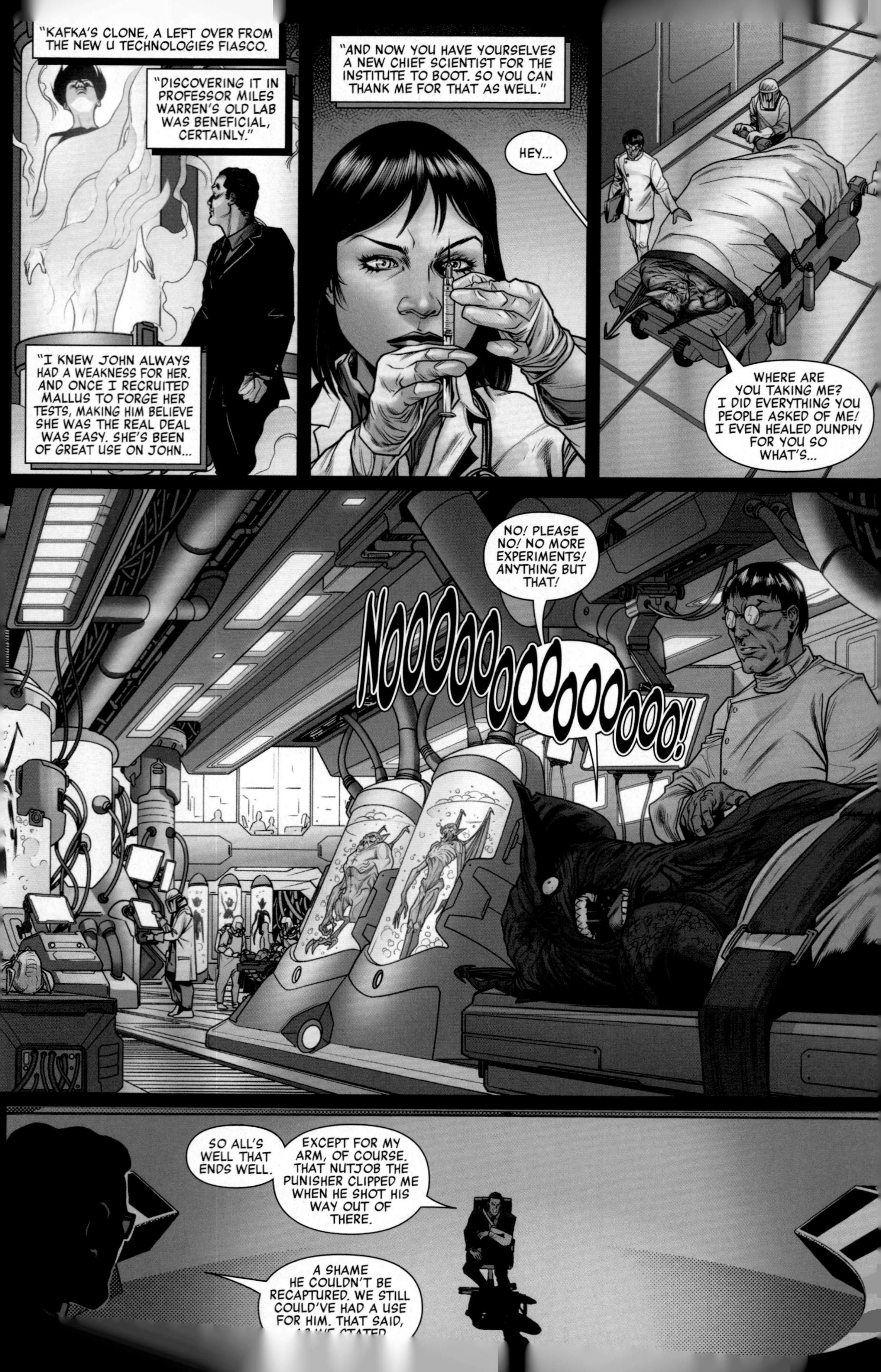
"KAFKA'S CLONE, A LEFT OVER FROM THE NEW U TECHNOLOGIES FIASCO.
"DISCOVERING IT IN PROFESSOR MILES WARREN'S OLD LAB WAS BENEFICIAL, CERTAINLY."
"I KNEW JOHN ALWAYS HAD A WEAKNESS FOR HER. AND ONCE I RECRUITED MALLUS TO FORGE HER TESTS, MAKING HIM BELIEVE SHE WAS THE REAL DEAL WAS EASY. SHE'S BEEN OF GREAT USE ON JOHN...
"AND NOW YOU HAVE YOURSELVES A NEW CHIEF SCIENTIST FOR THE INSTITUTE TO BOOT. SO YOU CAN THANK ME FOR THAT AS WELL."
HEY...
WHERE ARE YOU TAKING ME? I DID EVERYTHING YOU PEOPLE ASKED OF ME! I EVEN HEALED DUNPHY FOR YOU SO WHAT'S...
NO! PLEASE NO! NO MORE EXPERIMENTS! ANYTHING BUT THAT!
NOOOOOOOOOOOOOOO!
SO ALL'S WELL THAT ENDS WELL.
EXCEPT FOR MY ARM, OF COURSE. THAT NUTJOB THE PUNISHER CLIPPED ME WHEN HE SHOT HIS WAY OUT OF THERE.
A SHAME HE COULDN'T BE RECAPTURED. WE STILL COULD'VE HAD A USE FOR HIM. THAT SAID,

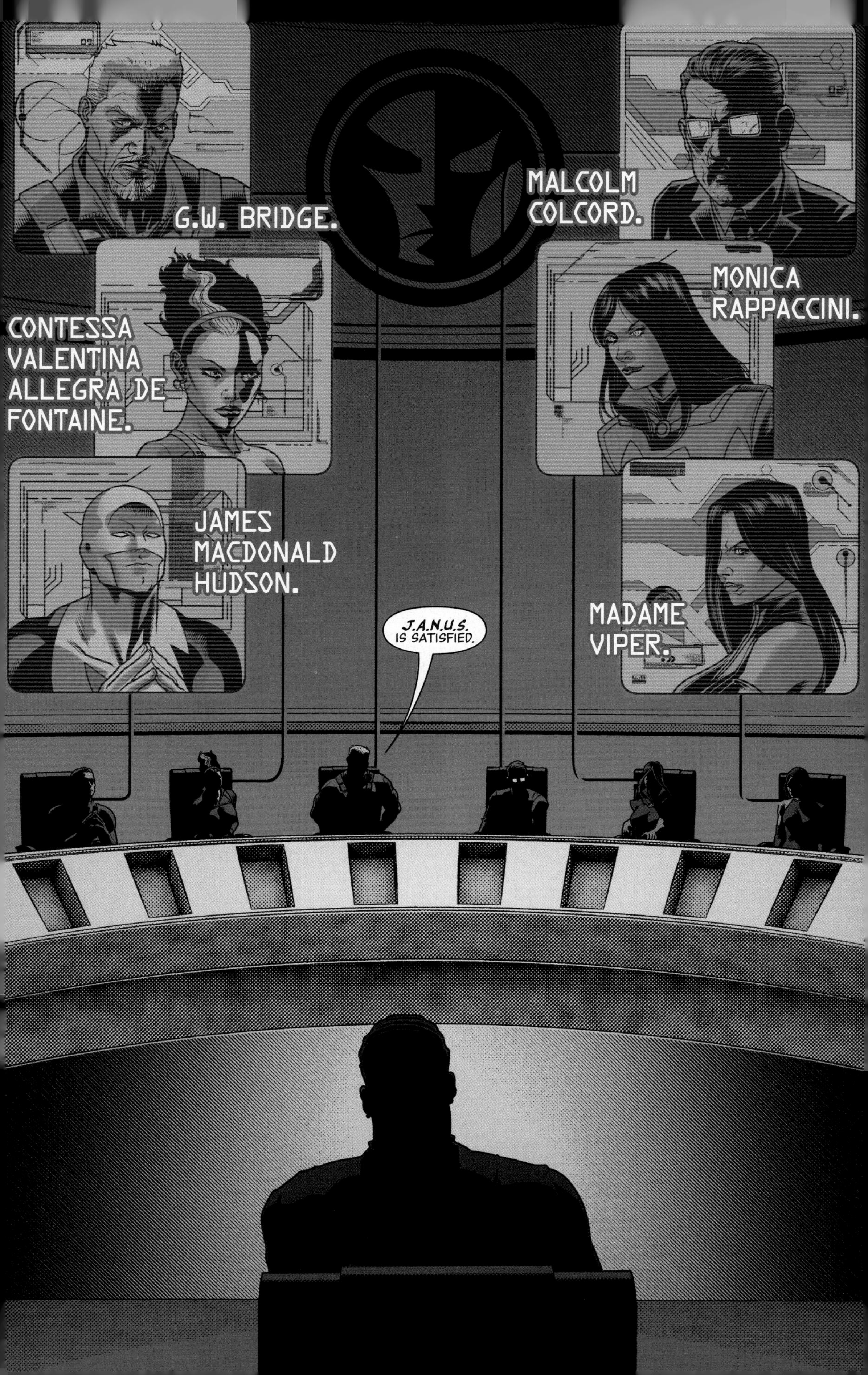
G.W. BRIDGE.
MALCOLM COLCORD.
CONTESSA VALENTINA ALLEGRA DE FONTAINE.
MONICA RAPPACCINI.
JAMES MACDONALD HUDSON.
MADAME VIPER.
J.A.N.U.S. IS SATISFIED.

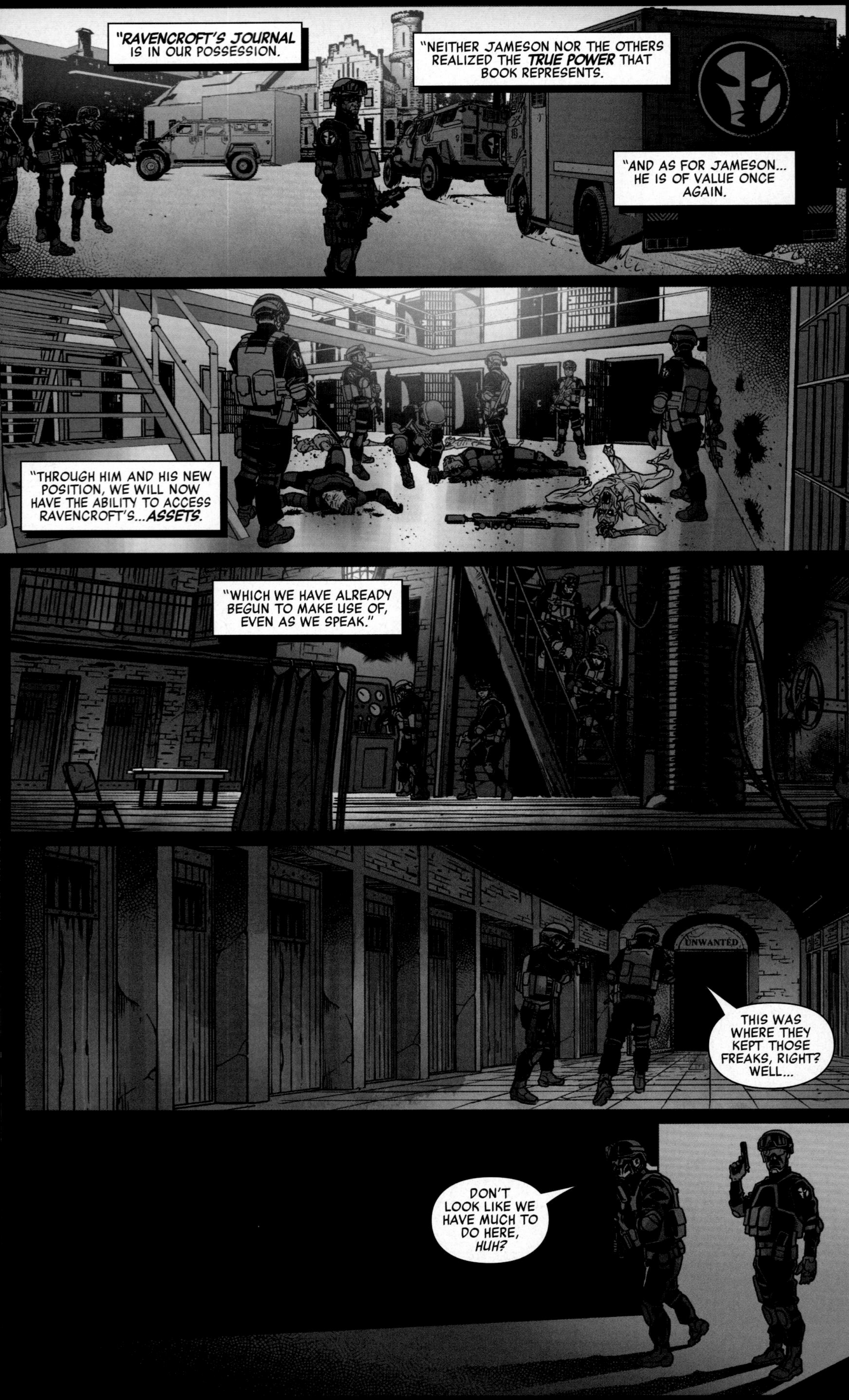
"RAVENCROFT'S JOURNAL IS IN OUR POSSESSION.
"NEITHER JAMESON NOR THE OTHERS REALIZED THE TRUE POWER THAT BOOK REPRESENTS.
"AND AS FOR JAMESON... HE IS OF VALUE ONCE AGAIN.
"THROUGH HIM AND HIS NEW POSITION, WE WILL NOW HAVE THE ABILITY TO ACCESS RAVENCROFT'S...ASSETS.
"WHICH WE HAVE ALREADY BEGUN TO MAKE USE OF, EVEN AS WE SPEAK."
UNWANTED
THIS WAS WHERE THEY KEPT THOSE FREAKS, RIGHT? WELL...
DON'T LOOK LIKE WE HAVE MUCH TO DO HERE, HUH?

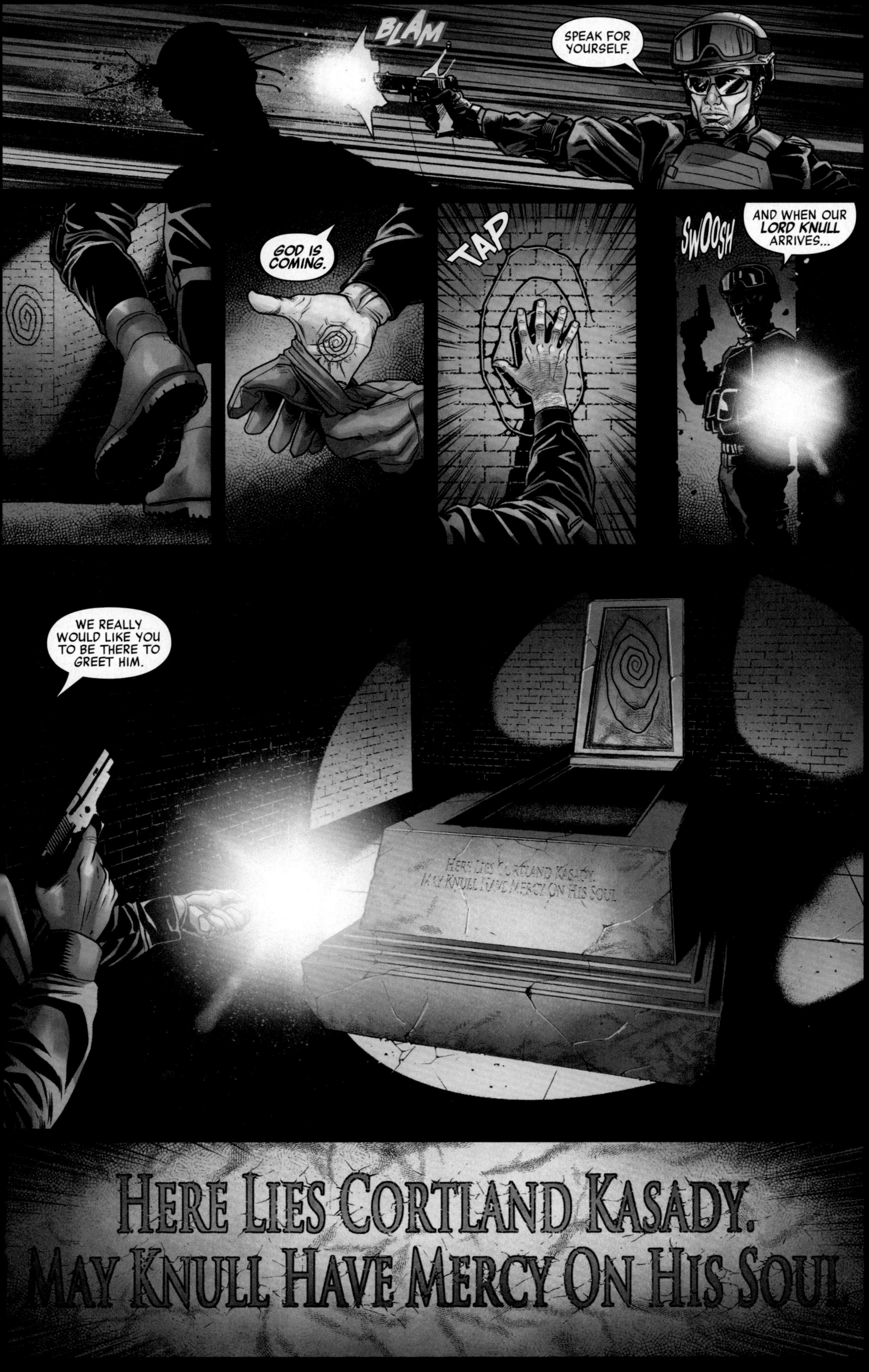
BLAM
SPEAK FOR YOURSELF.
GOD IS COMING.
TAP
SWOOSH
AND WHEN OUR LORD KNULL ARRIVES...
WE REALLY WOULD LIKE YOU TO BE THERE TO GREET HIM.
HERE LIES CORTLAND KASADY.
MAY KNULL HAVE MERCY ON HIS SOUL

CORTLAND KASADY
WILL
RETURN.

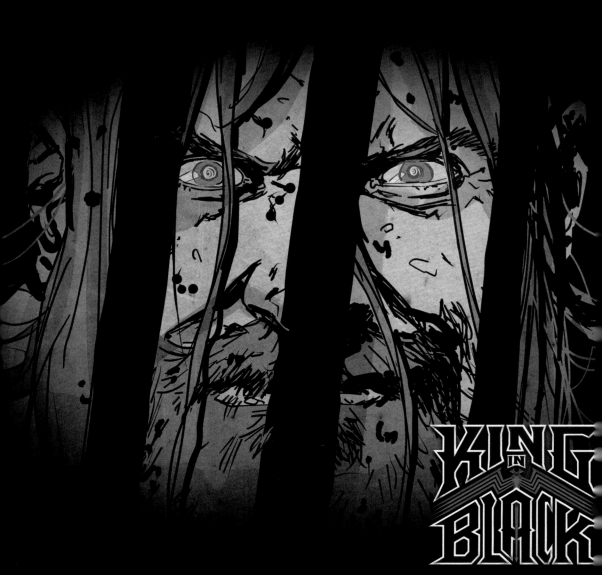

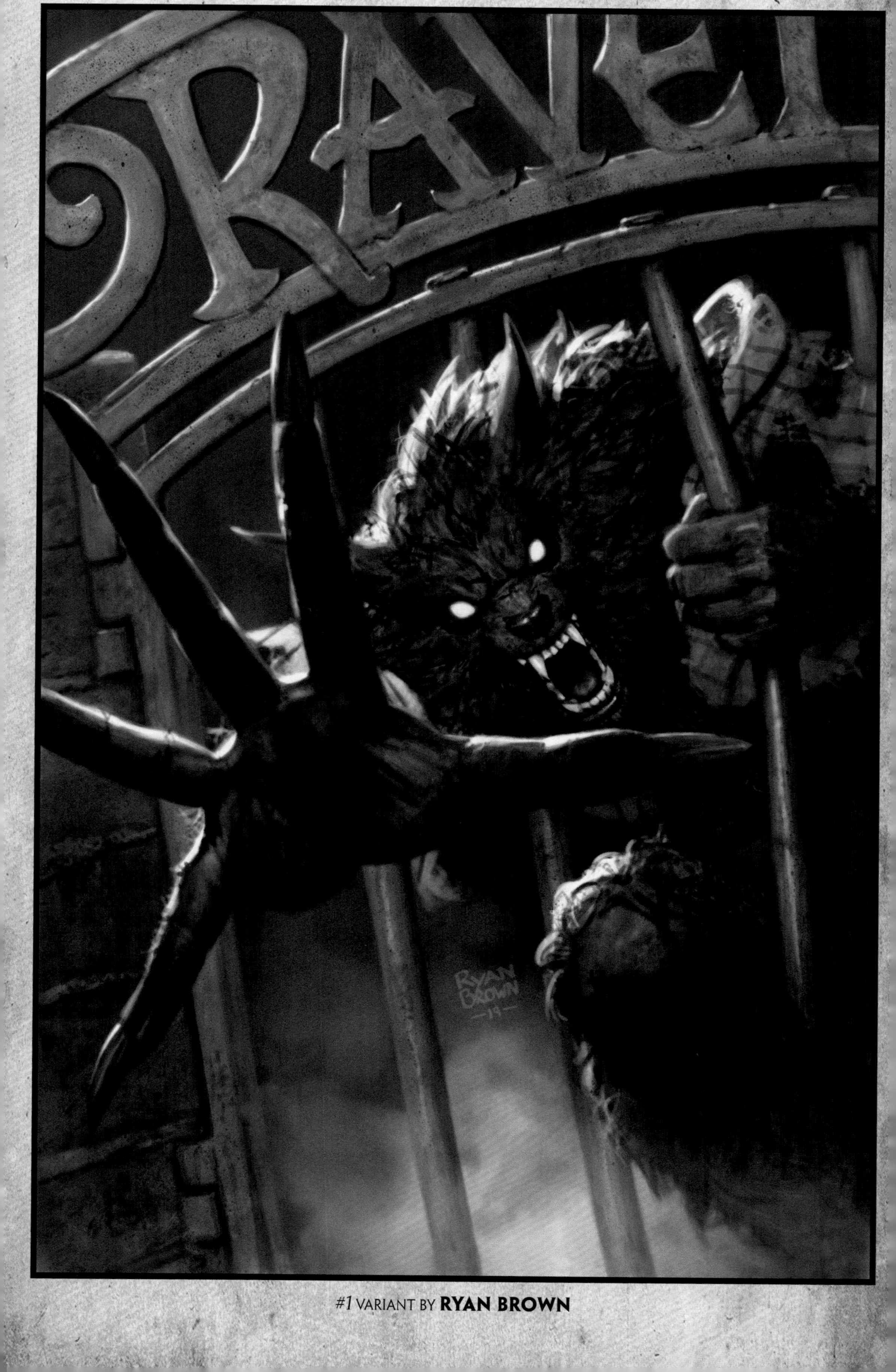
RYAN BROWN
-19-

#1 VARIANT BY **RYAN BROWN**

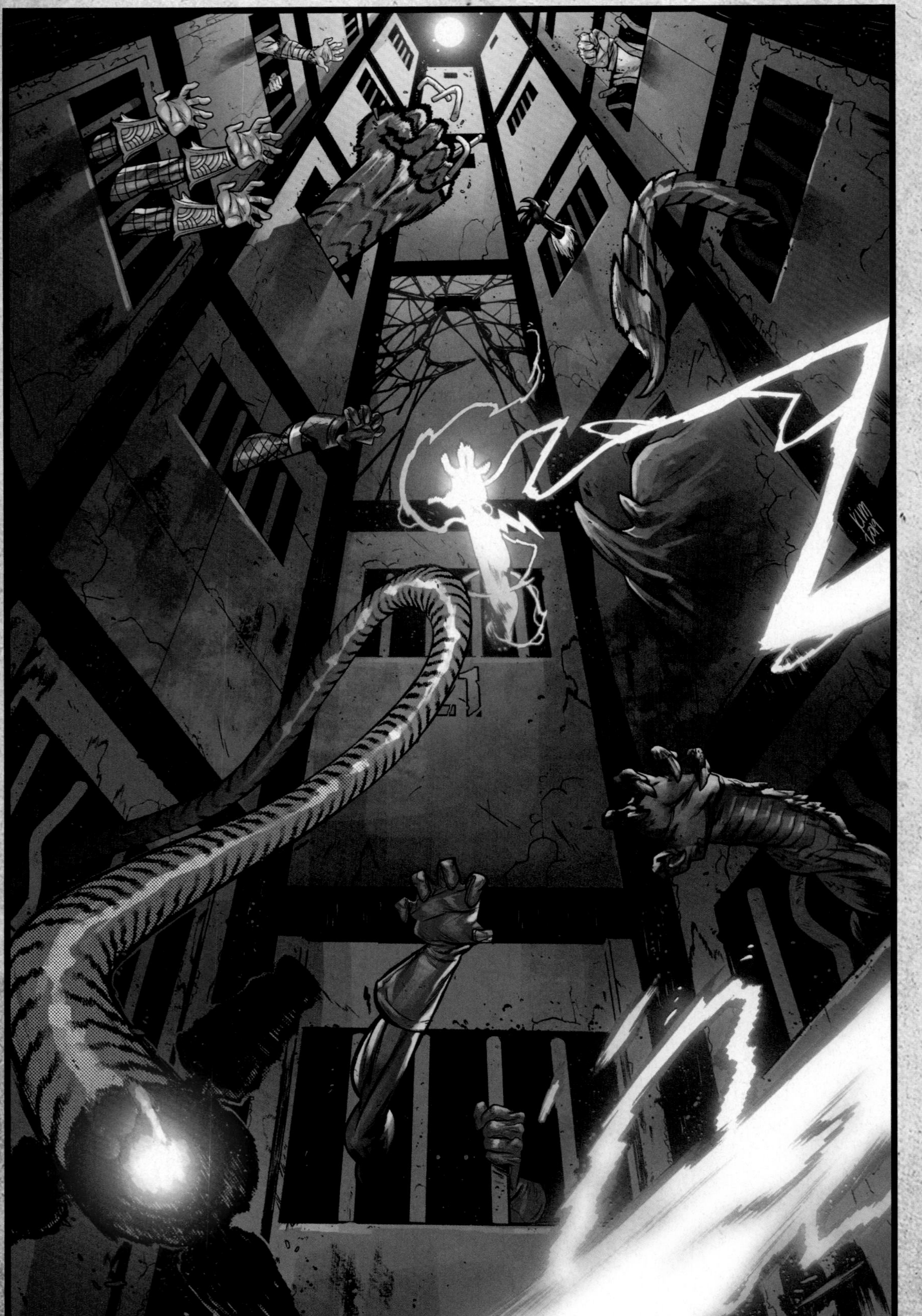
KIM 2019

#1 VARIANT BY **KIM JACINTO** & **RAIN BEREDO**

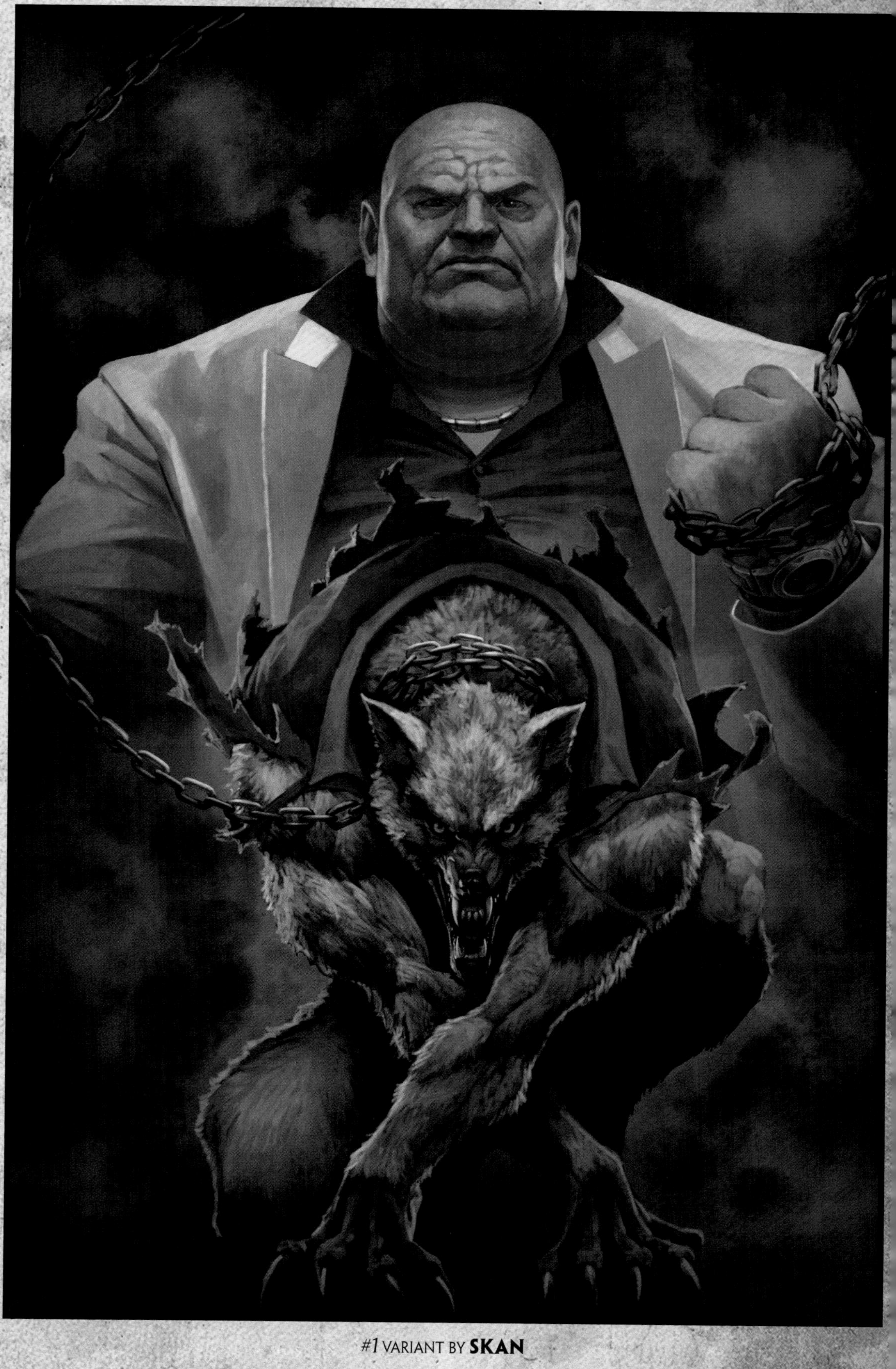

#1 VARIANT BY **SKAN**

#3 VARIANT BY **E.M. GIST**

#4 VARIANT BY **ARIEL OLIVETTI**